D1606131

Lure of the Arcane

Lure of the Arcane

THE LITERATURE OF CULT AND CONSPIRACY

Theodore Ziolkowski

The Johns Hopkins University Press
Baltimore

© 2013 The Johns Hopkins University Press
All rights reserved. Published 2013
Printed in the United States of America on acid-free paper
9 8 7 6 5 4 3 2 1

The Johns Hopkins University Press
2715 North Charles Street
Baltimore, Maryland 21218-4363
www.press.jhu.edu

Library of Congress Cataloging-in-Publication Data

Ziolkowski, Theodore.
    Lure of the arcane : the literature of cult and conspiracy /
Theodore Ziolkowski.
        pages cm
    Includes bibliographical references and index.
    ISBN-13: 978-1-4214-0958-0 (hardcover : acid-free paper)
    ISBN-13: 978-1-4214-0959-7 (electronic)
    ISBN-10: 1-4214-0958-5 (hardcover : acid-free paper)
    ISBN-10: 1-4214-0959-3 (electronic)
    1. Conspiracy in literature.   2. Secret societies in literature.
3. Secrecy in literature.   I. Title.
    PN56.C675Z56 2013
    809'.93355—dc23
                                        2012041101

A catalog record for this book is available from the British Library.

Special discounts are available for bulk purchases of this book.
For more information, please contact Special Sales at 410-516-6936 or
specialsales@press.jhu.edu.

The Johns Hopkins University Press uses environmentally friendly book
materials, including recycled text paper that is composed of at least
30 percent post-consumer waste, whenever possible.

For my wife
Yetta Goldstein Ziolkowski
to whom I have been bound for over sixty years
with cultlike devotion
and
in conspiratorial mystery

Contents

Preface

This book can be seen in part, I suppose, as an attempt to rationalize and justify my longtime practice at bedtime of reading mysteries or thrillers—books that some of my academic colleagues have uncharitably called "trash" but that I prefer to regard more tolerantly, along with such fans as W. H. Auden, T. S. Eliot, Jorge Luis Borges, Friedrich Dürrenmatt, and Umberto Eco as literary sociology, fictionalized politics, or aestheticized current events. Whether we share the cynical view or the loftier one, it has long been clear to me that readers and audiences for many centuries have been subject to the same proclivity for mystery, a susceptibility that accounts for the continuing popularity of many literary works that we now regard as classics, from Euripides' *Bacchae* to the present.

At the same time, the morning newspapers seemed to dwell increasingly during the first decade of the twenty-first century on stories about conspiracies: from plots by Al-Qaeda or the CIA to destroy buildings and airplanes to the controversies surrounding the cults of Scientology or Opus Dei, from the schemes of left-wing radicals to the counterplots of conservative extremists to undermine the government. These conspiracies in turn and in an unending cycle inform the conspiracy fiction and films that entertain many devotees.

My vague ruminations were catalyzed when my wife, Yetta, who has long provided the liveliest stimulation to my imagination, urged me to read George Sand's *The Countess of Rudolstadt* just at the moment when I was enjoying one of my contemporary thrillers at bedtime. The parallels between the two fictions struck me instantly and alerted me to similarities in other works familiar to me from world literature. As I began to think more systematically about the subject—the literary works and the historical circumstances that underlie them—I realized that I had already encountered one aspect of it almost fifty years ago in my first book, *The Novels of Hermann Hesse*. There, in a chapter on *The Journey to the East*, I had occasion to locate Hesse's novel in a tradition extending back to the German *Bundesroman* or "lodge novel" of the late eighteenth century, a genre revolving around a secret society that controls the hero and one of which Hesse was fully aware. I realized, too, that several of the works I had treated in my teaching and in other books over the years, notably on German Romanticism, also fit the pattern of "mystery" novels. At the same time, my ventures into the history of the genre— and this is precisely the joy and excitement of scholarship—led me into realms that I had not previously explored in detail: ancient mystery cults; the search for the Holy Grail; the practices of such postmedieval secret societies as the Rosicrucians, the Illuminati, and the Freemasons; and the *Protocols of the Elders of Zion*. Above all, I began to think about the reasons underlying our fascination with the arcane and the groups that exemplify it. This book is the result of that reading and those ruminations.

I would like to specify at the outset what this book is *not* about. On the one hand, it is not a history of the various movements discussed herein, from pagan religious cults down to postmodern conspiracies. These movements have been studied in an extensive and authoritative secondary literature, which I have used gratefully and acknowledged in my notes. Nor does it aspire to contribute to the already voluminous literature on conspiracy theory. On the other hand, it is not an attempt to provide ingenious new readings of the specific literary texts analyzed here as examples. Many of these works, masterpieces of world literature, have elicited elaborate commentary to which I have acknowledged my indebtedness.

My work is meant simply to identify specific texts, within the context of the secret societies or "conspiracies" activating them, as exemplary models for the lure of the arcane, as it has occurred repeatedly since antiquity within different societies and cultures: to illustrate, in other words, the diachronic appeal to many generations preceding our own of what is known today as "conspiracy fiction" and its progressive development as a genre. To this end it was often necessary to recapitulate works—some of which, despite their significance in their own periods, are not generally familiar and others that are no longer readily available—at sufficient length to establish the presence and illustrate variations of the basic pattern. While the continuity of pattern is often conscious for the writer, sometimes the same patterns turn up even in works in which no influence by earlier examples is probable—patterns suggested, it would seem, by the material itself. This study, in sum, falls most readily into the category known as genre history. In such studies it is not the (in any case impossible) goal to be bibliographically all-inclusive but, rather, to present significant examples that fairly represent the genre and its development.

Temporal or generic cross-reference occurs infrequently in most of the existing secondary studies. The histories of one secret society usually do not refer to the others, and the literary studies of specific periods—for instance, the Renaissance, German Enlightenment, or French July Monarchy—rarely look back or forward to similar literary manifestations in other periods. Thus Pierre-André Taguieff, in his massive *La foire aux "Illuminés"* (2005) restricts himself essentially to post-1970 views of the Illuminati and the impact of that cult on the late twentieth-century imagination. After submitting my manuscript I came across Jan Auracher's article "Erleuchtung und Bevormundung—Die Rolle der Geheimgesellschaften in den Bundesromanen von Friedrich Schiller und Dan Brown" (2010), which, while seemingly unaware of the longer historical continuity of the genre, notes the common pattern underlying Dan Brown's novels and the German lodge novel and correctly attributes their popularity to the reader's longing for mystery and the occult. The notable exceptions to this generalization are to be found not in scholarly studies but in such fictions as Robert Shea's and Robert Anton Wilson's *Illuminatus! Trilogy* or Umberto Eco's *Foucault's Pendulum*, both of which include much information about the history of various cults and conspiracies. With this book I hope to have made a persuasive case for the historical continuity of a specific genre—the fiction of cults and conspiracies—and for the significance of that genre as a reflection of the religious, political, and social concerns of the respective ages. I also hope, in the process, to have persuaded other fans of contemporary thrillers that our craving for mystery and adventure may be satisfied with equal gratification by a host of classics from the canon of world literature.

It is a pleasure, finally, to acknowledge those who have contributed in various ways to my project. I want to express my appreciation to Christian Staufenbiel, German specialist at the Cambridge University Library, for providing me with a copy of Heym's satire "Ein Interview mit den Weisen von Zion" from the library's

Stefan Heym Archive. As so often in the past, I have again benefited from the expertise of the Interlibrary Services of Princeton University Library in obtaining works not readily available in the stacks of Firestone Library or in our Rare Books collection. Matt McAdam, humanities editor at the Johns Hopkins University Press, expressed a gratifying and encouraging interest in my project from the outset and then guided it patiently and skillfully through the editorial process. In particular he found for its appraisal a knowledgeable reader, whose perceptive comments sharpened my work. The staff at the Press has assisted me at every stage with admirable professionalism. I am especially indebted to Melissa Solarz for her generous technical assistance with my manuscript. Joe Abbott edited my text with exemplary discernment and tact. Any mistakes or infelicities that remain are of course my own.

Just as a suggestion from my wife initially put me on to this topic, my son, Professor Jan Ziolkowski of Harvard University, gave me the idea for its conclusion when he asked me to review Yorick Blumenfeld's *The Waters of Forgetfulness* for *The Virgil Encyclopedia* that he is editing with his colleague Richard Thomas. My daughter, Professor Margaret Ziolkowski of Miami University, was able, with her knowledge as a Slavicist, to further my understanding of the *Protocols of the Elders of Zion*. My son, Professor Eric Ziolkowski of Lafayette College, from his field of religious studies, enhanced my insights into the relations between cults and religion. So this book, even more than others I have written, has turned out to be truly a family affair.

Lure of the Arcane

Introduction

Conspiracy Fiction

In September 2009 the publishing world heralded another major novel by Dan Brown, author of the international best sellers *Angels and Demons* (2000) and *The Da Vinci Code* (2003). Over one million copies were sold on the first day of publication and two million more during the first week. *The Lost Symbol* follows essentially the same formula as its two predecessors. Like them, it features Robert Langdon, the Harvard professor of symbology, who is joined by a lovely heroine with specialist skills (this time in the arcane science of noetics) to thwart a plot involving the efforts of a monstrous villain (this time a tattooed steroid-freak with a redeemer obsession) to recover a mythic object (this time The Lost Word as the key to the Ancient Mysteries) guarded by a secret society (this time the Freemasons rather than, as in Brown's earlier novels, the Illuminati, the Priory of Sion, or Opus Dei). Again, the plot takes us on an architectural tour of a national capital (this time not Rome and Paris but Washington, DC) with fascinating details about the Masonic symbols underlying the design and ornamentation of national landmarks: the Capitol, the Library of Congress, the National Cathedral, and the Washington Monument.

As usual in Brown's thrillers, the mystery involves anagrams, conundrums, and other clues hidden in works of art (this time Albrecht Dürer's *Melencolia* and a small model of the legendary Masonic Pyramid). The plot, condensed by urgent deadlines into a brief period (this time only twelve hours), is given a rather implausible dimension of national urgency that brings the CIA and its tyrannical director of security into the picture: the villain threatens to release to the media pictures of leading Washingtonians—the architect of the Capitol, the dean of the National Cathedral, the director of the Smithsonian, along with various senators and political figures—engaged in allegedly barbaric rituals and thereby to throw the government into turmoil. The Lost Word, which the villain had hoped in an ultimate consecration to tattoo onto his skull, turns out to be a copy of the Bible buried unattainably in the cornerstone of the Washington Monument.

Brown's novel, which remained on the best-seller lists for weeks, enjoyed considerable literary company.[1] That same year, 2009, saw the publication of several other successful thrillers based on essentially the same formula: a hero or heroine assisting a secret group to protect a mythic prize that is sought by villains.[2] Chris Kuzneski's *The Lost Throne* features three heroes coming to the assistance of a "Brotherhood" of monks from Mount Athos who are being murdered in their effort to protect the secret of hidden ancient treasure and books from an unscrupulous collector and his hired Spartan thugs. In Jim Marrs's *The Sisterhood of the Rose* the heroine links up with a group of women—including the mistresses of Hitler and Mussolini, Stalin's daughter, and the photographer Margaret Bourke-White—who band together to keep the great Treasure of Solomon, hidden centuries earlier by the Knights Templar, out of the hands of the Nazis.

These novels are often grouped together with those known loosely as "conspiracy thrillers."[3] But in conspiracy thrillers the secret society is usually a force of evil pursuing its own ends by illegal means but outwitted at the last minute by a hero with unusual talents acting alone or with a small group. In Daniel Levin's *The Last Ember,* for instance, the hero and heroine oppose a sinister Palestinian cohort wreaking havoc in Jerusalem and Rome in an effort to recover and destroy an ancient menorah proving the Jewish claim to the Temple Mount. In Dale Brown's *Rogue Forces* the U.S. president seeks to control a violent contractor known as "Scion" from pursuing his own interests in the Middle East for the benefit of the clandestine directors of his company. James Rollins's *The Doomsday Key* portrays a powerful group known as "The Guild," which cites reports by the Club of Rome to justify its use of genetic modification of food sources in order to control populations and the world. In Raymond Khoury's *The Sign* an elite coterie seeks first to prevent global warming, and ultimately to instigate a religious war of civilizations, by wielding scientific devices to legitimate a fake messiah who will preach their gospel. David Ignatius's *The Increment* features a powerful arms dealer who manipulates to his own advantage both the CIA and the British secret service when they seek to sabotage Iran's development of a nuclear bomb. In Brett Battle's *Shadow of Betrayal* an inner-government conspiracy known as "LP" schemes to terrorize a meeting of the G8 in order to frighten the United States into tightening its security measures. In Steve Berry's *The Paris Vendetta* a multinational cabal of financiers known as the Paris Club plots to manipulate the global economy for its own profit and is thwarted at the last minute by a small group including alienated members of the U.S. Secret Service and a Danish billionaire. In *The Hadrian Memorandum*, by Allan Folsom, the CIA orchestrates a menacing plot with violent mercenaries to seize a huge new oil field off the coast of West Africa—a plot frustrated at the request of the president by a onetime L.A. detective along with an operative of the Russian secret service and a former CIA agent.

In most of these examples the authors use headline-grabbing issues—conspiracies in Washington, the Israel-Palestine conflict, rogue contractors in Iraq, neo-Malthusian warnings about overpopulation, climate control, international concerns about Iran's nuclear plans, the terrorism threat at multinational conferences, global financial crises—to rationalize the intrigues of their secret groups and suggest their relevance to contemporary political concerns. To this extent the conspiracy thrillers differ from the novels à la Brown because the latter include an emphatically religious aspect transcending the political dimension.

Both types differ distinctly, in turn, from the genre of detective story after such classic models as those by Agatha Christie or Dashiell Hammett to the extent that they focus not on crimes aimed at individuals but on threats against nations or world civilization. The secret group seeks, whether for positive or self-serving reasons, to withhold certain knowledge from the world at large. The villain, whether operating against the secret society or, more commonly, as its agent, is opposed by an often alienated hero or heroine defending moral and social values with which the reader is expected to identify. All these thrillers may be distinguished, in turn, from such classic espionage novels as John Buchan's *The Thirty-Nine Steps* (1915) or Graham Greene's *Ministry of Fear* (1943), in which the threatening force is not an international secret society pursuing its own ends but, rather, agents for a specific wartime enemy.

Conspiracy Theory

All these novels belong to the category generally known as "conspiracy fiction," which can be seen as the literary counterpart to *conspiracy theory,* a term that appears to have been coined in 1909.[4] The phenomenon thrived in the twentieth century, when such political figures as Adolf Hitler and Joseph Stalin came to power as a result in no small measure of their shrewd and calculated manipulation of alleged conspiracies—of the Jews, the communists, or Wall Street, to mention only the most conspicuous examples. In the United States, Senator Joseph McCarthy owed his influence and notoriety largely to his pursuit through the House Un-American Activities Committee of purported communist conspiracies. The political assassinations of the 1960s—John F. Kennedy, Robert Kennedy, and Martin Luther King Jr.—which were attributed by many to conspiracies rather than to deranged individuals, helped to popularize the term, which in turn soon produced the coinage *conspiracy theorist.* A study in 1994 revealed that most of the survey respondents believed in one or more of several current conspiracy theories: that the Apollo moon landing was a hoax; that the AIDS virus was created in a government laboratory and deliberately spread in the gay and black communities; or that the FBI was involved in the assassination of Martin Luther King.[5]

There is no shortage in the twenty-first century of similar theories: for instance, that the tragedy of September 11, 2001, was carried out by agencies within the United States government for their own insidious purposes; that an Israeli plot produced the disastrous 2004 tsunami that wrought havoc in the Indian Ocean; that the murder of Princess Diana was planned by the royal family; or that Wall Street, in its multinational manifestations, seeks to manipulate the world economy for the benefit of its top investors. Scholars have not been slow to observe and analyze the phenomenon: in addition to the works cited in the notes to this chapter, for instance, the winter 2008 issue of the journal *New German Critique* was devoted wholly to articles investigating conspiracy theories from ancient Rome to the post-9/11 United States of America. A cartoon by Barbara Smaller in the *New Yorker* for June 14, 2010, depicts a worried-looking man crouched anxiously over his computer as his wife explains to a friend, "Where the conspiracy theories of the right overlap the conspiracy theories of the left, you'll find Richard."

In a classic essay Richard Hofstadter defined "the central preconception of the paranoid style [as] the existence of a vast, insidious, preternaturally effective international conspiratorial network designed to perpetrate acts of almost fiendish character"—acts directed not against the individual but "against a nation, a culture, a way of life whose fate affects not himself alone but millions of others."[6] More recently Michael Barkun analyzed conspiracy theory in greater detail as "the belief that an organization made up of individuals or groups was or is acting covertly to achieve some malevolent end"—a belief that is frightening because "it magnifies the power of evil, leading in some cases to an outright dualism in which light and darkness struggle for cosmic supremacy" but also reassuring because "it promises a world that is meaningful rather than arbitrary."[7] Barkun goes on to distinguish between "event conspiracies" that are discrete (e.g., the Kennedy assassination or terror attacks on airplanes), systemic (e.g., such international conspiracies as communism or multinational financial conglomerates), and superconspiracies (that is, event and systemic conspiracies linked by a guiding evil force). According to this classification most contemporary conspiracy thrillers are based on systemic conspiracies.

In the strictest sense only the second type of secret society may with any precision be designated as a conspiracy, which both by common and by legal definition is a secret agreement of two or more persons to commit an illegal act. Accordingly, the secret societies in the mentioned novels by Dan Brown, Chris Kuzneski, and Jim Marrs are not technically conspiracies.[8] But secret societies, as we will see repeatedly, are often accused of conspiracy even when their goals are, strictly speaking, perfectly legal. In Brown's novel, for instance, it is the villain's hope to malign the "good" secret society of the Freemasons as an evil conspiracy by publishing allegedly scandalous photographs of its members.

The Appeal of Mystery

Virtually all secret societies share as their attraction the promise to make sense of a world grown incomprehensibly chaotic and to provide a meaningful structure linking past and present. This meaning may reside in the "Lost Word" of Brown's novel; in the arcane lore of such orders as the Freemasons, Illuminati, Rosicrucians, Jesuits, or Templars; or in the teachings of such ancient religious cults as those of Demeter, Dionysus, or Isis. The secret knowledge that we possess within our own group or that we attribute to others is known technically as a mystery.

What do we mean by *mystery*? Etymologically the word is based on the Greek verb *muô* (to close or lock away), from which are derived the verb *mueô* (to initiate) and the noun *muêsis* (initiation). From these, in turn, stem the nouns *mustês* (initiate) and *mustêrion* (mystery). Accordingly the mystery is originally a secret doctrine to which only the initiates are privy: a doctrine that is "occult" (from the Latin and signifying "concealed"), "arcane" (from the Latin *arca*, signifying a chest in which something is hidden), or "esoteric" (from the Greek, meaning something concealed "most within"). In contrast to the public or exoteric religion that is accessible to everyone, the mystery is reserved for the initiates, a group often defined by the Latin word *cultus* (cult). In modern popular usage the term *mystery* has been broadened and trivialized far beyond its original and religiously profound meaning: to designate any unsolved problem (as in the contemporary murder mystery) or anything that is difficult to explain (as in "the mystery of the universe"). As expressed by one recent observer in an effort to explain the contemporary obsession with technology, "We may not believe in God anymore, but we still need mystery and wonder."[9]

One reason for the appeal of secret societies lies in what might be called the lure of the arcane. It is a basic human impulse to enjoy secrets, to be included in a special group that has privileged information about any subject that matters to the individual, whether government, finance, sports, the arts, or religion. In the mid-nineteenth century Thomas De Quincey wrote: "To be hidden amidst crowds is sublime—to come down hidden amongst crowds from distant generations is doubly sublime."[10] De Quincey was writing with a degree of cynicism about those who feel they are connected by "the grander link of awful truths which, merely to shelter themselves from the hostility of an age unprepared for their reception, must retire, perhaps for generations, behind thick curtains of secrecy." Yet his cynicism correctly identified a widespread phenomenon. A century later C. G. Jung observed that "there is no better means of intensifying the treasured feeling of individuality than the possession of a secret which the individual is pledged to guard. The very beginnings of societal structures reveal the craving for secret organizations."[11] This impulse accounts for the self-protective tendency among the young, but also among their seniors, to join teams, clubs, gangs, political parties, professional associations, and other circles.[12]

In a fundamental study published before the term *conspiracy theory* was coined, the German sociologist Georg Simmel identified some basic elements of secret societies.[13] They offer (a) exclusion against the broader social environment (b) by providing esoteric/exoteric meaning and (c) an intensification of the feeling of unity; (d) they demand absolute obedience (e) to unknown leaders; and (f) they achieve the sense of equalization by wearing masks or costumes. The collectivizing tendency has as its corollary the corresponding belief, especially in periods of social unrest and insecurity, that other groups must be responsible for the problems or conditions affecting us adversely—groups over which we have no control.[14] As Simmel points out, secret societies by their very nature are regarded by the existing central authority as hostile. Timothy Melley has called this belief "agency panic"—that is, "an intense anxiety about an apparent loss of autonomy, the conviction that one's actions are being controlled by someone else or that one has been 'constructed' by powerful, external agents."[15] (We will see that such agency panic is a common feature of conspiracy literature at least since Euripides.) In our eagerness to blame others for our problems, we feel an impulse to identify a specific enemy. Naming a conspiracy is simpler than undertaking the more complicated analysis of the motives and means of the institutions—financial, political, ideological, religious, military, and others—that constitute our society and easier than accepting the fact that a single deranged individual is responsible for an assassination or some other terrible act. The motivation depends on circumstances, but the impulse to seek conspiracies is universal and is not limited politically to left or right or socially to minority or majority status. Or on a more positive note: the popularity of millenarianism in its various religious, political, or social forms resides in no small measure in the reassuring feeling that history has a meaning or pattern and that present misery actually signals the imminent advent of the a new Golden Age, Paradise, or Utopia.

It is not necessary for the reader to give credence to the "mystery" or conspiracy in order to be interested. Most readers of contemporary thrillers do not "believe" in the sinister plots that Dan Brown and his fellow authors depict. Jane Austen, though widely read in the Gothic romances of her day, presumably did not regard as true their mysteries, which she satirized delightfully in *Northanger Abbey*. Similarly, the satire of Umberto Eco's *Foucault's Pendulum* depends, as we will see, on his extensive and skeptical acquaintance with conspiracy theories and conspiracy fictions from many centuries. Accordingly, the question of intent arises with considerable frequency: was the work meant as satire or as a serious critique?

In 1756 the young Edmund Burke published (anonymously) his first work, *A Vindication of Natural Society,* in which he spoke of "the lucrative Business of Mystery."[16] Burke was referring specifically to the "mysteries" held by "the Doctors of Law or Divinity," who used them to exploit a gullible public. It has been widely debated whether Burke's pamphlet was intended as a conservative's satire on the liberal belief in a natural as opposed to an "artificial" civic society as held by such contemporaries as Rousseau, or whether it was the serious attack of a youthful anarchist on the institutions of his society.[17] Certainly Burke had no love for the profession of law, which he had recently chosen to leave—an attitude that supports the second view. (The issue is still debated with regard to Burke's pamphlet, as it is in connection with such literary adaptations of secret societies as Euripides' *The Bacchae* or Goethe's *Wilhelm Meisters Apprenticeship* or, as we will see, the Rosicrucian manifestos and the alleged *Protocols of the Elders of Zion*.)

The Conspiracy Phenomenon

Contrary to the view expressed by many commentators focused on the present or recent past, our society today is not uniquely or even especially susceptible to the lure of the arcane and to the appeal of conspiracy as an explanation for current events.[18] To cite just a few examples to be discussed in the following chapters: the mystery cults of antiquity were cited by Greek rationalists as a factor in the decline of Athenian democracy and virtue; in the Renaissance it was widely rumored that the Rosicrucians instigated the Thirty Years' War for their own antipapal purposes; many in the late eighteenth century blamed the French Revolution on the Illuminati, who were believed to have fomented it as a vehicle to achieve their Enlightenment goals. The endurance and continuity of conspiracy theory is further suggested by the widespread imitations evident within the secret societies themselves. In the late twentieth century the anticommunist John Birch Society appropriated the cell structure of communism as the model for its national network of local chapters. A half-century earlier the anti-Catholic Second Ku Klux Klan (founded 1915) based its rituals, ranks, costumes, and crosses on practices of the Catholic Church.[19] For many European communists in the 1930s the party became a surrogate for the church, providing the faith as well as the structure of the religion they had forsaken.[20] The fabrication of the *Protocols* was based on earlier literary models. In the eighteenth century the Freemasons claimed the Egyptian cult of Isis as the historical source for their beliefs and rituals. The original Rosicrucians of the early seventeenth century derived their learning from Arabic sages. In classical antiquity the cult of Dionysus imitated the practices—notably the ecstatic dances—of earlier Asian worshippers. Although at many stages secret societies found their appropriate literary manifestation, it is important to realize at the outset that not every cult or order inspired a literary masterpiece and that not every period or culture brought forth its own literary variations.

The conspiracy phenomenon is ancient. People have believed in conspiracies presumably as long as there have been groups of at least three people in which one is convinced that the other two are plotting against him or her. In that sense one might look back as far as Eve and the serpent to find the world's first conspiracy. As we will see, the subject of the conspiracy varies considerably from age to age. Whereas recent generations have tended to find their conspiracies in politics and government, the past often sought its mysteries in religious cults or associations. In ancient Rome the senate sought to prohibit the cult of Isis lest its euphoric excesses undermine public morality and political stability. During the Middle Ages many rulers feared such powerful and mysterious religious orders as the Knights Templar.

All these factors help to account for the current popularity of conspiracy thrillers or, more generally, any fiction involving secret societies.[21] Popular fiction provides us with easy access to material that might otherwise require extensive historical, sociological, political, or psychological knowledge and research. As a German scholar recently put it more theoretically: such novels "demonstrate exemplarily the construction principle of conspiration-scenarios that reduce complexity by offering personalizing causal attributes for the confusing multiplicity of contingent sequences and series of events."[22] In addition, the appeal of the genre, which has broadened its scope from fiction to TV, film, and electronic games—all easily available on the Internet—resides to a great extent in its sheer entertainment value. The 1997 thriller-film *Conspiracy Theory* features a New York taxi driver who, obsessed by his theories, stumbles unwittingly into an actual governmental plot and is almost killed in the process (a plot anticipated, as we will see, by Eco's *Foucault's Pendulum*). We can observe from the safe remove of our theater seats or armchairs the machinations of conspiratorial groups and identify readily with the hero or heroine who unmasks and defeats them. We enjoy the "thrill" of grave threat—hence, of course, the name of the genre—without any personal danger or even discomfort. At the same time, we often learn something from these fictions because they are usually written by knowledgeable authors and often incorporate esoteric details about the various cults and secret societies they introduce. Although Euripides and Apuleius, Schiller and Mozart, do not provide us with the "Author's Note" and even bibliographies often appended to contemporary thrillers, they had firsthand knowledge of their arcane material, and their works often help scholars to understand past secret societies and conspiracies in their historical context. For instance, Apuleius's *The Golden Ass* includes the only extant depiction of the rituals of the Roman cult of Isis, and four centuries of Rosicrucianism are based on "manifestos" that are obviously literary fictions.

The following chapters trace the evolution of cults, orders, lodges, secret societies, and conspiracies through various literary manifestations—drama, romance, epic, novel, opera—down to the thrillers of the twenty-first century and observe how the lure of the arcane throughout the ages has remained a constant factor of human fascination as the content has shifted from religion by way of philosophy and social theory to politics and how, in the process, the underlying mythic pattern was gradually co-opted for the subversive ends of conspiracy.

CHAPTER ONE

The Mystery Cults of Antiquity

Classical antiquity was familiar with political conspiracies. The successful plot in 411 BCE to overthrow democracy in Athens and to establish the oligarchy of the so-called Four Hundred is one of the more notorious incidents of ancient Greek history. The Catalinarian conspiracy of 63 BCE in Rome resulted not only in the defeat and death of Cataline but also in four of Cicero's most eloquent orations. But these conspiracies, however important for rhetoric and history, rarely showed up in contemporary literature. Among extant Greek tragedies only Aeschylus's *Persians* had a contemporary historical subject, and it was taken from foreign, not domestic, affairs. While three of Aristophanes' comedies deal with political topics—the triad *Acharnians, Peace,* and *Lysistrata*—they do not feature conspiracies or mysteries. Similarly, although Horace and Catullus were personally close to the leading political figures of their day, they scrupulously avoided political topics in their poems; and, a few generations later, Juvenal was careful to satirize only the dead. The conspiracies and mysteries that caught the attention of writers along with their audiences and readers in Greece and Rome were religious in nature.

The Cult of Dionysus: Euripides' *Bacchae*

It has often occurred to me that the perfect bookends for one's shelf of Greek drama would feature images of Dionysus. Greek tragedy arose from the dithyrambs chanted in preclassical times to that popular deity; and it ended, as far as the extant texts are concerned, in 406 or 405 BCE with Euripides' posthumously performed *Bacchae,* in which Dionysus occupies one of the two central roles. More specifically, the images on our bookends should portray at the one end the bearded Dionysus, as revered by earlier generations (and as known from visual representations preserved on scores of mixing bowls and drinking cups), and at the other the beautiful, youthful, almost androgynous deity who emerged in rejuvenated form toward the end of the fifth century BCE and whom we recognize from later busts and statues.[1] In sum, Greek tragedy begins and ends with Dionysus, in whose magnificent theater on the south slope of the Acropolis the Athenian festivals known as the Great Dionysia were celebrated.

As one of the most heatedly debated and frequently performed Greek dramas and widely regarded as Euripides' most perfect work, *The Bacchae* is familiar today to many readers and theater audiences. According to the mythological background of the play, which is rehearsed in Dionysus's opening monologue and in the first choral song, or *parodos,* Dionysus is the son of Zeus and Semele, daughter of King Cadmus of Thebes. When Semele, being human, is destroyed by the exposed lightning-glory of Zeus, the god takes her unborn child into his own thigh and nurtures it to birth, concealing it from his possessive wife, Hera. Semele's three jealous sisters, denying that she had lain with a god, reported that her pregnancy resulted from a normal albeit illicit human union and that Zeus destroyed her for falsely claiming him as the father. Grown to maturity, Dionysus first establishes his religious sect in the Near Eastern lands of Lydia and Phrygia, where his mostly female worshippers or *maenads,* wearing fawn skin and carrying a *thyrsos* (a fennel staff crowned with ivy), roam the mountains in blissful groups known as *thiasoi,* dancing ecstatically *(oreibasia),* singing Bacchic hymns, and performing ritualistic orgies *(orgia)* characterized by *sparagmos* (the dismemberment of living beasts) and *omophagia* (the consumption of raw flesh).

As the play begins, Dionysus, disguised as a foreigner and accompanied by a chorus of female Asiatic worshippers, has recently arrived in Thebes, where, as punishment for their disdain of his mother, Semele, he has maddened his three aunts—Agaue, Ino, and Autonoe—dressed them in his ritual attire, and sent them off to Mount Cithaeron with the other women of Thebes to sing and dance in his honor. When Agaue's son Pentheus—who as Cadmus's grandson has inherited the kingship—returns to Thebes from a journey abroad, he is chagrined to learn that the women have left their homes and families to celebrate Bacchic revels in the mountains, where he suspects that they also engage in illicit sex. Even his grandfather Cadmus and the blind seer Tiresias have succumbed to the lure of the foreign wizard. Cadmus orders his men to find and arrest the pretender and to fetch the women down from the mountains. They return with the smiling and seemingly docile stranger but report that the women have escaped their chains and fled back to Mount Cithaeron. When the arrogant Pentheus tries to imprison the long-haired and effeminate alien, he is misled by his growing madness and mistakenly tries to fetter a bull, whereupon the prisoner escapes and, by supernatural means, causes the palace to burn and collapse.

Pentheus, finding the stranger again at ease outside the ruined palace, determines that he shall not escape a second time. At this moment a messenger arrives to report the startling events on the mountain: the bacchantes, led by Agaue and her sisters, drove away the men who tried to capture them, dismembered their flocks and herds with their bare hands, and rushed down to the plains, where they ransacked the villages and kidnapped the children. When the men took up arms against them, the women defeated them with their thyrsus staffs. Increasingly infuriated, Pentheus vows to lead his troops against the raving women, but the stranger dissuades him, saying that they can be overcome peaceably. He persuades Pentheus to disguise himself as a maenad—with a wig, long linen skirts, fawn skin about his shoulders, and a thyrsus—and then leads him up the mountain to spy on the revelers.

When from the glen where they conceal themselves Pentheus is unable to see the women, the god magically bends down a tall fir tree and lets Pentheus, seated on its branches, ascend to a lofty vantage point. But the women, who are quietly singing their hymns and replenishing the ivy garlands on their thyrsus rods, catch sight of him before he can observe their activities. Rushing over, they hurl stones and branches at the elevated Pentheus but are unable to reach him with their missiles. So they violently uproot the whole tree, causing Pentheus to fall to the ground, where in a frenzy they tear him limb from limb. Agaue, failing in her madness to recognize her own son, wrenches his left arm from its socket while her sisters and the other maenads seize and scatter other parts of his body. Finally Agaue impales his head on her thyrsus and carries it in triumph down the mountain and into the city of Thebes, parading it proudly in the mistaken belief that it is the head of a young lion.

In the final scene the horrified Cadmus, who has gathered his grandson's scattered body parts, confronts his manic daughter and gradually leads her to an awareness of her dreadful offense. The gods now punish the entire royal house, driving them into exile for the disrespect they all displayed by failing to acknowledge Dionysus's divinity and Zeus as his father. Dionysus appears on high in his true epiphany and proclaims that Cadmus and his wife, transformed into snakes, shall lead foreign armies against the Greek cities until, following the destruction of Delphi, they are defeated. As the play ends, the sobered Agaue wanders off with her followers to join her sisters, saying that she will go anywhere but back to Cithaeron with its terrible memories. In its own brief coda the chorus praises the unanticipated wonders accomplished by the gods.

The Bacchae is remarkable for several reasons. In the first place, unlike most other Greek tragedies, it is based not only on myth but also on an early historical event: the introduction into pre-Homeric Greece of the Eastern religion of Dionysus.[2] (Nietzsche and other nineteenth-century scholars mistakenly believed that Dionysus was a relatively recent addition to the Greek pantheon.) It is generally accepted that the cult of Dionysus in its primitive form—winter dances of frenzied maenads in the mountains with ritual *sparagmos* and *omophagia*—was no longer practiced in Athens at the time of Euripides.[3] According to present understanding the Dionysiac festivals in that sophisticated city were "occasions for old-fashioned country gaiety and a little old-fashioned country magic, as at the rural Dionysia; or for pious and cheerful drunkenness, as at the Feast of Cups; or for a display of the civic and cultural greatness of Athens, as at the City Dionysia."[4]

Toward the end of the fifth century BCE, however, civic life in Athens was severely disrupted by plague and the effects of the Peloponnesian War.[5] According to Thucydides the plague produced "unprecedented lawlessness" (bk. 2, 53) while the revolutions in city after city accounted for "a general deterioration of character throughout the Greek world" (bk. 3, 83).[6] The insecurity of the populace, nurtured by a loss of faith in the old gods, opened the way for a virtual invasion of such foreign deities as the Phrygian Cybele and Sabazios, the Minoan-Mycenaean Rhea or Meter, the Thracian Bendis, and others.[7] Four centuries later the historian Strabo listed this phenomenon among the leading characteristics of the times. "Just as in all other respects the Athenians continue to be hospitable to things foreign, so also in their worship of the gods; for they welcomed so many of the foreign rites that they were ridiculed therefor by comic writers; and among these were the Thracian and Phrygian rites."[8] At the same time, in reaction to the atheism of skeptical rationalists, these decades witnessed a series of notorious trials for impiety—Aspasia, Anaxagoras, Alcibiades, and Protagoras, among others—culminating in the condemnation of Socrates.[9] These developments, which produced a general transvaluation of values, significantly shaped what has been called Euripides' "theater of ideas."[10] More specifically, in his description of the ecstatic abandon of the primitive bacchantes Euripides confidently expected his audience to recognize the dangers inherent when a disintegrating civilization opened itself to the excesses associated with the various contemporary foreign cults that he condemned.[11]

In the second place, this final example from the canon of Greek tragedy contains several features that are conspicuously archaic. Notably, the chorus of Asiatic women as spokesperson for the Dionysiac religion in its various aspects assumes a more dynamic role here than in any drama since Aeschylus's tragedies a half-century earlier. Moreover, as one of the two protagonists Dionysus, not content with the role of deus ex machina to which deities were traditionally relegated, moves into the center of the dramatic action.

Finally, the tragedy involves an unusual amount of grotesque comedy. The two old men, Cadmus and Tiresias, present an almost clownish appearance as, dressed in fawn skin and crowned with ivy, they clumsily strike the ground with their thyrsus staffs and limp off to join the maenads in their mountain orgies. Later, having accepted the stranger's suggestion, the severe Pentheus looks no less absurd than his elders when he emerges from his palace clad in women's garments: the stranger tucks up a curl protruding from his wig like a girl primping her friend; Pentheus looks coyly over his shoulder to see if his pleats drape properly over his heels; and he attempts awkwardly to raise and lower his thyrsus in time with his right foot. When we see him for the last time, the dictator has been transformed into a buffoon.

Interpretations of *The Bacchae* have most often focused on the question of Euripides' attitude regarding the Dionysiac religion.[12] Many older commentators, arguing that the bestial actions of the Theban women in their mountain orgies do not exemplify the positive, even euphoric, view advanced by the Asiatic chorus in its *parodos* and first ode, believed that the elderly poet, at the end of his life, shifted from the rational skepticism of his youth and maturity to a wholehearted embrace of Dionysiac bliss (the so-called parodos theory).[13] More recent critics have tended to emphasize the gruesome actions of the Theban maenads in the mountains and the vengeful justifications of the chorus in its later odes, concluding that the poet intended his play as a rational warning against all religious extremism (the so-called propaganda theory).

Both approaches involve analyses of the two protagonists and the positions they represent: Dionysus, whose emblems include wine and ivy, embodies the vitality of nature *(physis)* and the human emotions, while Pentheus exemplifies

the civilized order *(nomos)* of the city and a blasphemous, even atheistic rationalism that curtly rejects all that the god represents. Both aspects are reflected in
further polarities in the action—for instance, the women who desert their looms
and shuttles in the city for the thyrsus staffs in the mountains. However, both
protagonists reveal conflicts in their character. Dionysus, whose promise of bliss
turns out to be the illusory product of drugged ecstasy,[14] forsakes the benign tranquility *(hesuchia)* that typifies his earlier behavior and reveals a cruel and vindic-
tive brutality, signaled by the frequent animal images of serpent and bull used to
characterize him, in his determination to force Thebes, even against its will, to
learn and respect the rites of his worship. At the same time, Pentheus's initial
ruthless self-control, which represses all human feeling, cracks as he reveals a
voyeuristic eagerness to watch the maenads at play (and, he thinks, at sex) in the
mountains. Accordingly, our view of the two characters shifts in the course of
the action. Our initial sympathy for the seemingly delicate and effeminate Dionysus at the mercy of a harsh Pentheus yields to compassion for all the members
of the House of Cadmus as the god takes his gleeful revenge: Pentheus in his
dreadful dismemberment, Agaue in the shocking consciousness that she has
massacred her own son, and Cadmus in his transformation into reptilian form
and expulsion from his city.[15] Moreover, the play would not offer genuine dramatic conflict or have true tragic impact if the two leading figures could not be
seen in some sort of dialectical balance.

For the purposes of this discussion, however, it is necessary to emphasize a
wholly different aspect of the play. We know that "secrecy was radical" in the
various cults, from the traditional Ephesian mysteries to the more recent foreign
cults[16]—so radical, indeed, that Aristophanes makes fun of it in *The Frogs* (esp.
lines 314–419), where Dionysus himself spies on the chorus celebrating the secret
rites of the Eleusinian mysteries. Precisely that secrecy is stressed in *The Bacchae*.[17] When Pentheus initially interrogates the captive stranger, he asks about
the rituals of Dionysus. The disguised god responds that those rituals are "not to
be disclosed" (line 472: *arrhêt'*) to the uninitiated and that it is not permitted by
law or custom (line 474: *ou themis*) for Pentheus to hear about them. Later Agaue
urges the maenads to shake Pentheus down from his tree to prevent him from
reporting the god's "secret dances" (line 1109: *chorous kryphaious*).

At the same time, it is Pentheus's desire to leave the security of the city and to
gain that secret knowledge that causes his downfall. In this connection we must
keep in mind the fact that Pentheus does not hear the early songs of the Asiatic
chorus and therefore knows nothing of the bliss promised to the followers of

Dionysus; he knows the Dionysiac rites only at secondhand from the various reports of the more questionable activities of the Theban women in their mountain orgies. From the beginning, moreover, it is evident that his eagerness is not a purely objective quest for knowledge or insights into a cult but is exacerbated by what an early critic called his "libidinous desire for witnessing secrets" *(libidinosa spectandorum secretorum cupido)*.[18] His very first speech betrays his suspicion that the Thracian women have run off to the mountains to service men illicitly in hidden places (lines 222–23). He concludes his opening tirade with the remark that nothing good can come of their festivities once women have tasted a bit of wine (lines 260–62). A few moments later he argues that Dionysus is "defiling their marriage beds" (line 353). When the stranger explains that his god's rites usually take place at night, Pentheus indignantly objects that nighttime is treacherous and corrupting for women (line 487). Later Pentheus imagines the women "like birds in a thicket in the most pleasant snares of the love-couch" (lines 957–58). Up on the mountain, complaining that his sight cannot reach them from the glen, he insists that he wants to "see the shameless conduct" (line 1062: *aischrourgian*) of the maenads. His voyeurism is emphasized by frequent occurrences of verbs for seeing, and when he has accepted the stranger's invitation to disguise himself as a maenad in order to witness the women's activities, forms of the word *kataskopos* (spy) and *kataskopê* (spying) are used by three different voices to designate Pentheus. Initially, he says that he simply wants to reconnoiter the scene (line 838: *molein eis kataskopên*) before dealing with the women. Then, when he emerges from the palace in his disguise, the stranger tells him that he looks just like a maenad, "a spy on your mother and her troop" (line 916: *kataskopos*). Finally, the now gloating chorus rejoices at the vengeance that will overtake the "maddened spy" (line 981: *lussôdê kataskopon*). It is his prurient inquisitiveness that undermines his reason and rational control and leads to his cruel death. Like the proverbial cat, Pentheus is killed by his curiosity.

While *The Bacchae* reflects the specific debate in the late fifth century regarding the role of foreign ecstasy-cults during the breakdown of Athenian civilization and presents a casebook study of a rational mind giving way to repressed emotions, it is not unreasonable to see in it a more general warning against the all-too-human desire to gain insight into secrets and arcane knowledge. For his part Dionysus clearly intends to spread his influence and thereby undermine the rational basis of existing society. Meanwhile, the audience is titillated at a safe remove by the spectacle.

From Chorus to Cult

If we accept the definition of a cult as "the system of a specific ritual and prayers for a single deity or a set of deities,"[19] then the followers of Dionysus in *The Bacchae*—the chorus of Lydian women and the murderous maenads on Mount Cithaeron—do not yet constitute a cult in any rigorous sense of the word. Their worship, to be sure, is centered around a specific deity. But only the Lydian chorus refers to any ritual practice; the women on the mountain simply run wild in their *oreibasia*. Only the Asian chorus appears in their opening songs to be familiar with some part of the myth associated with the ritual: Dionysus's birth. The Theban women worship Dionysus, wear his fawn skin, and carry his thyrsus but say nothing about his myth—and how could they, having been only recently driven by madness into their activities? Neither group, in sum, represents anything resembling systematic cult worship. This lack of cult status is immaterial as far as Pentheus is concerned: he is motivated principally by his political concern about the undermining of his authority by the foreign stranger and his lustful desire to observe the secret activities of the women on the mountain, whether or not they were systematized into a cult.

That is not to say that cult worship was unknown in Euripides' Athens. The Eleusinian mysteries, which emerged from the prehistoric worship of a mother- and earth-goddess named Demeter, developed by the late sixth century BCE from a local cult in Eleusis administered by noble families into an Athenian state cult with its own priests *(hierophantes)*, official torchbearers, and herald.[20] Every autumn the great celebrations took place during which thousands of Athenians and visitors set out on a pilgrimage along the sacred road to Eleusis. Most of the pilgrims were not initiates into the mysteries but simply observers of the public celebrations that involved white garments, holy objects borne in a special container *(cista mystica)*, and the sacrifice of a small pig. The actual initiation *(teletê)* into the mysteries took place in secret with rites *(dromena)* and words *(legomena)* that were both *arrhêta* (unspeakable) and *aporrhêta* (absolutely forbidden)—and, hence, largely unknown to the public then and still to scholars today.[21]

In the course of the fourth and third centuries BCE the Dionysiac orgies, which had hitherto been celebrated in loose associations such as the *thiasoi* of Theban women on the mountain, began to acquire firmer contours as a cult.[22] As we already know from Tiresias's speech in *The Bacchae*, Dionysus, the god of wine and all natural fluids, was welcomed as the necessary complement to Demeter, the goddess of grains and the dry products of the earth: the symbols of nature and culture, respectively. The inevitable result was what has been called the "bourgeoisification" *(Verbürgerlichung)* and "domestication" of the orgiastic cult and its removal from the mountains into the cities.[23] During the Hellenistic period the religions of Dionysus and Demeter, who were readily identified with the Roman deities *Liber* and *Ceres,* began to make their way into the Roman Empire and, to the extent of that identification with the existing religion, were tolerated and accepted.

The Romans, however, did not welcome the simultaneous invasion of the cultic worship of Dionysus, as it had developed in Lower Italy and Etruria. This was not because, in their generally ecumenical attitude toward public religions and private cults, they regarded private cults per se as a threat to traditional religion. Rather, they feared the Dionysiac cults because they encouraged a decay of morality and a sense of democratic equality among their initiates, who were often drawn from the politically unrepresented classes: notably women, slaves, and the plebeians. The rulers regarded these new cults, in contrast to the traditional cults that constituted Roman religion, as a threat to the existing social and political order.[24] Thanks to Livy's *History of Rome* (39.8-19) we have a lively, almost novelistic, account of the events that led in 186 BCE to the prohibition of the Dionysian cults—an account colored by Livy's own moral views and by his sense, familiar from Euripides, that the Bacchic cult represents chaos in contrast to the order of the state.[25]

A certain Greek, we are told, arrived in Etruria (modern Tuscany) as "a priest of secret nocturnal rites" (8.4-5: *occultorum et nocturnorum antistes sacrorum*). Following their initiation, men and women alike participated in feasts featuring wine, which destroyed all modesty and led them to practice promiscuous couplings (8.7: *stupra promiscua*) of every sort. (We recall that Pentheus worried about the corrupting effect of wine on women.) Soon the Etrurian evil made its way into Rome like a contagious disease. At first the evil was concealed within the vastness of the city, but at a certain point the consul Postumius heard about it.

A young man named Aebutius, having lost his father, was brought up by his mother and stepfather, who squandered his inheritance. To prevent him from taking any future actions against them, they decide to corrupt and blackmail the youth by initiating him into the Bacchic rites. Aebutius is devoted to a freedwoman and noble courtesan named Hispala, who formerly as a slave had been required by her mistress to attend the secret rites. Now she warns Aebutius against them, saying that the initiates become the victims of the priests and their disgraceful practices (10.8: *infanda*). When Aebutius, taking her advice, refuses to go along with his mother's plot, she and the stepfather throw him out of the house. When he tells his virtuous aunt Aebutia what happened, she urges him to report the matter to the consul Spurius Posthumius Albinus. The consul orders Hispala to reveal everything to him, promising her protection for her testimony about the nocturnal Bacchanals in the grove of Stimula (a goddess identified with Dionysus's mother, Semele). Though she fears that the cult members will tear her apart if she testifies, Hispala eventually relates everything: the origin of the mysteries, which were originally restricted to women and celebrated each year for three days; the expansion of the cult to include men and initiation rites for five days each month; and their obscene practices. To regard nothing as wrong or immoral (13.11: *nefas*), she says, was the chief doctrine of their religion.

As soon as Hispala completes her testimony, she is moved under protective guard into a safe house, and the consul takes the matter to the Senate, which is alarmed lest the conspiracies and nocturnal meetings (14.5: *coniurationes coetusque nocturni*) involve some betrayal or danger to the state. After the Senate issues its edict against further gatherings of initiates into the Bacchic rites—*Senatus consultum de Bacchanalibus*—Posthumius addresses the people of Rome, explaining the severity of the decree and its cruelty by stating that "there has never before been so much evil in the republic" (16.2-3: *numquam tantum malum in re publica fuit*). Rewards are offered for all information leading to the arrest of initiates, whose number according to Livy amounted to some seven thousand men and women. Those who did not flee were arrested and either executed or imprisoned. Hispala and Aebutius were rewarded handsomely for their information, which had brought the actions of the Dionysiacs to public attention.

The fierce repression of the cults and the denial of official veneration did not, however, preclude the popularity of Dionysus/Bacchus as god of wine in Roman culture. The frequency of his image in mosaics, along with depictions of cultic practices in the famous frieze in the Villa dei Misteri near Pompeii, provides adequate testimony for his lively survival. For our purposes, however, we must now turn from Dionysus to another foreign deity whose cult was not only condoned but became wildly popular in Rome as the sophisticated counterpart to the more plebeian god of wine.

Egyptian writings and images nowhere provide a connected narrative of the myth of Isis and Osiris, benevolent and just ruler of the Realm of Death and the most exalted of the Egyptian deities, but Plutarch's later treatise *De Iside et Osiride* (c. 115 CE) gives a reasonably accurate account synthesizing the various sources (chaps. 12–21).[26] Briefly: Osiris was the son of the Great Mother Nut, who, while married to the sun god Ra (or Re), conceived him through extramarital intercourse with the earth god Seb (or Geb). Eventually Osiris became king of Egypt, where he brought men out of their animal-like existence by training them in agriculture, giving them laws, and teaching them to worship the gods. When Egypt had been civilized, he left it under the rule of his sister and wife, Isis, while he himself set out to indoctrinate the other nations of the world. On his return he was murdered by his brother, Set, the incarnation of evil, who enclosed him in a beautifully wrought chest and set him adrift on the Nile. Isis eventually traced the chest to the Phoenician city of Byblos, where it had become enclosed within the trunk of a huge tamarisk tree, which in turn had been cut down and used as a pillar for the roof of the king's house. Isis managed to recover the chest with Osiris's body and took it back to Egypt. Set, discovering the chest, cut his brother's body into fourteen pieces, which he scattered across the land. Isis, with the help of Anubis, scrupulously collected the various body parts—all except the phallus, which had been tossed into the Nile and eaten by fish and which she replaced with an artificial member.

Isis and Osiris had a son, Horus, whom according to Plutarch they conceived while still brother and sister in Nut's womb. According to a variation of the myth the conception took place after Isis recovered and, in the form of a hawk, brought the dismembered body of her beloved brother and husband back to life—a scene frequently portrayed on monuments and papyri. However, her love, while it had the power to wake the dead, could not save Osiris from the netherworld. Despite his revivification by the winged Isis, Osiris was condemned to live out his life in the underworld and to become its god. On at least one occasion Osiris returned briefly to the world above to train Horus to regain the throne in battle with Set and to instruct him in his role as future king of Egypt.

This myth, which occupied a central place in ancient Egyptian religion, was brought to the Greco-Roman world following Alexander the Great's conquest of Egypt, and Isis was welcomed as a tutelary deity who offered guidance and protection for the dead on their road to the underworld. The goddess, who was identified with Demeter but also with the Greco-Roman goddesses of the underworld (Persephone/Proserpina) and of love (Aphrodite/Venus), provided a set of religious associations quite different from those of Dionysus or most other deities of Greece and Rome. Her cult spread rapidly in the Hellenistic states and notably within the urban bourgeoisie.[27] The worship was brought from Memphis to the island of Delos in the third century BCE by Greek-speaking devotees and, a century later, after the sack of the island in 88 BCE by the Persians, taken from there by Roman merchants to Italy, where it was disseminated by the usual trade routes. Initially the Senate sought by repeated edicts to prohibit the cult for many of the same moral and political reasons for which it had rejected the cult of Dionysus.[28] Amusingly, as in the case of the Dionysiac cult, it was again a sex scandal, as reported by the historian Josephus in his *Antiquities of the Jews* (18.3.2), that highlighted what many believed to be the shameful practices taking place in the temple of Isis at Rome in the early first century CE.[29]

A virtuous beauty named Paulina, though married happily, was desired by the unscrupulous Decius Mundus. When he failed in his attempt to buy her favors with the huge sum of two hundred thousand Attic drachmae for a single night of lovemaking, his maidservant Ide, "one skillful in all sorts of mischief," proposed another device. Knowing that Paulina was a devoted worshipper of Isis, she approached the priests of the temple and offered them fifty thousand drachmae if they would tell Paulina that she was desired by the god Anubis. Honored by this allegedly divine request, Paulina went to the temple, where, under the cover of total darkness, she spent the night with Mundus, assuming that he was the god. She spread the word of her divine honor to her husband and friends, who were greatly impressed. But two days later Mundus confronted her with the insulting revelation that he had possessed her for only fifty thousand drachmae instead of the two hundred thousand he had offered her. Paulina confessed "the wicked contrivance" to her husband, who immediately reported it to the emperor, Tiberius. After an examination of the facts, the emperor ordered the priests as well as Ide to be crucified, banished Mundus, demolished the temple of Isis, and in 19 CE prohibited the worship of the goddess. Again, as with Livy's tale of Aebutius and Hispala, the historical accuracy of Josephus's story of Paulina is less important than its exemplary value as an indication of public beliefs regarding the cult of Isis in the first decades of that century.

The rapid assimilation of Egypt into the Roman Empire during the imperial decades and the ensuing Egyptomania in Roman high society—high-class Roman hetaerae often served in the temples[30]—caused the worship of Isis to be approved as a *sacrum publicum* during the reign of Caligula (37–41 CE). During the next two centuries new temples were erected to the goddess, and her festivals were admitted to the Roman calendar and spread throughout the empire.[31] A symptom of the widespread interest in the cult can be seen in Plutarch's treatise (c. 120 CE). With the gradual victory of Christianity, the worship once again died out.

The Cult of Isis: Apuleius's *The Golden Ass*

Against this historical background we can now turn to the second major example from antiquity, in which the quest for forbidden knowledge involves a true cult and not simply a loose coven of frenzied women. Apuleius's *Metamorphoses,* better known as *The Golden Ass,* the only detailed account of a mystery cult surviving from classical antiquity, while not wholly autobiographical, appears to be based on the author's firsthand experiences with magic and cults—although there is no evidence that he was ever initiated into the cult of Isis. Born c. 123 CE at Madaurus in North African Numidia, Apuleius was educated at Carthage, Athens—where he was initiated into various cults[32]—and Rome and then returned to Oea (modern Tripoli) in North Africa, where he married Pudentilla, the wealthy widowed mother of an old friend. When jealous relatives accused him of winning her hand by means of magic, Apuleius defended himself successfully, as he relates in his *Apologia,* and was acquitted. Moving to Carthage, he achieved renown as a philosopher and rhetorician and was appointed chief priest of the province, where he died at an uncertain date.

His novel or, more accurately, romance *The Golden Ass* is related by Lucius, who at the outset is traveling on business from Corinth to Hypata (modern Ypati) in Thessaly. (Much later he is identified without explanation as "a poor man from Madaurus" [11.27: *Madaurensem . . . pauperem*].) Along the way he hears from fellow travelers stories of a witch who transformed men into various beasts: beavers, frogs, rams. At the same time, several experiences expose his curiosity and naive credulity—a trait that accounts for many of his future adventures. At Hypata he bears letters of recommendation to a certain Milo, with whom he lodges. His cousin Byrrhaena warns him against Milo's wife, Pamphile, who is known to be "a magician of the first order and master of every necromantic spell" (2.5: *maga primi nominis et omnis carminis sepulchralis magistra*). But Lucius, not unlike Pentheus, succumbs to an overwhelming curiosity (2.6: *curiosus alioquin*) to learn about sorcery and immediately rushes back to Milo's house, where he solicits the help of the maid Fotis (or Photis) in his endeavors. In the course of their erotic encounters Fotis reveals to him "the arcane mysteries" (3.5: *arcana . . . secreta*) of her mistress, who in magical ceremonies uses cuttings of their hair to win the attention of handsome young men who appeal to her. In addition, she can transform herself into an owl and fly to her trysts. Lucius, "ardently desirous of learning more about magic" (3.19: *coram magiae noscendae ardentissimus cupitor*), persuades Fotis to let him secretly observe one of those transformations.

He is so smitten by what he sees that he implores her to obtain for him some of Pamphile's magic ointment. Fotis obliges but mistakenly gives him an ointment that transforms him into an ass rather than a bird. She assures him that he can easily change himself back simply by eating some roses. But he is repeatedly prevented from doing so, and the next few books relate the adventures (after the fashion of the erotic and often scurrilous Milesian tales mentioned in the first sentence) that he experiences and witnesses and hears while in the body of an ass. (The most famous of these is the story of Cupid and Psyche, which takes up most of books 4 through 6.)[33] In this opening section, then, Lucius's adventures, with their frequent reversals of fate, amount virtually to a comic parallel to Pentheus's tragic fate. Again there is no cult involved; again the hero is drawn into his misfortune by his curiosity to witness the magical and sexual practices of a woman; but instead of the dismemberment that Pentheus suffers, Lucius undergoes only his transformation into an ass and the repeated beatings of the various owners through whose hands he passes.

At length Lucius is delivered from his unfortunate circumstances. Returning with a new owner from Thessaly to Corinth, he is now famous, having been taught various human tricks by an earlier master. Thanks to this renown, he is chosen to take part in the public punishment of a female poisoner: he is expected to have sex publicly with the woman in the great theater before wild beasts tear her apart and eat her. Unwilling to pollute himself in this manner and to be exposed to public ridicule, Lucius stealthily escapes and runs down to the nearby town of Cenchreae, the Aegean seaport of Corinth, where he falls asleep on the beach. From this point on, all of book 11, the final book of *The Golden Ass,* is devoted to the cult of Isis and Osiris.[34]

When Lucius the ass wakes up to a glorious full moon, he plunges his head into the sea seven times to purify himself and then prays to the goddess—whether she be Ceres, Venus, Diana, or Proserpina—to end his travail and transform him back to his human shape. Then he falls asleep again, whereupon, in a scene that could be either waking or dreaming, the goddess, moved by his prayer, appears and introduces herself as "the natural mother of all things, mistress and governess of all the elements, the initial progeny of worlds, chief of the powers divine, queen of all that are in hell" (11.4), and so forth.[35] Known to different peoples under different names, she is called by her true name only by the Egyptians: Queen Isis *(reginam Isidem).* She promises Lucius that she is prepared to help him if he commits his life to her worship. She announces that on the following day her priests will dedicate a new ship to her as an offering for the fresh season of navigation and that Lucius should attend and eat the roses carried by the chief priest in his right hand—the roses that, as he has long known, will effect his restoration to human shape.

Lucius follows her orders and, the next morning, watches the great procession from the town to the harbor. It is led by a parade of eleven strange figures—a soldier, a hunter, a transvestite, a gladiator, a magistrate, a philosopher, and others—that apparently recapitulate the various adventures of his past and, in their comic aspect, are hardly specific to the cult of Isis.[36] What follows, however, appears to be an accurate description of the public aspect of an actual Isiac ritual. Women carrying flowers and mirrors and young men with candles and torches, all dressed in white and singing, are followed by musicians and various temple officials calling for the way to be cleared for the goddess. Then follow the true initiates—women with anointed hair and men with shaven heads, all dressed in shining white garments. The high priests—the so-called shrine-bearers (11.17: *pastophores*)—bear various relics sacred to the goddess: a gold lantern, sacrificial pots, a palm tree fashioned of gold, the caduceus of Mercury, an open left hand as a token of equity, a winnowing fan, and a vessel for wine. They are followed by the dog-headed divine messenger Anubis, a cow representing the Great Mother, a priest carrying the secrets of the cult in a chest, and another bearing a vessel engraved with hieroglyphs and Egyptian images. When the high priest appears, holding in his right hand the timbrel (the *sistrum* typical of the Isis cult) and garland of roses, Lucius approaches and consumes the flowers. He immediately loses his animal form and recovers his naked human shape. The priest, ordering garments to cover him, tells him that his transformation had been "the sinister reward for his unfortunate curiosity" (11.15: *curiositatis improsperae sinistrum praemium*) and urges him, in order to enjoy future security, to join the cult, become a voluntary minister, and serve the goddess. The ceremony ends at the shore, where the various cult objects are deposited in a boat designed after the Egyptian model that, following its consecration, is launched without crew into the sea.

Up to this point we have witnessed the public or exoteric solemnities of the cult of Isis: ceremonies, like the procession from Athens to Eleusis, that any passerby might readily have witnessed.[37] It concludes with the purely fanciful magical act that completes the plot initiated in book 3 by Lucius's curiosity. In fact, the novel might well have ended at this point with Lucius's happy restoration. But, continuing for roughly a year longer, it depicts Lucius's three successive inductions to ever higher degrees in the esoteric cult of Isis.[38] The significance of these pages has been much debated, a debate that reminds us immediately of the discussion surrounding *The Bacchae:* did it mark the author's conversion to religion or his satirical critique of it? Here the debate varies between similar extremes. Some scholars argue that the novel is fundamentally to be taken as a serious religious text, a view that assumes a radical break in the tone and thrust of the narrative of books 1 through 10; while many insist that it is pure comic satire and nothing else.[39] Still others believe that with his authorial ambivalence between cult and comic Apuleius intentionally left the decision up to the reader.[40] Without entering the debate among classicists and historians of religion but considering these concluding passages from our specific point of view, we quickly ascertain that Lucius, while talking a great deal, actually betrays absolutely nothing about the secrets of the cult of Isis. Rather, he titillates the imagination of his readers by repeatedly promising insights that he then fails to deliver.

After the priests return to the temple, restore the relics to their proper places, and declare the season open to sea fare, Lucius visits with friends and relatives. He then rents a house within the premises of the temple, where each night the goddess appears, urging him to be initiated into the secrets of her religion (11.19: *sacris suis . . . initiari*). But Lucius, out of what he calls his "religious awe" *(religiosa formidine)*—actually, his concern about the rigors of her cult—hesitates. When the chief priest (11.20: *summus sacerdos*) appears to him in a dream, correctly foretelling that his lost belongings will arrive from Thessaly, Lucius is impressed by that sign and asks to be initiated. The priest insists that he must wait until he receives a proper command from the goddess because such instruction is a serious matter "corresponding to a voluntary death" (11.21: *ad instar voluntariae mortis*). So Lucius waits for some time until Isis appears again in a vision to proclaim that his time is at hand and that the high priest, Mithras, will be the "minister of his sacrifices" (11.22: *sacrorum ministrum*). He meets the priest, who tells him that he will now "be introduced to the most holy secrets of the religion" (11.22: *piissimis sacrorum arcanis insinueris*). From the innermost shrine of the temple he shows Lucius "certain books written with unknown characters" and decorated with images of strange beasts and "interpreted to me such things as were necessary to the use and preparation of mine order." Lucius then charges his companions to buy the things he needs. (Harrison argues that the repeated references to the cost of initiation are another sign of Lucius's naiveté and the satire of religion.)[41] After washing and purification the priest takes Lucius back into the temple and gives him "a charge of certain secret things unlawful to be uttered" or, more literally, "secretly entrusted me with certain things that transcend utterance" (11.23: *secretoque mandatis quibusdam quae voce meliora sunt*).

(We note that we, the readers, have still learned nothing.) He orders Lucius to fast for ten days. On the day of dedication priests of Isis arrive from all over, presenting Lucius with gifts. Then all noninitiates are ordered to leave, and Lucius is led to the inmost shrine of the temple (11.23: *sacrarii penetralia*). At this point the narrator tells the studious reader that we would no doubt like to know what was said and done there and assures us that he would gladly tell us "if it were lawful for you to hear" *(si liceret audire)*. In compensation, however, he tells us generally that he approached the underworld and the gates of Proserpina, saw the sun shine brightly at midnight, and encountered the gods of the underworld and the heavens. Then he warns us that we (having learned nothing!) must conceal what we have heard.

When morning comes he emerges from the temple in a fine garb that he is not prohibited from describing since many noninitiates saw him at that time. A great celebration takes place, at which Lucius delivers an oration to the goddess Isis. Then, without a further word of explanation, he packs up his belongings and, following the command of the goddess, sets out for Rome. He arrives, he tells us precisely, on the evening before the Ides of December and goes straightway to the great temple of Isis in the Campus Martius. There, to his great astonishment—for he believes that he has already been adequately initiated (11.27: *plenissime initiatus*)—he is ordered in his dreams to receive a new consecration. He reasons that, although initiated into the cult of Isis, he is not yet a member of the order of Osiris, which requires an entirely different ceremony. He goes to a priest of that order, who tells him he had been notified of the visit of a "poor man from Madaurus," whom he should initiate into the mysteries. Lucius, impoverished from the costs of his first initiation in Cencreae, sells what little remains to him and makes some extra money by arguing cases in the law courts. Then he again fasts for ten days, shaves his head, and is inducted into "the nocturnal ceremonies of the great god" (11.28: *principalis dei nocturnis orgiis*). (Again we note that Lucius has paid money to the temple and that we, the readers, have learned nothing new. In addition, exposed with his shaved head to the ridicule of the Romans, he reminds us of Cadmus and Pentheus in their maenadic garb.)

To his amazement the goddess appears to him yet again, saying that his initiation into a third order is required: an honor worthy of rejoicing since so few are summoned more than once. Again, and in a correspondingly brief passage (since we now are familiar with the routine), Lucius goes to the priest, fasts for more than ten days, and buys the necessary accoutrements. A few days later Osiris, "the ruler of the greatest" (11.30: *maximorum regnator*), appears to him in his dreams and announces that Lucius should now win glory as an advocate in the courts and that he should not serve the mysteries as a priest but within the ancient college of *pastophores,* an office that Lucius with his shaven crown executes with great joy for the next five years—and no doubt to the profit of the cult.

It is difficult, given the lack of any true insight into the teachings of the Isiac cult, to agree with the reasoning of those who regard book 11 as a religious manual. It is easy, in contrast, to appreciate the arguments of those who see in Lucius the naive and comical victim of shrewd priestly maneuvering—especially since the high priest of Isis bears a name associated with the enormously popular cult of Mithras. As in *The Bacchae* it is persuasive to see Lucius's physical and spiritual metamorphoses as an argument against undue curiosity: first into the machinations of the Thessalian witch Pamphile and later into the mysteries of the cult of Isis. The first causes him to lose his humanity, the second to forsake his worldly possessions and individuality and to put his forensic talents at the service of the cult. In neither case do we have reason to believe that he learns any true secrets— certainly the reader does not.

In sum, both Euripides and Apuleius achieve the popularity of their respective works in part by appealing to precisely that same trait of human nature and cynicism that responds in the twenty-first century to conspiracy theories and to the works of Dan Brown and his fellow conspiracy-novelists.[42] For we must always remember that Euripides' audiences were, and are still, not for the most part Dionysiac enthusiasts, any more than Apuleius's readers were or are Isiac worshippers at any stage of initiation.

CHAPTER TWO

The Order of Knights Templar in the Middle Ages

The lure of the arcane appears to be magnetic. Just as mythic or historical figures such as Gilgamesh, Heracles, or Parzival are often surrounded by tales and adventures borrowed from altogether different sources, one mystery often attracts another. Thus, for instance, in the twelfth century the mythic unicorn became associated with the equally mythic carbuncle stone that glows in the dark.[1] The animal and the stone had led separate mythic existences for centuries. But when in Christian bestiaries and lapidaries the unicorn—for its purity and its reputed capture only by a virgin—and the carbuncle—for its healing power and luminosity in the dark—began to be taken as symbols for Christ, they were soon brought together. In Wolfram von Eschenbach's *Parzival* (482,24–483,1) we learn, for instance, that the carbuncle grows under the horn of the unicorn:

ein tier heizt monicirus:

. . . .

wir nâmen den karfunkelstein
ûf des selben tieres hirnbein,
der dâ wehset under sînem horne.
[There's an animal called unicorn:

. . . .

we took the carbuncle stone

from the same animal's headbone
that grows there beneath its horn.]

It is therefore hardly a surprise when that same poet combines two other hitherto separate mysteries of the early thirteenth century: the Knights Templar and the Holy Grail.

The Order of Knights Templar

Although Jerusalem was captured by the First Crusade in 1099, the route to the Holy City was still by no means safe for pilgrims, who could be assaulted by robbers on the way from the coast, by Egyptians coming from the south, and by Turks lurking in the north.[2] King Baldwin II and the Patriarch of Jerusalem welcomed it in 1118, therefore, when Hugues of Payens (Champagne), who was born in a chateau only a few miles north of Troyes, offered his small band of knights— their initial number is traditionally given as nine—to protect pilgrims seeking to visit Jerusalem, the River Jordan, Galilee, and other places sacred to Christians. The king provided the knights, who were dedicated to monastic poverty and chastity, with quarters in his palace in the al-Aqsa mosque on Jerusalem's Temple Mount, reputedly the site of the Temple of Solomon, and the group quickly became known as "The Military Order of the Knights of the Temple of Solomon" or, for short, Knights Templar. Ten years later Hugues, as its first Master, traveled to Europe to publicize the order (which in the meantime had grown to about thirty), to recruit more knights, and to obtain broader authority for his order than that of the Patriarch of Jerusalem. He was successful that same year at the Council of Troyes, where his countryman and friend St. Bernard of Clairvaux— himself a former knight and the most prominent theologian of the age—gave the order his enthusiastic endorsement and drafted the first Rule of the Poor Knights of Christ and of Solomon's Temple *(Regula pauperum commilitonum Christi Templique Salomonici)*: seventy-two clauses outlining in essentially Cistercian terms the rules governing the beliefs and behavior of the knights, specifying even such details as diet, clothing, and speech. The knights could not own chests with locks, hunt with hawks, or without permission receive letters from parents or friends. Paragraph 70 emphatically proclaimed the rule of chastity: "The company of women is a dangerous thing, and the devil has turned many men from the path to paradise by providing female company."[3] With Bernard's backing the order rapidly expanded, gaining financial support through donations of money, slaves, buildings, and estates—initially in France but soon thereafter in England and Spain, where the assistance of the Templars against the Moors was eagerly accepted.

A few years later Bernard offered further moral support to the Knights of the Temple with his treatise "in praise of the new knighthood" (*Liber ad Milites Templi De Laude Novae Militiae* [1135]), which provided a theological justification for "holy violence" or just war, arguing that "the knights of Christ fight the battles of their Lord in safety, not fearing to have sinned in killing the enemy, nor fearing for their own deaths, since neither dealing out death nor dying, when for Christ's sake, contains anything criminal but rather merits glorious reward."[4] Upon Hugues's death in 1136 he was succeeded as Master by the Burgundian nobleman Robert de Craon, and a subtle shift took place in the order's ethic. Whereas Hugues admired the monastic environment of Clairvaux and adhered to the religious ideals of his friend St. Bernard, Robert's orientation was more courtly, knightly, and chivalrous; he was also a skilled administrator and organizer. It was at this juncture that the order became a true synthesis of monk and knight, of church and court, of mysticism and chivalry—the unique combination for which it became renowned.[5] At the same time the charter of the order was broadened by the papal bull *Omne Datum Optimum* (1139) of Innocent II, which placed the order directly under the authority of the pope and, reaffirmed several times in the course of the century, assured the jurisdictional and economic independence of the Templars from both local church and local government. The order, now virtually a state within a state, was permitted to bury its dead in its own cemeteries and, from 1147 on, to wear the insignia with which its image entered history and heraldry: the red cross on a white background.

Paradoxically, while the wealth of the order both in the West and Outremer (its territories "beyond the sea") rapidly expanded, its actual military accomplishments, while often spectacular, were not politically significant. The Second Crusade of 1148–49 was a failure despite acts of great heroism by the Templars: courageous but often foolhardy, they were accused by their critics of acting rashly and taking risks simply for the sake of glory and booty. Although they acquired a number of castles in Jerusalem and Syria extending from Gaza to Antioch, their reputation was tainted by growing accusations of pride and avarice. Although many of the Templars remained illiterate, some learned Arabic and were able to function as translators in transactions with the enemy. Allegedly, they accepted payment from the Syrian Assassins to avoid direct military conflict with them. It was also rumored that they carried out treacherous acts—in 1173, for instance, killing a Syrian envoy traveling under safe conduct of the king and patriarch of Jerusalem—in order to prevent a peace alliance that threatened to undermine their entire existence, which depended on war. Their martial reputation was further damaged in 1187 when they were decisively defeated and slaughtered by Saladin at the Battle of Hattin—a humiliating defeat that led to the fall of Jerusalem and, in 1191, to the shift of the order's headquarters, along with that of the Latin Patriarch, to Acre and to the occupation of Cyprus. As their influence in the East waned, their power shifted to Europe.

While they fought without strategic sophistication, often outmaneuvered by the Arabs and notably by Saladin, they enjoyed enormous tax- and tithe-free success in finance and commerce, becoming as bankers to popes and monarchs more of an international financial organization than a military force. During the twelfth century their promissory notes provided the principal and safest means of transferring money from country to country while their castles and manors offered secure deposit vaults for goods and treasure. Their wealth was such that they could lend money to prospective pilgrims for their trips; convey them in their fleets; then house, feed, and protect them upon arrival in the East—all for considerable profit.

The envy and hostility aroused by the privileges granted through papal bulls, by their vainglorious deeds, and by the secrecy of their order led increasingly to resentment among the clergy, the nobility, and the populace, including charges of heresy, blasphemy, sexual license and sodomy, usury, and treason. It was rumored that their initiation rites required the initiate to spit on the cross, deny Christ, and kiss the backside of the officiator. Disputes with their knightly competitors in the East, the Hospitallers, intensified. Archbishop William of Tyre in his informative chronicle never tired of criticizing the Templars in the Holy Land for forsaking the original ideals of the order. As early as 1160 Pope Alexander had to issue a bull prohibiting people from dragging Templars from their horses and otherwise abusing them.[6] By 1207 even their papal advocate Innocent III issued a bull *De Insolentia Templariorum*. As Henry Osborn Taylor remarked in his classic work *The Medieval Mind*, "among the laity the gap between the ideal and the actual may best be observed in the warrior class whose ideals accorded with the feudal situation and tended to express themselves in chivalry."[7] The knights were no worse than other classes, he continues; but the contrast between their professed ideals and the feudal reality was glaring. "Feudalism itself presents everywhere a state of contrast between its principles of mutual fidelity and protection, and its actuality of oppression, revolt, and private war." Taylor summarizes that the history of the Templars "shows the necessary as well as inevitable secularization of a military monastic order."[8]

At the beginning of the thirteenth century, in sum, the Knights Templar enjoyed a remarkably mixed reputation of admiration and envy, of respect and suspicion.[9] As I suggested in connection with the ancient mystery cults, what matters here is not the historical truth, which still today remains unclear and in dispute, but rather the beliefs commonly held among contemporaries. Still praised in many quarters for their early reputation for poverty, chastity, and bravery—the very model of the monastic knight—they were censured and feared for a variety of more worldly sins believed to be concealed by the secrecy of their order. As the age of chivalry along with the Crusades waned in the course of the thirteenth century, the order lost its raison d'être. The criticisms led ultimately in 1312 to its suppression, and two years later the last Master, James of Molay, was burned at the stake—ostensibly for blasphemy but in actuality for reasons of realpolitik: King Philip IV wanted to seize the order's vast resources to cover his enormous debts. (In fact, he failed because the forewarned Templars had already hidden their treasure.) In the meantime, and in subsequent centuries, the secrecy surrounding the order fostered rumors and generated the lure of the arcane: among others, the association of the Templars with another mystery of the age, the Holy Grail.

The Legend of the Grail

The quest for the Grail, having never ended, is pursued by scholars today at least as avidly, and often as fiercely, as by the knights of yore. Very little is certain regarding the Grail—not its etymology, its shape, its function, its seekers, and most assuredly not its source. According to the most widely accepted etymology, Helinand of Froidmont's thirteenth-century *Chronicon,* the French word *graalz* or *graal* was derived from the Latin vocable *gradalis,* designating a large flat dish on which food delicacies with their sauces were arranged in graded ranks for service to the wealthy: *scutella . . . in qua pretiosae dapes cum suo jure divitibus apponi gradatim.*[10] As first described in poetry by Chrétien de Troyes, the Grail, albeit a platter made of gold and encrusted with jewels ("de fin or esmeré . . . pierres prescïeuses"), contains neither lamprey nor salmon (that is, no foodstuffs) but only a single host wafer ("une sole oiste").[11] In other works and depictions it is described or portrayed as a chalice, a ciborium, a cup, or a stone. In some texts it holds, as we have seen, only a wafer for a single individual; in others it magically feeds multitudes whatever food and drink, hot and cold, they may desire. It is sought generally by all the knights of King Arthur's Round Table but most notably by Lancelot, Galahad, and Parzival. But it is above all the source of the Grail for which the quest goes on.

The origins of the Grail have been sought as far afield as in Jewish legend, in Iranian myth, and in Caucasian epic tales.[12] Essentially, however, three principal theories have contended for acceptance. The earliest believers in the Middle Ages attributed the Grail to Christian tradition. According to Helinand's *Chronicon* the *gradalis* was a "bowl or dish from which the Lord dined with his disciples" (*de catino illo sive paropside, in quo Dominus cenavit cum discipulis suis*).[13] Helinand based his definition on the fictitious account in Robert de Boron's late twelfth-century Old French prose romance *Joseph d'Arimathie*, which amounts virtually to "a new apocryphal gospel."[14] According to Robert, who based his work on both canonical and apocryphal gospels, the Grail was the vessel used at the Last Supper; later Joseph, having obtained the treasured object from Pontius Pilate, used it to collect the drops of blood oozing from the still bleeding body of Christ when he and Nicodemus removed it from the cross and washed it.[15] Robert goes on to relate how the vessel was brought to Britain, where it was rapidly assimilated into local folklore.

Jessie L. Weston, dissatisfied with the theories of Christian legendry and folklore and inspired by James G. Frazer's *The Golden Bough*, argued in *From Ritual to Romance* (1920) that the Grail story stemmed anthropologically from "an ancient Ritual, having for its ultimate object the initiation into the secret of the sources of Life, physical and spiritual," and dedicated to a deity of vegetation.[16] Weston's classic work, which has received widespread attention thanks to the acknowledgment in T. S. Eliot's notes to *The Waste Land* (1922), provided the initial impulse for Roger Sherman Loomis's investigations; but in the course of several books and articles from 1927 on he eventually rejected her anthropological theory and became the most vociferous advocate of the Celtic origin. In a late summa he stated his final conviction that the Grail legends "form a branch of the Arthurian cycle"; that "the starting-point of the Grail tradition was Ireland" and that the Irish sagas passed over to Wales, where they were absorbed into similar local traditions; that the Grail castle was "originally a Celtic Elysium"; and that the transmission of Celtic legend to the non-Celtic world was "accomplished almost entirely by the cousins of the Welsh, the bilingual Bretons."[17]

We have no need to engage in the disputes among medievalists regarding the sources of the legend, whether Christian, anthropological, or Celtic. What matters here is the simple fact that, by the late twelfth century, belief in the Grail existed—a belief no doubt enhanced by the contemporary obsession with holy relics stemming from the Crusades and reaching its peak following the fall of Jerusalem in 1191, when such relics became rarities. The Grail was first—that is, before Robert de Boron—introduced into the so-called *matière de Bretagne* by Chrétien de Troyes in *Le Conte du Graal* (c. 1180), his final and longest, albeit uncompleted, romance, where it constitutes a central symbol, although it had not yet assumed its subsequent associations: it is once called "a sacred object" (v. 6425: "sainte chose"), but its sanctity appears to derive more from the host it bears than from its own history, which is never mentioned. Perceval fails initially in his quest because, when he first sees the jewel-encrusted vessel carried by a lovely damsel past the table where he is dining with the Rich Fisherman ("le riche Pescheor") into another room, he fails in his naiveté to ask who is served from it. He later learns that it is his own uncle, father of the Fisherman, who is nurtured by the consecrated wafer that is brought to him each day in the Grail. Chrétien's account of Perceval breaks off at this point, and we never learn from him what happens if and when Perceval returns to the Grail Castle. For our specific purposes: Chrétien never identifies the knights of the Grail Castle with the Templars— oddly enough, it would seem, since he was a fellow countryman of Hugues de Payens, as well as Bernard of Clairvaux. That task awaited his German successor, Wolfram von Eschenbach.

The Cult of the Grail in Wolfram's *Parzival*

Wolfram claims to have a better source than Chrétien for his knowledge of the story: a Provençal "Master Kyot," who became acquainted with the marvels of the Grail in a work by the "heathen" (that is, Arab) Flegetanis that he found in Toledo.[18] According to Flegetanis, the skilled astrologer who read the secret in the stars, the "thing called the Grail" (454,21: "ez hieze ein dinc der grâl") was brought down from heaven by a troop of angels, who left it on earth to be guarded by "a baptized progeny" (454,27: "getouftiu vruht") bred and dedicated to a pure life.[19] This Grail is not a vessel but a stone—also known as "Lapsit exillîs" (a pseudo-Latin phrase whose meaning is still unexplained)—with wondrous powers. By virtue of this stone, for instance, the Phoenix, having been burned to ashes, is reborn more brightly than before. Moreover, however ill a mortal may be, he cannot die for a week after he has beheld the stone. Anyone who should look regularly at the stone in the course of two hundred years would keep a complexion as fresh as in his youth. The marvelous power of the stone is restored each year on Good Friday, when a dove descends from heaven with a small wafer, which it deposits thereupon and by virtue of whose power the stone produces all food and drink that the earth bears—but of paradisal excellence.

This Grail is kept at a place called Munsalvaesche in a building described as a castle *(burc)* or, more frequently, a palace *(palas)* of enormous wealth. Wolfram takes pleasure in portraying the elaborate fixtures: cups and dishes of gold, rich carpets, beds of aloes wood adorned with precious stones and with posts of viper's horn, brocade cushions, and silk mattresses. But he makes the point most effectively by stating that Parzival, when he becomes King of the Grail at Munsalvaesche, and his brother Feirefiz, dividing between themselves the wealth of West and East, are the richest men on earth (796,22–25). The term *tempel* occurs only once (816,15), to designate the room within the palace where the stone is kept and from which it can be removed only by a virgin. It is attended by a company of men and women who come to Munsalvaesche as children from many countries and must remain chaste as long as they remain on the premises. However, both women and men go out into the world from time to time—the women publicly and the men secretly—to marry in the hope of producing children who will in turn go to Munsalvaesche and serve the Grail. (We learn shortly before the end of book 16 that Templars who take on such foreign service must forbid people to ask their name or lineage: an anticipation of the story of Parzival's son Loherangrin, the Swan Knight, who must leave his wife in Brabant when she learns his name.) No one can reach the Palace of the Grail who has not been proclaimed by heaven as destined for it by an inscription that appears along the top edge of the stone—a name that disappears as soon as it has been read. Moreover, the stone is not visible to non-Christians: Parzival's heathen half-brother Feirefiz must be baptized before he can behold its wonder. Clearly, Wolfram's "grâl" is quite different from the bejeweled host-bearing platter of Chrétien or the ancient holy vessel of Robert de Boron.

The Palace of the Grail at Munsalvaesche is protected by a "knightly brotherhood" (470,19: "ritterlîchiu bruoderschaft") who must remain chaste (493,24: "mit kiuscheclîchen güeten") and forgo women's love. Only the king and those who are sent out into the world may enjoy marriage and sexual love. Constantly in search of adventure, the knights ward off anyone seeking without divine proclamation to approach the stone: knights whom Wolfram—for the first time and unlike either Chrétien or Robert de Boron—regularly denotes as Templars *(templeise)* and who must refrain from frivolity (473,3: "lôsheit") and maintain humility (473,4: "diemuot") in their lives. The name first occurs when Parzival, before he has attained sufficient maturity, unwittingly strays into the forbidden territory. (On the earlier occasion when he visited Munsalvaesche [bk. 5], he did so on the invitation of the Rich Fisherman, but in that passage the knights are not yet called Templars.) He is warned by a Templar in shining armor that Munsalvaesche does not permit anyone to approach so near without fighting a battle to the death. Parzival defeats the Templar and appropriates his horse but fails on this occasion to find his way to the Palace of the Gral.

From these and other indications, then, we conclude that Wolfram's grâl is a sacred object and constitutes the center of a cultlike society whose secrets and powers are known only to chosen initiates. A celebration of the cult in the presence of the King of the Grail and his knights is elaborately described in book 5. The great door to the hall is thrown open, and a procession of twenty-four handsomely clad ladies and maidens enters, bearing golden candelabras, ivory trestles, candles, a tabletop of precious stone, and a pair of silver knives. The princess enters bearing "the wish of paradise, a thing called the Grail" (235,23: "daz was ein dinc, daz hiez der grâl"), and sets it on the table before the king. The four hundred knights, seated at a hundred tables and served by almost twice that number of pages, receive from the wondrous stone, each according to his desire, food both hot and cold and beverages of every kind. Following the meal, the procession leaves the room with the stone as ceremoniously as it entered.[20]

The guardians of the Grail, the "templeise," resemble the historical Templars in several senses. As we have seen, they inhabit a palace and not Solomon's Temple; and their symbol is the turtledove, not the red cross on a white field. Yet both are knightly monkish orders; both orders enjoy vast wealth in their palaces; both require an initiation; initiates to both are sworn to secrecy; and both are said to worship an idol (Wolfram's "grâl"-stone and the various idols that the Templars were accused of venerating).[21] To this extent Wolfram's "templeise" not only reflect the positive values attributed initially to the Templars; even the negative aspects—the wealth, the secrecy, the idolatry—are given a positive twist. (The fact that the knights of Munsalvaesche are not yet designated as "templeise" in book 5 suggests that Wolfram's own views changed in the course of the lengthy composition and that he only gradually came to identify the Templars with the Holy Grail.)

Finally, it needs to be stressed that the Templars are contrasted with the knights of King Arthur's Round Table, who in all their knightly virtue are utterly worldly and secular as opposed to the saintly protectors of the Grail. The two groups represent the medieval poles of knighthood and religion, church and state, the realms through which Parzival journeys on his quest for the Grail.[22] It is important to understand that at no point does Wolfram suggest that either of the two realms is defective or superior to the other. The realms of religion and knighthood as he first experiences them are imperfect: the primitive Christian community that his mother, Herzeloyde, has created in the forest of Soltane and the arrogance and cruelty exhibited by members of Arthur's court when he first irrupts into it.[23] But both worlds are ultimately redeemed by heroes motivated by unsullied knighthood and pure religious compassion: Gawan and Parzival. We might reasonably conclude that Wolfram's principal concern was for the dangers of an oversecularized knighthood that was losing all sense of its original religious values.

Parzival's Quest

Parzival's quest takes up less than half of Wolfram's verse epic, *Parzival* (completed c. 1210), which is generally regarded as one of the masterpieces of medieval literature. The first two of its sixteen books relate the adventures of Parzival's father, Gahmuret; seven books (7–8, 10–14) follow the adventures of the Arthurian knight Gawan; the remaining seven books (3–6, 9, 15–16) are devoted to Parzival. The contrast between the two medieval institutions—Round Table and Gral, state and religion—is exemplified on an individual level by the careers and adventures of the two knightly heroes.[24]

Parzival's quest gradually reveals itself as a medieval parallel to Lucius's quest for initiation into the cult of Isis. When Parzival arrives in Terre de Salvaesche and meets a gentleman fishing in a lake, we already know a great deal about him. He is the son of King Gahmuret and Queen Herzeloyde, rulers of several kingdoms. Gahmuret—who has already sired an older son, the speckled Feirefiz, from the black queen Belacane of Zazamanc—has been killed before the walls of Baghdad. When she receives the news, Herzeloyde disposes of her wealth and kingdoms and retires into the forest solitude of Soltane, forbidding her trusted attendants ever to mention "knighthood" in the presence of her son, lest he follow in his father's footsteps and suffer a similar early death. Parzival is raised as a true naïf, ignorant of his father, his heritage, even his own name, but skilled as a huntsman and sensitive to the sweet sounds of the birds. His formal instruction in religion is equally neglected although his mother leads an exemplary proto-Christian life: she tells him only that God is brighter than the day while the lord of hell is black and treacherous, lacking the primary knightly quality of loyalty or trustworthiness *(triuwe)*. So when in his teens he encounters in the forest four knights in glittering armor, he thinks in his simpleminded literalness that they are gods. When they laughingly inform him that they are only knights, he hears the fateful word for the first time and urgently inquires how one becomes a knight. From King Arthur, they tell him, surmising from his radiant if ragged beauty his noble heritage.

Reporting this encounter to his chagrined mother, Parzival implores her to permit him to seek out King Arthur and to obtain knightly honors for himself. With a heavy heart she gives her consent, but not without imparting four bits of advice, which her son takes literally to heart: cross streams only where the water is clear; greet everyone courteously; accept gratefully the advice of any experienced gray-haired man; and seize every opportunity to take a lady's kiss and her ring. On the following morning, clad in the fool's habit in which his mother has dressed him, he sets off so excitedly that he fails to notice that Herzeloyde falls dead of sorrow behind him.

Following a stream to a clear and shallow ford, he sees a beautiful noblewoman asleep beneath an awning. Heeding his mother's words in the most literal sense, he leaps upon the lady, stealing both her kisses and her ring—an act that provokes dire consequences for the lady Jeschute with her husband. Later he comes upon another woman, grieving over her dead lover, who turns out to be his cousin Sigune. Recognizing him from his words, she reveals to him his name and heritage.

The next day, passing a knight whose splendid red armor arouses his envy, he arrives at King Arthur's court. Impressed with the youth's appearance despite the fool's garments he wears, Arthur promises to equip him as a knight. But Parzival demands the armor of the Red Knight he has seen outside. Putting aside fears for the lad's safety, Arthur promises him that he may have it if he can win it. Despite his inexperience, and to everyone's astonishment, Parzival succeeds in slaying the knight with his hurled javelin—the first and only killing that he will commit—and strips the knight of his armor.

Parzival arrives that evening at the castle of Prince Gurnemanz. Recognizing the youth's quality despite his rough ways, the elderly gentleman takes him under his tutelage for two weeks and teaches him the rules of knightly and courtly culture, which Parzival takes as literally to heart as his mother's precepts: to practice compassion, humility, and moderation; to be manly and brave; to spare those he has defeated in battle; to cleanse himself after battle so that he may be attractive to women; and, fatefully, not to ask many questions (171,17: "ir ensult niht vil gevrâgen"). With these lessons in mind, Parzival rides off to the kingdom of Brobarz, where he liberates the beleaguered city of Belrepeire and wins the hand of its queen, the beautiful Condwiramurs (bk. 4). After a time, however, he takes leave of his beloved wife in order to visit his mother and go in search of further knightly adventure.

Arriving at a lake, Parzival asks directions from a handsomely clad gentleman who appears to be fishing (bk. 5). The fisherman sends him to his nearby castle, where Parzival is welcomed by a crowd of knights who relieve him of his arms, provide him with water for washing, and bring him fresh garments. Even though both the kingly fisherman and his knights are "sorrowful" (225,18 and 228,26: "trûreg"), Parzival is well treated and invited to the evening meal. The dinner is anything but a festive occasion. His host, seated before a roaring fire and clad in heavy garments despite the warm season, invites the guest to sit beside him. Immediately a page dashes in bearing a lance bloody at its tip, whereupon everyone in the vast hall weeps in lamentation. Carrying the lance around the hall, the page rushes back out again. Then the cult procession, as earlier described, takes place.

While all these wonders occur, Parzival sits quietly and, keeping in mind the courtly precepts learned from Gurnemanz, doesn't utter a word. If he remains here as long as he stayed with Gurnemanz, he reflects, surely his questions will eventually be answered. A page brings in a handsome sword. Telling Parzival that he had often borne the sword in battle before God devastated his body, the king presents it to him. Again Parzival restrains his questions out of courtesy. When the tables are cleared, the gathering disperses and Parzival is conducted to his bedchamber.

The next morning Parzival is astonished to discover that the castle is deserted. He dresses himself, finds his horse and weapons, and rides out of the castle. Suddenly a page, raising the drawbridge behind him, curses Parzival for neglecting to ask his host the question that would have brought him a great reward. A short time later he again encounters his cousin Sigune, who informs him that he has been at Munsalvaesche, the castle of the Grail, and that its lord is Anfortas, who, grievously wounded in battle, must spend his time in a reclining position. She takes it for granted that Parzival asked the question that would have relieved the suffering king and granted Parzival all he could desire here on earth. Dismayed to learn of his omission, she too curses him and spells out the terms of his mission: You should have taken pity on your host by asking about his suffering. Though Parzival is still alive, he has lost all hope of heavenly bliss and knightly honor.

Departing sadly, Parzival makes his way via various adventures back to King Arthur's court, where he is formally invited to become a knight of the Round Table. As he enjoys the felicities of the knights and ladies, the hideously ugly sorceress Cundrie rides in on her mule and warns King Arthur that the fame of the Round Table has been blemished by the presence of Parzival, who brought sorrow on the fisherman through his lack of compassion and, by his silence, great sin upon himself. With all the rhetorical power at her command—she speaks all languages, including Latin, Arabic, and French—she curses Parzival and condemns him to hell before riding off as abruptly as she appeared.

Parzival tries to explain to the company his behavior at Munsalvaesche, recalling Gurnemanz's admonition to avoid bold questions (330,5: "vrêvellîche vrâge"). Assuring them that nothing is more important to him than to win back his honor and their esteem, he takes his leave. When his new friend Gawan wishes that God may help him in his quest, Parzival asks the same question he had put years earlier to his mother: What is God? Were he almighty, he would not have brought Parzival such shame. Although up to this point he has sought to serve God, he now abjures that service. With these bitter words Parzival rides away from King Arthur's court and, for the time being, out of the narrative, which now turns to Gawan.

At this point we might pause to ask why such a seemingly innocent omission, motivated by good breeding, should be regarded as a failure of knightly *triuwe* (Sigune at 255,15) or even as sin (Cundrie at 316,23). Some scholars speak of a fall from innocence when Parzival killed the Red Knight. Some cite the self-centeredness and lack of ethical maturity that let Parzival desert his mother, pounce on the lady Jeschute, and ignore the grief of his cousin Sigune. Others point to his superficial understanding of knighthood, which at this point is still focused on such externalities as rules of behavior and glittering armor. Still others blame the emotional immaturity that prevents him from making autonomous decisions. And we should keep in mind the folktale element underlying the plot, which often involves magical questions.

As we follow in books 7 and 8 the adventures of Gawan, Parzival for several years roams the world in his attempt to regain his honor and win glory. Finally (bk. 9), four and a half years later, and after yet another encounter with his cousin Sigune, who tells him that the Castle of the Grail is not far away, he meets an elderly knight, who informs him that the day is Good Friday. Parzival rides on, thinking that God, if he truly rewards those who have striven with knightly merit, will perhaps come to his aid today. He arrives at Fontane la Salvaesche, the abode of the hermit Trevrizent, from whom Parzival now finally learns the mysteries of Munsalvaesche.

Trevrizent, it emerges, is the brother not only of Anfortas and Repanse de Schoye of Munsalvaesche but also of Herzeloyde—and therefore the uncle of Parzival, who is thus related to the family in charge of the Grail. He relates to his nephew the story of the miraculous stone and the inhabitants of the Palace. Anfortas, as king of the Grail, is forbidden to seek any love other than that specified by the writing on the stone. In his youth he violated the rules of the order and, while jousting in honor of his lady, was wounded in the testicles by a poisoned lance. A physician removed the lance head, but the wound festered so severely that it could be cured by none of the remedies known to the medieval world (which Wolfram recounts with considerable pleasure). The pain can be temporarily relieved by inserting the tip of the lance into the wound, whereby the heat of the poison draws the frost from his body. This matter then hardens on the lance tip so solidly that it can be removed only by the two silver knives. Because the wound's stench is so terrible that Anfortas must cleanse himself daily in the lake, he has come to be known as "the fisherman."

At this point his narrative reaches the moment of Parzival's first arrival at Munsalvaesche. A message had appeared on the stone that a knight would arrive and, if he should ask a specific question—"My lord, what causes your distress?" (484,27: "herre, wie stêt iuwer nôt?")—the king would be healed. Should anyone forewarn the visitor, the results would fail, but success would entitle him to become the new King of the Grail. But the visitor failed, Trevrizent heard. At first Parzival cannot bring himself to confess his sin, but finally he admits that the visitor was none other than himself. Trevrizent is dismayed. Parzival was betrayed by his God-given senses, he says, which should have alerted him to the significance of the sights, sounds, smells, tastes, and feelings offered to him by the cult ceremony at the Castle of the Grail. Parzival must now add that sin of omission to his two other involuntary sins: responsibility for the death of his mother and the slaying of the Red Knight, who turns out to have been his cousin.

Parzival remains for two weeks with his uncle, who finally absolves him from the sins of which, albeit unwittingly, he is guilty. The absolution is possible because at this point Parzival, through his own spiritual suffering, has reached the emotional maturity and moral integrity necessary to accept his responsibility and to express remorse for his sins. In other words, he has begun the process of internalizing the religious and knightly values that hitherto he had understood in a superficial and purely mechanical manner.[25] In sum, Parzival has undergone what might be viewed as three degrees of initiatory preparation: his mother's instruction, Gurnemanz's tutelage, and Trevrizent's teaching. He is now prepared for the final initiation.[26]

The Fulfillment

Again Parzival's quest is interrupted by Gawan's adventures. When he finally arrives at the Castle of the Grail for the second time (bk. 16), it is almost anticlimactic since we have already learned the foregone conclusion. Escorted by Cundrie and his brother Feirefiz, whom in the meantime he has encountered, he arrives at Munsalvaesche, where the ailing Anfortas has been kept alive by his weekly exposure to the Grail. After the mournful king has greeted the two brothers, Parzival kneels three times in the direction of the sacred stone and then, turning to Anfortas, poses the at-this-point purely ritual question: "Uncle, what ails you?" (795,29: "oeheim, waz wirret dir?"). From this moment on things move quickly. Anfortas is restored to his full health and vigor, and Parzival is acknowledged by the Templars as their king and lord.

Parzival rides out to convey the joyous news to his uncle Trevrizent in the nearby hermitage. Then he gallops on to meet the entourage escorting Condwiramurs and their two sons from distant Brobarz. Making over all his secular lands to his infant son Kardeiz and entrusting him to guardian knights, Parzival and Condwiramurs take the other son, Loherangrin, with them to become Parzival's eventual successor at the Castle of the Grail. At a great celebration the stone is again brought in by Repanse de Schoye and set before the new King and Queen of the Grail. Feirefiz is mystified at the proceedings because, as an infidel, he is unable to perceive such a sacred Christian miracle as the Holy Grail; but he is smitten with love for Repanse de Schoye. Following his baptism the next day, he wins both her hand in marriage and the ability now to see the wondrous stone. After twelve days of festivities they return to his lands in the East, where Repanse de Schoye bears a son named John, later to be known as Prester John. Wolfram concludes with a brief recapitulation of the later life of Parzival's son, Loherangrin.

Again, then, we find a hero in quest of a secret society that promises a higher knowledge. Parzival is not motivated, as is Pentheus, by sociopolitical worries and a lust for sexual titillation; like Lucius, he is entranced by the seeming magic that he witnesses and must proceed from his initial naiveté to a more mature wisdom before he may be admitted to the cult: that is, to the kingdom of the Grail. As in both earlier works, the secret society portrayed here has its basis in historical reality: the Knights Templar held in early thirteenth-century Europe a position of mystery akin to that of the mystery of Dionysus in fifth-century Greece and the cult of Isis in first-century Rome.

Like the two earlier authors, Wolfram was writing his work in a period of considerable political and social turmoil. The tension between church and state, Grail and Round Table, had been mounting for several centuries. The church declared the primacy of the papacy in the western Roman Empire while the state insisted that the consecration of the popes and investiture of bishops was valid only if approved by the emperor and other temporal rulers. The controversy between spiritual and secular powers came to a preliminary head toward the end of the eleventh century in the so-called Investiture Contest, when Pope Gregory VII demanded that that church have full authority over the secular sovereigns. His demand was denounced by King Heinrich IV, who in turn was excommunicated by the pope. In an effort to save himself from deposition by the princes who sided with the pope, in 1077 Heinrich made his humiliating barefoot pilgrimage to Canossa in the northern Apennines to obtain release from the ban. The controversy was finally resolved at the Concordat of Worms in 1122 when Pope Calixtus II and Emperor Heinrich V divided the powers of investiture between church and state. It was during this period that the Templars were rising to power under the authority and protection of a succession of popes and were exempted from secular authority.

The power of the German emperors was further eroded in favor of the papacy until 1152, when Friedrich Barbarossa was elected to the kingship without the pope's approval. Eugenius II, needing the assistance of the new sovereign in order to maintain his own temporal power in Rome, gave way. His successors, however, renewed the struggle, forcing Barbarossa in 1176 to kneel and acknowledge the supremacy of the Holy See. In the early thirteenth century it was the ambition of Innocent III to consolidate all power, both secular and temporal, under the church—to be at once pope and emperor, *caput ecclesiae* and *caput mundi*. (We recall that, though a supporter of the Templars, he also denounced their arrogance in his bull of 1207.) And precisely during the period when Wolfram was writing *Parzival*, he seemed to be succeeding in his dream. As a result, Wolfram's Germany was weakened by internal strife as rival kings contended for the imperial throne. Moreover, following the failure of the Third Crusade (1189–92), Europeans largely renounced their hope of reconquering Jerusalem. As a result the Fourth Crusade (1202–4) moved against Constantinople and, through its conquest, fostered the division of the eastern and western churches.

It was against this background and in this sense of social unrest that Wolfram wrote his version of the quest for the Holy Grail—a version that provided a new source for the Grail (a stone brought down from heaven by the neutral angels; or initially guarded on earth by those same angels) and its cult (the Knights Templar).

Within our specific context Parzival's quest can be seen as a three-stage process of initiation leading to his admission into the Order of the Templars, an organization that, contrary to at least some contemporary opinion, he portrayed in the light of its original conception: as the ideal of knightly monasticism.[27] The object of the quest is still essentially religious in nature although in the Middle Ages the pagan deities, Dionysus and Isis, have now given way to the Christian God and their cults to a more highly organized churchly order. Above all, Wolfram satisfies the lure of the arcane in an audience eager to hear more about the secrets of the Templars and the Grail.

CHAPTER THREE

The Rosicrucians of the Post-Reformation

The Climate of the Times

The second half of the sixteenth century witnessed an intensifying crisis in German history. While much of Europe suffered from wars and revolutions, during the sixty years from the Peace of Augsburg in 1555 to the outbreak of the Thirty Years' War in 1618 Germany enjoyed an extended peace.[1] But the accord was deceptive, concealing as it did a period of escalating tensions in religion, politics, and society.[2] As the Protestant reform movement following Luther's death in 1546 lost much of its energy and deteriorated into denominational bickering, the Catholic Church began to recover its vigor with the active assistance of the newly founded order of Jesuits (1534), which by 1540 had established itself in Germany. The negotiations at Augsburg had resulted in a policy that came to be known as *cujus regio, ejus religio,* according to which each land's ruler determined its religion. Religious intolerance and strife between Protestants and Catholics grew apace.

As the integrity of the Holy Roman Empire disintegrated, its once centralized authority gave way to a patchwork comprising dozens of often petty principalities whose independence and wealth were enhanced by the widespread expropriation of church properties. As the local rulers gained in authority, their courts tended to develop despotic social structures, causing the peasantry and incipient middle class to lose in prosperity and independence. As a consequence the economic situation in many lands worsened.³ Several years of miserable crops caused by bad weather devastated the peasantry, and the merchant class in many inland principalities suffered from the shift of the economy to overseas trade, which favored the coastal lands.⁴ In the law courts, which had operated since 1495 according to the reformed Roman law of the Holy Roman Empire, Protestant defendants often complained that the decisions were "too Catholic." When the Catholic resurgence had gained such momentum that the Reichstag was contemplating the restoration of church properties, many Protestant princes of the small German territories decided in 1608 to form a Protestant Union for their mutual support—a move that generated in response the constitution of a Catholic League. In 1612 the more tolerant Emperor Rudolf II was succeeded by his brother Matthias, a strong supporter of the Counter Reformation. By 1618 the denominational strife among the German principalities and within Europe at large had become so fierce that a general war broke out, fought principally on German soil and devastating Germany for thirty years.

By the beginning of the seventeenth century the social insecurities and general anxiety produced by this situation had generated predictable results. Dismayed by their sociopolitical disenfranchisement, confused by the various schisms that dominated the religious scene, and finding their traditional beliefs challenged by developments in modern science—notably the Copernican Revolution, which displaced humankind from the center of creation—many people at the turn of the seventeenth century turned to the various esoteric and utopian movements that had emerged in the course of the sixteenth century.⁵

Mysticism had been a strong current in German religious thought ever since the time of such late medieval mystics as Meister Eckhart, who, proclaiming direct access to God through prayer and meditation, prepared the ground intellectually and spiritually for the sixteenth-century humanists who rediscovered various classical sources proclaiming the essential dualism of macrocosm and microcosm. The Hebraist Johannes Reuchlin (1455–1522), with his influential work *De arte cabalistica* (1517), helped to popularize the teaching of Jewish kabbalah: that God is accessible to our understanding through ten emanations (Sephiroth) extending down through every level of his creation in the great Tree of Life. Agrippa—Heinrich Cornelius Agrippa von Nettesheim (1486–1533)—turned in his *De occulta philosophia* (1531) to the Neoplatonism that had been rediscovered in Italy by Marsilio Ficino and Pico della Mirandola: the idea that the individual soul partakes of the universal spirit but, in order to achieve ultimate unity, must first purify itself of all earthly elements. The teachings of the alleged Hermes Trismegistus were spread through translations of the *Corpus Hermeticum,* initially by Ficino (1471) but soon rendered into German by Sebastian Franck (1542). Here the Gnostic dualism of Neoplatonism was paralleled by the view that the macrocosm of spirit and matter is mirrored in the microcosm of soul and body, realms ruled respectively by God and the demiurge. These various schools offered complements to or even surrogates for a traditional Christianity that in its Protestant and Catholic forms seemed to be increasingly meaningless in the modern world.

Neoplatonism and Hermeticism found an allegorical parallel in alchemy and astrology, which by offering a physical analogy to the process of spiritual purification fascinated many contemporaries—and continued into the twentieth century to obsess such thinkers as Rudolf Steiner and Carl Gustav Jung.[6] In contrast to mysticism, which looked inward, alchemy and astrology appealed to modern minds attracted by the new sciences because they proposed to detect the divine in the world of nature. (Alchemy's appeal was essentially spiritual: its principal contribution to the development of modern chemistry appears to be distillation, an important stage in the alchemistic process.) Paracelsus (Theophrastus Bombastus von Hohenheim [1493–1541]) sought to understand the microcosm in its earthly aspect through alchemy and in its divine aspect through astrology. Several leading German alchemists such as Andreas Libavius (1555–1616) dedicated themselves to the practical medical uses of alchemy; Heinrich Khunrath (1560–1605) regarded the alchemical quest for the Philosopher's Stone allegorically as an attempt to understand the wholeness of the macrocosm; Michael Maier (1569–1622), arguing a direct correlation between heaven and earth, hoped to transform the external world through the discovery of the Philosopher's Stone.[7] These developments, which took place mainly among private scholars not associated with the largely denominational universities, were accompanied on another level by hordes of charlatans—the false alchemists and astrologers, the soothsayers and prophets such as, notoriously, the historical Doktor Faust—who gave alchemy its undeservedly bad name and caused Dante to relegate them to the eighth circle of his Inferno (29.73-139).

By the turn of the seventeenth century, as the various social, political, and religious tensions were reaching the breaking point, millenarian prophets emerged to proclaim the imminent apocalypse, a new Golden Age, a Great Reformation, or the end of time.[8] Following the teachings of the great medieval scholar Joachim da Fiore, who declared that human history progressed in three stages—the era of the Father (ruled by Law), the Son (ruled by the Gospels), and the Holy Spirit (the imminent future)—many such millenarians were convinced that the third stage was at hand. The appearance in 1604 of a spectacular supernova near the conjunction of Mars, Jupiter, and Saturn—an astronomical phenomenon that was discussed by Johann Kepler in *De stella nova* (1606)—affirmed to many viewers that the end or at least the New Order was at hand.[9]

Andreae's *Chymical Wedding*

Among the various responses to the general intellectual climate and the social malaise, the most immediately influential and controversial was the Rosicrucian movement. It is widely assumed by scholars today that the Rosicrucian manifestos of the early seventeenth century constitute in reality a grand fiction. Nevertheless, many readers of the past four centuries have accepted them as valid and taken the ideas and views expressed in them as the basis for various movements still today calling themselves "Rosicrucian," including notably the followers surrounding the German anthroposophist Rudolf Steiner, the Golden Dawn familiar to readers of W. B. Yeats, and in the United States the *Fraternitas Rosae Crucis,* the *Societas Rosicruciana in America* (SRIA), and the Ancient and Mystical Order Rosae Crucis (AMORC).[10] I am concerned here, however, not with the later history and development of Rosicrucianism but exclusively with the enormous excitement aroused by writings that may in fact have been no more than a hoax perpetrated by a group of students and young intellectuals at the University of Tübingen in the first two decades of the seventeenth century.

Almost exactly four centuries after their original publication, considerable uncertainty still surrounds the origins of Rosicrucianism and the manifestos on which it is based. The key writings embrace three anonymously published documents: the two actual manifestos—known as the *Fama* (1614) and the *Confessio* (1615)—and a much longer companion piece entitled *Chymical Wedding of Christian Rosencreutz* (*Chymische Hochzeit: Christiani Rosencreutz* [1616]). Almost everything about these three documents, apart from their actual dates of publication, is obscure. When were they written? Who wrote them? Were they reporting historically on persons and a movement that already existed, or did the movement come into existence as a result of their publication? Are they to be taken seriously or satirically?

According to the most reliable authorities, including the author himself, the *Chymical Wedding* was written sometime soon after 1605 by a young student of theology, Johann Valentin Andreae (1586–1654).[11] Andreae, grandson of a prominent Lutheran theologian who became chancellor of the University of Tübingen and son of a less accomplished parson with a weakness for alchemistic charlatans, spent most of his life in the Lutheran principality of Württemberg. Born in Herrenhausen, just west of Tübingen, the sickly child grew up and was home-tutored there and in Königsbronn (almost sixty miles to the northeast) until 1601, when his father died. His mother, an energetic and resourceful woman (to whom her son dedicated an enlightening biographical account)[12] moved her family of seven children to Tübingen so that her four sons could receive their educations at the university. In 1607, when they had all completed their studies, she relocated to Stuttgart, where she became manager of the Court Apothecary.

Andreae, a highly intelligent and voracious reader, made excellent use of his studies, receiving by the time of his *baccalaureus* in 1603 and his master's degree in 1605 a strong liberal education. During these years he lived at home and, unlike many students of the age, engaged in no carousing: until 1605, he tells us in his *vita,* he never drank a glass of wine outside his home and limited his companionship primarily to two older friends who contributed profoundly to his education outside the university—notably, the physician Tobias Hess (1568–1614), a friend with whom his father had carried out alchemistic experiments; and the lawyer Christoph Besold (1577–1638), who knew nine languages, owned a remarkable library, and in particular was well informed about Near Eastern culture and its religions.[13] In 1605 Andreae began the formal study of theology but early in 1607, as a result of a still undocumented scandal involving several other students, was expelled from the university. After expressing his appreciation for his beloved alma mater in an informative farewell address, *Vale Academiae tubingensi* (published 1633),[14] Valentin's long suppressed wanderlust found satisfaction in several years of itinerant roaming. In 1607 he traveled to Strassburg, Heidelberg, Frankfurt am Main, and several other towns along the Rhine, broadening his circle of acquaintances and exploring various libraries. In 1608 he moved to Lauingen on the Danube (the birthplace of Albertus Magnus on the border of Württemberg and Swabia) to tutor and mentor two young noblemen in school there. In 1610 he returned to Tübingen, but when a plague that year forced the university to move temporarily to other towns, Andreae set out once again—this time to Switzerland to perfect his knowledge of French and to inform himself about Calvinism and, beyond that, to Paris and (possibly) England. After a few months back in Tübingen the ambitious young man traveled in 1612 to Italy, where he visited Venice, Padua, Verona, and Rome.

Back in Tübingen later that year, he finally obtained a fellowship to live as a *stipendiarius* at the famous *Stift* (the theological seminary where almost two hundred years later the triumvirate of Hegel, Schelling, and Hölderlin would be roommates) and prepared himself for his ecclesiastical career. By 1614 he had successfully passed the examinations and was awarded a deaconship, the lowest post in the Lutheran church hierarchy, in the town of Vaihingen, just north of Stuttgart. From that moment until his death forty years later Andreae moved up through the ecclesiastical ranks of Württemberg: 1620 chief pastor (*Spezialsuperintendent*) in Calw (later Hermann Hesse's hometown); 1639 court preacher in Stuttgart; 1650 director of the Lutheran school at Bebenhausen (where later Schelling was educated); and in 1654, a few months before his death, to the honorific position of abbot of Adelberg (where Kepler had studied)—a five-stage sequence that he summarized as: Laboratorium, Directorium, Oratorium, Purgatorium, and Refrigerium.[15] By the end of his career Andreae was widely regarded as the leading Protestant theologian of Germany.

Andreae was an incredibly prolific author, having more than one hundred publications to his credit in the course of his life.[16] But his literary—that is, nontheological—works embracing poems, plays, and satires were written mostly before his assignment in 1620 to a position of significant pastoral responsibility in Calw. A great admirer of Erasmus, he wrote a still entertaining satirical Latin play entitled *Turbo* (1616), which displays certain similarities to the earlier folkbook of *Doktor Faustus* (1587): the perturbed and disturbed hero, Turbo, accompanied by his sensible and down-to-earth servant Harlekin, is driven by *curiositas* and *vanitas* to experience first the pedantry of the various faculties, then the vagaries of society and the disappointments of love in Paris, and finally the charlatanry of the alchemists. His *Mennipus* (1617), which is subtitled "a mirror of our inanities" *(inanitatum nostratium speculum)*, contains a collection of one hundred short, biting satires on such topics as "The Pedagogues," "The Master of Fine Arts," "The Pulpit Speaker," "Image of a True Evangelical Teacher," and "The Education of a Prince."

We know from many of his writings, including the eulogy to his mother, that he was contemptuous of the alchemists and charlatans who had befuddled his susceptible father. He speaks of "the deceivers who tried to sell [his father] various products of their arts" *(impostores, qui varias artes venditabant)* and of "a worthless mob of alchemists injurious to our family" *(inutilem chymicorum, & rei familiari noxiam turbam)* that led his father by the nose.[17] In light of his satiric temperament and early contempt of alchemists, we should approach the

Chymical Wedding of Christian Rosencreutz with considerable caution. It is the only one of the three early Rosicrucian texts of which in his *vita* Andreae later acknowledged authorship. But even there he called the work a *ludibrium*—a "jest" or "fantasy" written in 1605 when he was only nineteen years old—and expresses his astonishment that it should have been taken seriously and honored by elaborate interpretations: evidence, he concludes of "the inanity of the curious" *(inanitatem curiosorum)*.[18] The interpretations have continued unabated into the present.[19]

The notoriously difficult text, incorporating many literary allusions and autobiographical details, has been characterized as a fairy tale,[20] a novel,[21] a fantasy,[22] and even science fiction. In any case it has much less to do with Rosicrucianism than with alchemy. *Chymical wedding* is a technical term for a stage in the alchemistic process to produce the Philosopher's Stone: the chemical coagulation of material in the conjunction of sulfur and quicksilver (mercury) that results in cinnabar (vermilion) and symbolizes the conjunction of sun and moon, mind and soul. So from the title page on we know that the wedding described in the fiction will represent an alchemistic process, either literally or symbolically or both. The colon preceding the name in the original title *(Chymische Hochzeit: Christiani Rosencreutz)* makes it clear that it does not involve the wedding *of* Christian Rosencreutz—whose name is often spelled *Rosenkreutz*—but is a work by him about a wedding he attends.

The long, often confusingly inconsistent account proceeds sequentially over a period of seven days. (The number seven, representing the seven stages of the alchemistic process, constitutes an important structural element in the account.)[23] The first-person narrator is an elderly hermit, whose age, gray hair, and beard are repeatedly mentioned in the course of the narrative and set him apart from most other figures. On the Thursday before Easter in the year 1459 (a date that we learn much later) he receives an invitation, signed by *Sponsus et Sponsa* (the two betrothed) and delivered by a lovely messenger, to a wedding that is to take place in the immediate future. (The appearance on the invitation of an image reproducing John Dee's famous *hieroglyphic monas* prompted Frances Yates to argue the central importance of John Dee in the thought of Andreae and his Tübingen friends,[24] a view that has been largely rejected;[25] it is entirely possible that the image was added by someone other than Andreae, such as the Strassburg printer, who specialized in alchemy, or by the acquaintance who provided a copy of the manuscript to the printer.) Following a dream involving a rope to salvation let down seven times from heaven, Christian sets out the next day (II) and after various adventures reaches the palace, where at the first gate he hands over his invitation and introduces himself as "the Brother of the Rosy Red Cross." Proceeding through two more gates, he is given new shoes, groomed by barbers who leave his long gray hair intact, and joined by other invitees, who are welcomed by a lovely virgin who introduces herself as their "President."

On day III the young woman, whose name, as we learn from a numerical conundrum, is Alchimia (74),[26] requires the large group, which ranges from great kings and emperors to charlatans and lowly hermits, to undergo a test of their worthiness: each one is weighed in a golden Scale of Virtue with up to seven weights, whereby most—including vainglorious kings and pretentious alchemists who boast that they can manufacture the healing stone—fail, are punished, and sent away while Christian and a few others who pass are admitted into the Order of the Golden Fleece and Lion. The next morning (IV) their Virgin guide leads the group up 365 steps to a room where they meet three royal couples—an old king with a young queen, a middle-aged black king with an aged spouse, and two young ones—with whom they dine and watch the performance of a play with seven acts. (The action of the play roughly symbolizes the action of the novel itself.) Afterward, in a most bloody wedding act, the three royal couples are beheaded and, with their blood separately bottled, placed in coffins; their Moorish executioner is decapitated and his head put into a small chest. Alchimia tells the astonished guests that it is their responsibility to revive the kings and queens through their alchemy. That night Christian sees seven ships with the six royal coffins and the small chest, illuminated by the light of seven souls, sail away across the sea.

The next morning (V) Christian explores forbidden parts of the palace, where in an underground mausoleum illuminated only by the light of mystic carbuncle stones, he finds a grave with the perfectly preserved body of Venus. Because he dares to admire her naked beauty, in punishment Cupid pricks his hand with his arrow—a fateful gesture because it signifies Christian's earthly human side and makes it later impossible for him to attain the highest realm of perfection and condemns him to remain on earth. After a false burial of the six coffins at the palace, Alchimia conducts the alchemists, accompanied by seven virgins, in seven ships (arranged in a pentagonal formation) across the sea to an island with the Tower of Olympus.

The sixth day is filled with the alchemistic procedures that are supposed to bring the kings and queens back to life. As the alchemists gradually ascend the first six floors of the tower, they produce at each stage a product in the life-restoring

alchemistic process: an essence of stones and plants; a distillation brewed from
the Moor's head and the bodies of the six kings and queens; a snow-white egg
generated from that distillation in a golden globe, from which, after being warmed
in a copper vessel, a magical bird emerges; after it is fed the blood collected earlier from the decapitated bodies and undergoes various color changes (according to the alchemistic stages), the bird is decapitated on an altar displaying seven
symbolic items, incinerated, and its ashes collected. At this point Christian and
three others are singled out and conducted up through the seventh level to an
attic room with seven domes, where under the supervision of a wise old man
they mix the ashes with the specially prepared essence of stones and plants into
a dough, which they pour into two small molds and bake in an oven. When they
open the cooling molds, they discover two tiny homunculi made of human flesh.
When they sprinkle the forms with drops of the bird's blood, they quickly grow
to normal human size. Then in a mystical ceremony the still lifeless bodies are
covered with cloth, surrounded with blinding lights, and have wreathed trumpets
placed in their mouths.

During this entire process Christian alone realizes that his companions are
being deceived by an illusion: they believe that their alchemy and fire from the
wreathed trumpets have brought the young king and queen back to life when,
in fact, Christian alone saw a "bright stream of fire" (115: "ein hellen Fewrstrie-
men") from heaven shoot through an opening in the ceiling and into the lifeless
bodies. When the bodies come to life, they are clothed in royal garb and are accompanied back down the stairs.

On the last day the alchemists are informed by their mistress Alchimia that
they have now been elevated to Knights of the Golden Stone. In a vast fleet the
alchemists sail back to the palace with the royal entourage, where Christian, in
deference to his long gray beard and venerable age, is seated next to the young
king. When they reach the first gate, the elderly gatekeeper, once a famous astrologer, hands the king a petition asking to be relieved of his duties. It turns out
that he, too, like Christian, had once viewed the naked Venus and had thus been
condemned to guard the gate until another sinner volunteered to relieve him. At
a great banquet a page reads aloud the five articles governing the conduct of the
new Knights of the Golden Stone, and Christian signs the book, providing for
the first time his full name and the date of 1459 (thus locating the action of the
account 150 years in the past). At this point the king tells Christian that he knows
that Christian succumbed to the beauty of Venus and must guard the gate until
another sinner comes to relieve him—something that will not happen before the

birth of the king's future son. After the others have taken their leave, Christian is led with two other elderly gentlemen, the old man from the Tower and the king's astrologer, into a splendid chamber with three beds and . . . At this point the work breaks off and ends with the brief notation of the alleged editor that two pages are missing from the manuscript and that Christian, who had feared he must remain as guardian of the palace gate, has returned home.

Obviously, the work with its multiple sevens amounts in large measure to a satire of alchemy.[27] Christian is a detached observer when the false alchemists fail their test in the Scales of Virtue and when the various alchemistic procedures are conducted on the sixth day; and it is suggested that the revivification of the young king and queen, if not an act of God, is an illusion produced with various magician's tricks. The narrative has nothing to do with the Rosicrucians: the only orders mentioned are the Orders of the Golden Fleece and of the Golden Stone, the latter evidently a reference to the traditional alchemists' quest for the Philosopher's Stone. At the same time, it is this text that first provided the full name of Christian Rosencreutz, reputedly the founder of the order. (The name itself has been persuasively explained as an allusion to the heraldic shield of the Andreae family, which bears a red X-shaped St. Andrew's Cross with four roses in the interstices. When Christian sets out, he is wearing a white linen cloak strapped crosswise with a blood-red band and a hat sporting four red roses.) And the text includes at one point an encrypted date, 1378, which was subsequently reputed to be the birthdate of Christian Rosencreutz, making him eighty-one years old.

The work, now generally accepted as a fiction,[28] was long regarded by many Rosicrucians as a true account of an episode from the life of a "historical" Christian Rosencreutz.[29] As to why Andreae waited ten years to publish this youthful *jeu d'esprit,* various reasons have been advanced: that it was given to the publisher without his knowledge and even against his wishes; that, at the beginning of his professional ecclesiastical career, he published it to repudiate the two "Rosicrucian manifestos," which had been wrongly attributed to him and which, he feared, might damage him professionally; that, by portraying Rosencreutz as a "Christian Everyman" skeptical of alchemistic nonsense, he published it in an effort to "christianize" the Rosicrucian movement.[30]

The Manifestos

The *Chymical Wedding* was written several years before the manifestos, which are usually dated around 1610, whose authorship Andreae never acknowledged, and which are never mentioned in the earlier text.[31] Whether Andreae wrote them or whether they emerged as a collaborative project from the group of young Tübingen friends surrounding him, Andreae's youthful *ludibrium* provided the impetus, as well as the name of the hero (indicated only by initials) in the *Fama*, which may be regarded as the founding document of Rosicrucianism and which is the central text to be considered in the present context.

The *Fama*—its complete title is *Fama Fraternitatis, Deß Löblichen Ordens des Rosenkreutzes / An alle Gelehrte und Häupter Europas geschrieben* (Report of the Brotherhood of the Laudable Order of the Rosy Cross, addressed to all the scholars and leaders of Europe)—was sandwiched on publication between two other works: the *General Reformation of the Whole Wide World,* a section translated by Andreae's friend Christoph Besold from the satire on such human foibles as avarice, ambition, and hypocrisy by Traiano Boccalini (*Ragguagli di Parnaso* [1612]); and a *Response* to the *Fama* by the Tyrolese teacher and alchemist Adam Haslmayr, which had been published two years earlier and for which Haslmayr, on the indictment of the Jesuits, had been imprisoned and then condemned for four years to the galleys. (Haslmayr's response is of particular significance because it proves that the *Fama* was circulated widely in manuscript copies for several years before its publication.)

The *Fama*, which is much shorter than the *Chymische Hochzeit,* comprises three parts: the life of Frater (Brother) Christian Rosencreutz, who is identified only by his initials as "Fr. C. R."; the discovery 120 years after his death of his secret mausoleum; and the general invitation to others to join the movement he founded.[32] In the first sentence the authors, who introduce themselves as "Brothers of the Fraternity of the R. C.," state that in recent times God has allowed knowledge both of his Son and of nature—that is, of the macrocosm and microcosm—to expand so significantly that a new age appears imminent even though it is opposed by "the old enemy" in the form of enthusiasts and malcontents. It was the hope of such a General Reformation that inspired Brother C. R. to his endeavors.

C. R. was a German of noble birth, who because of his family's poverty was placed at age five in a monastery, where he learned both Latin and Greek. In his early teens he undertook with another brother a pilgrimage to the Holy Sepulchre. When that brother died en route in Cyprus, C. R., rather than turning back, continued on to Damascus, where, because of illness, he remained for a time, impressing the Turks with his medical skills. At age sixteen, having heard much about the wise men in Damcar (Damar, in Yemen), he traveled to that city, where he perfected his knowledge of Arabic, mastered the skills of mathematics and physics, and translated into Latin their *Liber M.* (presumably *Liber Mundi,* or book of the macrocosm). After three years and on the advice of his mentors in Arabia—because, as the tale implies, the Arabic scholars, unlike the Europeans, freely shared and exchanged their knowledge—he journeyed across the Red Sea to Egypt, whence he sailed to Moroccan Fez, where he added "Magia" and the kabbalah to his other Arabic learning and began to comprehend the image of the macrocosm as reflected in humankind, including all human institutions: religion, government, medicine, language, and so forth. After two years in Fez he crossed to Spain with his new learning and treasures—including various forms of nature unknown in Europe—anticipating a warm reception by scholars. Instead, the scholars in Spain and other European lands, resentful of C. R.'s knowledge, which they regarded as harmful to their lore and insulting to their reputations, ignored or disparaged him. Even though the world was already pregnant with great premonitions (20: "mit so grosser Commodion schwanger"), it had to await the moment when a new flame in the *Trigono igneo* (an allusion to the supernova of 1604, which appeared in the constellation of three stars) would ignite the ultimate spiritual conflagration.[33]

Returning to Germany, he built himself a simple habitation, where he studied and integrated the knowledge he had acquired.

After five years his desire for a General Reformation—he lived a century before Martin Luther—caused him to invite three brothers (all identified only by their initials)[34] from his former monastery to join him in the common enterprise: they produced an extensive *Vocabularium* of magical terms, wrote down the first part of the great *Liber Mundi,* and constructed a grand House of the Holy Spirit (21: "Gebäw Sancti Spiritus"). But as their medical responsibilities increased—the sick came in great crowds to Sancti Spiritus—they added four more members to their group. When they had arranged matters so that the work at home could proceed smoothly and all had mastered the exoteric and esoteric philosophy of the order, they decided that they should no longer restrict themselves to their monastery. Agreeing that their order should remain secret for 120 years, five brothers departed into various lands with their new skills and knowledge, leaving two at home with C. R., and reassembled once a year back at Sancti Spiritus to report on their progress and discuss the future. Although free of illness, they were all mortal and eventually, having named successors, died and were buried in secret, leaving the places of burial unknown to this day. In a document known as their *Confessio* the authors promise to reveal the reasons why they are now finally willing to open their brotherhood and its mysteries, together with the vast fortune required. "For Europe is pregnant and will bear a strong child, which must have a large inheritance of money" (23).

The present generation of the brotherhood—that is, the authors of the *Fama*—did not know when Brother C. R. died or where he was buried but only the names of his successors down to the present. Following the death of a brother in Gallia Narbonensi (Narbonne, in France), his successor arrived to inform them that the brotherhood would soon no longer need to remain secret but could be revealed to the entire German nation. The following year, while undertaking a repair in Sancti Spiritus, he uncovered a brass memorial plate engraved with the names of all the brothers. Seeking to shift it to a more suitable location, he disclosed a large nail, which, when he tried to remove it, exposed a hidden door bearing the inscription: *Post CXX. Annos Patebo* (In 120 years I shall be revealed), which they took as a sign that it was time for a spiritual-intellectual door to the world outside to be opened. Opening the door, they found a heptagonal chamber magically illuminated and containing a sepulcher with various mystical and holy inscriptions in Latin and covered by an altar bearing the inscription: *Hoc Universi Compendium vivus Mihi Sepulchrum Feci* (25: During my lifetime I built for myself this sepulcher as a model of the universe). The entire mausoleum displayed symbolic aspects on ceiling, floor, and walls. Each wall held a case containing books, including C. R.'s *Itinerarium* and *Vita,* and various objects: mirrors with certain properties, little bells, lighted lamps, and other items. Removing the top of the altar, they found C. R.'s body, perfectly preserved and holding a book concluding with the statement that he had become more than a hundred years old and that his body had been removed from the sight of the world for 120 years. Within another altar they found C. R.'s *Minutus Mundus* or "microcosm"—a model corresponding in its movements to the movements of the macrocosm. Replacing the altar on the tomb and leaving the model in place, they closed and sealed the door to the burial chamber, awaiting the response of the world to their *Fama.*

The brethren were confident that a General Reformation of things both human and divine was about to take place because there had been a sign in the heavens of a bright light (apparently a reference to the supernova of 1604), causing others to join their fraternity and make the fortunate beginning of the Philosophical Canon predicted and desired by Brother C. R. So that every Christian might know what beliefs they held, they proclaimed their pure belief in Jesus Christ—

quite distinct from that professed by the enthusiasts, heretics, and false prophets who were thriving in Germany—and the sacraments of the first renewed church (that is, the Lutheran reformation). They also proclaimed their allegiance to the Holy Roman Empire and the Fourth Monarchy (as heralded in the book of Daniel). Their philosophy was nothing new, they maintained, but rather the same as that proclaimed since Adam by Moses and Solomon, as well as such Greek thinkers as Plato, Aristotle, and Pythagoras in a great sphere of knowledge, all of whose parts were equidistant from the center. They explicitly rejected the teachings of the gold-making alchemists and charlatans who exploited the credulity of the people, repeating with Brother C. R. that *aurum nisi quantum aurum* (gold is nothing but gold). They promised to list in a catalog the many books and images that had been put forth in the name of Alchemy to the detriment of God's glory (29: *in Contumeliam gloriae Dei*) so that learned men might take note and resist the various tricks of the great enemy. In conclusion they bid the learned men of Europe to read, examine, and contemplate their *Fama* and the accompanying *Confessio* and to respond individually or collectively to their exhortation. Even though they could not yet reveal their names, they were confident that the messages from outside would reach them either by word of mouth or in writing. Meanwhile their House of the Holy Spirit would remain untouched, unseen, undestroyed, and hidden from the wicked world *sub umbra alarum tuarum Jehova* (under the shadow of thy wings, Jehovah). At that point the *Fama* ends; the *Confessio Fraternitatis*, a brief statement of the generally antipapal and reformative beliefs and goals of the brotherhood, which is irrelevant to our purposes, was published separately a year later.

In sum, we have been introduced to a hero whose name we know (from the subsequently published but previously written *Chymical Wedding*); but this Christian Rosencreutz is quite different from the elderly, bearded hermit monk of the *ludibrium*. From hints in the text we can date his birth to around 1380: the discovery of his corpse and the following composition of the *Fama* is dated to 1604 by the reference to the great supernova; since he was to remain hidden for 120 years, his death took place in 1484; and since he lived more than one hundred years, he was born roughly a century earlier. (We learn from the *Confessio* that he was actually born in 1378—a date that is also encrypted in the *Chymical Wedding*.) The path of his first years—youth and early manhood—is related in considerable detail, and the stages of his later life and activities, both practical and philosophical, are recapitulated. Finally, we learn about his death and, 120 years later, the discovery of his body and the dissemination of his teachings. Essentially they call for the integration of new scientific findings into Christianity while battling alchemy, which perverts that effort.

For our purposes the details of the brotherhood's teaching are not germane: they reflect a generally antipapal but broadly Christian and humanistic attitude characteristic of many Renaissance intellectuals. The exhortation, as we will see, elicited a broad response from readers who took it literally. But the parallels between the *Fama* and the earlier works considered, as well as those still to be taken up, are striking. At the beginning of each we witness a quest: Dionysus's journey from Asia to Greece, Lucius's peregrinations from Greece to Rome, Parzival's quest,[35] and Christian's journey to Damascus and, by way of North Africa and Spain, back to Germany. In each case the hero's quest revolves around a cult/order/society: the practices of Dionysus's maenads on Mount Cithaera; the cult of Isis into which Lucius is initiated; the court of the Fisher King where Parzival finally arrives; and the brotherhood that Christian establishes. As in the contemporary conspiracy novels, the cult in each case is one that arouses suspicion and even fear among outsiders: hence in the *Fama* the reluctance to mention names and the need to keep their secret for 120 years. The listener or reader is not indoctrinated into the secrets of the various cults. Yet although we are not initiated, we are attracted and entertained in each case by the lure of the arcane: it piques our interest simply to hear about them. For these reasons it makes sense to include the *Fama* in our series of secret societies, regarded as it is by most readers as a pure fiction—an adventure story followed by initiation into an order that was widely regarded by contemporaries as a threat to existing society.

But this original Rosicrucianism differs radically from the other cases, in which an actual historical group gave rise to the fiction. Here, in contrast, the fiction gave rise to the movement. In this case a company of young men in Tübingen, using ideas associated with various contemporary esoteric trends—principally alchemy and astrology, Hermetics and kabbalah—invented a cult and its founding hero for their own purposes. Whether we agree with Rudolf Steiner and other latter-day Rosicrucians who take the fictions seriously, or whether we choose to regard them as satires on prevailing alchemistic charlatanry and unrealistic utopian dreams, the fact remains that Christian Rosencreutz's "brotherhood" was invented and not based on an existing cult. No one has expressed the general principle more clearly than C. G. Jung, who observed that "when no valid secrets really exist, mysteries are invented or contrived to which privileged initiates are admitted."[36]

The Response

We can appreciate the controversy and anxiety aroused by the three Rosicrucian writings if we consider the reception of this *first* or original Rosicrucianism in the years 1612 to 1622, which has without exaggeration been called a "media event."[37] Indeed, it might well be compared to the excitement generated by Dan Brown's *The Da Vinci Code*—the millions of copies sold, the film adaptation, the various exegeses taking the fiction seriously, and the critics who savaged it—with considerable precision. Whereas later readers, such as Herder,[38] Goethe, Rudolf Steiner, and Carl Gustav Jung were attracted principally by the *Chymische Hochzeit*, the initial excitement was aroused by the *Fama* and *Confessio*. We have already seen that Haslmayr was punished by the Jesuits in 1612 for his positive response to the antipapal *Fama*—an early signal of the controversy that awaited the pamphlet. By 1625 more than four hundred responses had appeared, a few in manuscript but mostly published, seeking to establish contact with the brotherhood or commenting on its exhortation. Thus one writer "inspired by the love of truth" (*veritatis amore incitatus*) addressed a one-page appeal to the "magnificent and illustrious masters, doctors of wisdom, and brothers of the society R. C." (*Magnificis et Clarissimis Dominis Sapientiae Doctoribus Fratribus Collegii R. C.* [1614]), and another wrote a "letter to the Christian brothers of the Rosy Cross" (*Epistola ad Fratres Christianos a Cruce Rosea* [1614]), wishing them increase and divine protection.[39] The original printing of March 1614 was followed in the next three years by six further editions, as well as several pirated editions. In 1615, for instance, the *Fama Fraternitatis* and *Confessio* were reprinted in Frankfurt am Main together with several responses and a "Discourse on the General Reformation of the Whole World" ("Discurs von allgemeiner Reformation der gantzen Welt").[40]

Many of the broadsheets and pamphlets were positive, issued by enthusiasts seeking support for their esoteric tendencies. But numerous voices were raised in opposition to what they regarded as a sinister conspiracy—to overthrow the government, to undermine religion, and so forth. From 1617 to 1620 a conservative house-tutor in Nürnberg, Friedrich Grick, writing under the pseudonym Irenaeus Agnostus, brought out more than a dozen critiques, such as his "thesaurus of faith: a necessary report and warning to the novices or young aspiring disciples who have been accepted and initiated by the highly laudable fraternity of the Rosy Cross" (*Thesaurus fidei: Das ist: ein notwendiger Bericht, uund Verwarnung an die Novitios, oder junge angehende Discipel, welche von der hochlöblichen*

Fraternitet deß Rosen Creutzes auff- und angenommen [1619]).[41] Scientists and theologians of every denomination joined in. In 1623 the astronomer Johannes Kepler issued a "discourse on the great conjunction or meeting of Saturn and Jupiter in the fiery sign of Leo" *(Discurs Von der Grossen Conjunction oder Zusammenkunfft Saturni unnd Jovis im fewrigen Zeichen deß Löwen),* in which he took issue with the authors of the *Fama* and others who believed that the supernova signaled a rebirth of Germany.[42] The Lutheran Johann Hintnem entitled his critique a "mirror of ambition" *(Speculum Ambitionis* [1620]); the Calvinist Philipp Geiger issued a "brief and well-meant warning against the Rosicrucian vermin" *(Kurtze und Trewhertzige Warnung, für dem Rosencreutzer Ungezifer* [1621]); and the Catholic Sigismund Dullinger, under the pseudonym S. Mundus Christophori F., spoke of "bacon on the trap: ruses and deceptions of the newly arisen brotherhood or fraternity of the Rosy Cross" *(Speck auff der Fall, Das ist: List und Betruch der Newentstandnen Bruderschafft, oder Fraternitet dern Vom Rosencreutz* [1618]).[43]

No one had ever encountered an actual member of the brotherhood, but soon secret societies calling themselves Rosicrucians were founded all over Europe, such as a group of alchemists at The Hague in 1622 who wore at their meetings a golden band from which a golden cross and a rose were suspended.[44] Elsewhere itinerant con artists and mountebanks sought to mystify the common folk in the name of Rosicrucianism.[45] In 1622 citizens of Paris could read placards advertising "deputies of the Rosy Cross" *(Nous Depoutez de la Rose-Croix),* who, visible and invisible, were sojourning in the city in order to teach "without books or signs" and who spoke the language of the country, wherever they might be, in order to save men from deathly error.[46] Frances Yates even attributed the disastrous Bohemian venture of Elector Friedrich V of the Rhine Palatinate to the influence of the Rosicrucians.[47] Following the notorious 1618 Defenestration of Prague, which brought the Bohemian Protestants into open rebellion against the Catholic Habsburg monarchy and triggered the Thirty Years' War, Friedrich V, regarded as the most prominent Protestant ruler, misguidedly accepted the invitation in 1619 to become king of Bohemia—the "Winter King" since his reign lasted only a few months and led not only to his failure in Bohemia but to the defeat and devastation of the Palatinate itself.

Andreae, though he had not yet acknowledged his authorship of the *Chymical Wedding* and (presumably) coauthorship of the *Fama* and *Confessio,* felt compelled to add his voice to the growing chorus. In his "Tower of Babel" *(Turris Babel sive Judiciorum de Fraternitate Rosaceae Crucis Chaos* [1619]) he surveyed what he called the "chaos of opinions on the brotherhood of the Rosy Cross": twenty-four scenes in which a personified Fama conducts discussions with various alchemists and adherents of the movement, exposing Andreae's own skepticism and scorn regarding the often irrationally exuberant responses to the Rosicrucian texts.[48] In various other writings down to his late *vita* he made clear his contempt of alchemy, reaching back to his childhood experiences with the alchemists who deceived his father, and kept a careful distance from developments surrounding the Rosicrucian movement. As I have already noted, he finally acknowledged authorship only of his youthful "jest," *The Chymical Wedding*. In a 1620 collection of pieces on "the destructive power of idle curiosity on those interested in the idiosyncratic" *(De curiositatis Pernicie Syntagma Ad singularitatis Studiosos)* he spoke in one section of "the deception of a certain Rosicrucian brotherhood" that constitutes "without doubt a noose and bone of contention [Stein des Anstoßes] for the curious of this age."[49] The fairy tale, he continues, "contained something that could stir the appetite of the soothsayers, the calculating exegetes, the spendthrifts, the microcosmicists, the enthusiasts, the kabbalists, and in general all the curious." The clergy feared that a new apostasy was going to flood the world; the people trembled lest some Arab army seek colonies in Europe; the learned community deplored a destructive barbarism.

Despite the initial wave of enthusiasm and apprehension, that first manifestation of Rosicrucianism died out in the early 1620s, partly as a result of disagreements among the new followers about its goals and partly because of accusations of heresy. Other determining factors were the rapid rise of scientific rationalism, which undermined alchemy and other esoteric fads, and the Thirty Years' War, which had devastating consequences for life in Germany. The movement was revived in the eighteenth century in the form of the Asiatic Brethren and the Order of the Golden and Rosy Cross, later in England as the Hermetic Order of the Golden Dawn,[50] and in various hypostases in the twentieth century. But these later manifestations all remained largely peripheral to the mainstream of intellectual and political life. The writings of the first Rosicrucian brotherhood, in contrast, belonged to the principal social and spiritual currents of the early sixteenth century and engaged the minds of virtually every leading figure of the age. The phenomenon, and notably the *Fama,* constitutes a remarkable example for the sheer power of ideas. Without a trace of an actual institution or movement behind them the Rosicrucian writings had a tremendous impact simply because they caught so well the chiliastic longing of the times for a "General Reformation" of religious, social, and political life in Europe—the lure of the arcane.

In the progression from cult to conspiracy the Rosicrucians marked a pronounced step from the pagan cults and the religious Order of the Knights Templar to a secret society—one founded consciously as the result of a quest but constituted in such a manner as to be self-perpetuating. In this novel society the lure of the arcane was represented by the promise of an occult wisdom that extends well beyond its (antipapal) religious aspect to embrace more generally the scientific and philosophical knowledge of the Renaissance—although, as is common in such narratives, from Euripides to Dan Brown, we are given no insight into the particulars of the teachings. Here, moreover, and especially in the widespread response to the manifestos we find perhaps the first hints of conspiracy.

CHAPTER FOUR

The Lodges of the Enlightenment

The Cult and Culture of Secret Societies

In his influential study of structural transformations of the public sphere during the Enlightenment, Jürgen Habermas argues that secret societies belonged— along with dining clubs, salons, academies, and coffeehouses—to the important new institutions of the emerging bourgeois élite comprising merchants, bankers, businessmen, and intellectuals.[1] More elaborately, in his brilliant inquiry into "the pathogenesis of the bourgeois world" Reinhard Koselleck analyzed the function of secrecy within those societies.[2] He maintained that the secret societies raised the spiritual inner-world created by those new bourgeois institutions of the En- lightenment to the level of a *mysterium* analogous to the mysteries of church or the arcane policies of the state. The content of the mystery mattered less than the fact of its secrecy (and hence our lack of knowledge about the "secrets" underly- ing many secret societies).

Essentially, secrecy had a protective function and shielded members against the absolutist state. In addition, it brought about a commonality among mem- bers: all those who shared the secret were equal, regardless of social status. It created a clandestine realm within the state in which the freedom of the bour- geoisie could be realized before it became, through revolution, a political fact. Two movements in particular seized the public's attention and imagination: the

Freemasons and the Illuminati, who "won their contours in the public-political consciousness in the first place as mythos."[3] (The Rosicrucians continued in various modifications to thrive into the eighteenth century. The Jesuits, whose order was forbidden by the pope in 1773 on the demand of absolutist states believing that the order was intriguing or actively conspiring to influence government or even to seize power, enjoyed a powerful underground existence.)

Freemasonry in its modern "speculative" form—as distinct from the medieval guilds of actual "operative" stonemasons—arose in England following the establishment in 1717 of the first Grand Lodge and its official Constitutions of 1723.[4] Thanks to its guiding principles—freedom, equality, fraternity, and tolerance—and its democratic organization, which opened membership to all social classes and faiths, the movement spread rapidly among liberal thinkers of Enlightenment Europe. The meetings provided a forum for public discussion and activity in a society hitherto dominated by the elitist culture of absolute monarchies: meetings that revolved around discussions of an ethical and philosophical nature, scrupulously avoiding politics and sectarian religion, and that afforded security and confidentiality thanks to the oath of silence taken by its members. More specifically, the reputation for occultism that accrued to the Freemasons, the Illuminati, and other secret societies during the Enlightenment was a specific response to the weakening of Christianity and the loss of religious faith.[5]

The meetings, at which the individual members regarded themselves as stones in the great temple of humanity that they were building, were organized by a Worshipful Master assisted by wardens, a treasurer, an archivist, a master of ceremonies, and other officers. The initiates, or Apprentices, progressed by tested achievement through the level of Journeyman or Fellow Craft to the highest stage of Master, acquainting themselves along the way with the secrets and symbols of the order—notably the mason's square and compasses—and acquiring their own accoutrements: apron, gloves, and an emblem, along with passwords and handshakes by which members could recognize one another. (The lodges of strict observance or Scottish Rite practiced a more elaborate hierarchy of degrees.)

The first German lodge was established in Hamburg in 1737 by Freemasons who had already been initiated in England. New orders rapidly sprang up in Dresden, Berlin, Bayreuth, Breslau, Frankfurt an der Oder, Frankfurt am Main, and elsewhere so that by 1754 Germany could boast of nineteen lodges. In Prussia Freemasons enjoyed a privileged status thanks to the membership of Frederick the Great, who was initiated in 1738 while still crown prince and who established lodge headquarters at his palaces, first in Rheinsberg and later in Charlottenburg.

As a result of its democratic ideals and practice of secrecy the movement, often regarded by outsiders as a revolutionary conspiracy, was soon opposed by political and religious leaders. Absolutist governments feared Freemasonry because they suspected that the order planned by surreptitious means to overthrow existing monarchies and establish a democratic world order. The Catholic Church believed that its members preached deism and even worshipped Satan. By 1740 the order had been widely prohibited—in, for example, the kingdom of Naples, Poland, Holland, France, Spain, Portugal, and elsewhere. In 1738 and again in 1751 it was declared illegal by the papacy and forced to lead a covert existence in many cities, a fact that contributed to the reputation of conspiracy.

The Illuminati, who unlike the international Freemasons enjoyed their short heyday principally in Germany and Switzerland, arose in partial response to a crisis in Freemasonry in 1776, when the lodge was split by a quarrel between the regular orders and those of strict observance.[6] During the ensuing confusions an occult mystical-spiritualistic movement emerged among some of the Freemasons, a movement known as the Order of the Gold und Rosy Cross ("Gold- und Rosenkreuzer," not to be confused with the Rosicrucians of the seventeenth century, with whom there was no direct connection), which believed in kabbala, alchemy, and magic.[7]

When a representative of this group showed up at the formerly Jesuit university of Ingolstadt and tried to enlist students, Adam Weishaupt (1748–1830), a non-Jesuit professor of philosophy and church law, assembled some of his brightest students in a discussion group known initially as the Perfectabilists. Taking as their symbol of wisdom the owl of Minerva, they pursued essentially the same ideals as traditional Freemasonry—liberty, equality, fraternity—but, in distinction from the other movement, had a specifically political agenda: to educate people through ethics and enlightenment to a level at which government of any sort would no longer be necessary and, in the process, to infiltrate government with members of the order. Within a few years and notably through the administrative skills of Baron Adolf von Knigge (1752–96), who as an experienced Freemason was early attracted to Weishaupt's group, this loose association acquired a more formal structure and a rapid expansion presided over by a committee known as the Areopagus.[8] Its members enjoyed secret names (Weishaupt was Spartacus; Knigge was Philo) and the seventy towns and cities over which its more than two thousand members were spread had their own designations (Ingolstadt became Eleusis). The order's strict obligation *de silentio,* which went so far as to require members to return any letters from the leadership along with their responses, was undersigned by all who accepted membership, including Goethe, who was inducted in 1783 into the Weimar lodge.[9] Years later, in 1815, when his son was promoted to Journeyman in Weimar's Masonic lodge, Goethe wrote a poem entitled "Secrecy" ("Verschwiegenheit"), in which he extolled the society's practice of discretion:

Niemand soll und wird es schauen
Was einander wir vertraut:
Denn auf Schweigen und Vertrauen
Ist der Tempel aufgebaut.[10]
[No one should and will see
what we have confided in one another:
For upon silence and trust
the temple is built.]

In 1784 Knigge was excluded from the Illuminati because of disagreements with Weishaupt on secrecy, which he regarded as incompatible with the individual's responsibilities toward bourgeois society. As members of that society, he felt, its leaders have the duty to understand the goals of all social organizations and to know whether they are harmful to the state. He went on almost immediately to satirize secret societies in his novel *The Story of Peter Clausen* (*Die Geschichte Peter Clausens* [1783–85]). Then, in his hugely popular book of manners *On Social Dealings with People* (*Ueber den Umgang mit Menschen* [1788]), he included an entire chapter "On Secret Societies and Dealings with Their Members." From his close involvement with several societies he knew what he was talking about. "Among the many harmful and harmless amusements with which our philosophical century concerns itself belongs the great number of secret associations and orders of the most varied sort," he begins.[11] "Nowadays in all classes one will meet few people who—drawn by the desire for knowledge, the urge for activity, sociability, or sheer curiosity—have not been members of a secret brotherhood at least for a certain period of time." He goes on to warn young men not to join such societies or, if they have already done so, not to allow themselves to be carried away by the more absurd enthusiasms and the sectarian spirit that prevail in such orders. In 1795 the revolutionary journalist A. F. G. Rebmann classified the impulse to idealize the world through secret societies as "the disease of our century."[12]

Like the Freemasons, and for essentially the same political and religious reasons, the Illuminati were soon prohibited during the reactionary hysteria of these immediately prerevolutionary years—1784 in Bavaria and 1785 in all Catholic lands by papal edict—and shifted their base to the northern Protestant states. The prohibition was followed by persecutions, house searches, and confiscations, which resulted in the seizure and publication in 1787 of alleged "Original Writings" of leading members, and triggered in turn a veritable Illuminatiphobia. The French Revolution was widely blamed on the conspiratorial machinations of the Illuminati and Freemasons, as in such muckraking works as John Robison's *Proofs of a Conspiracy against All the Religions and Governments of Europe, Carried On in the Secret Meetings of Masons, Illuminati, and Reading Societies* (Edinburgh, 1797) and, that same year, the Abbé Barruel's *Mémoires pour servir à l'histoire du Jacobisme* (Paris, 1797).[13] In fact, an American scholar of the period has argued persuasively that revolutionary faith in Europe of the late eighteenth and early nineteenth centuries was "shaped not so much by the critical rationalism of the French Enlightenment (as is generally believed) as by the occultism and proto-romanticism of Germany."[14] A British historian has demonstrated with great sophistication that the influence of secret societies (with particular reference to the "panic" produced by the Illuminati) is based not on what they actually accomplish but on what outsiders believe of their intentions..[15]

The Lodge Novel

The widespread fascination with secret societies was most conspicuously reflected in the enormously popular *Bundesroman* or "lodge novel"[16] in late eighteenth-century Germany—the German counterpart to the Gothic novel in England, which tended in contrast to revolve around a demonic figure rather than a secret society. As demonstrated by Marianne Thalmann in her definitive study, the lodge novel is a fictional type with distinctive characteristics.[17] It emerged during the latter half of the eighteenth century at the time when such arcane orders as the Freemasons and Illuminati, as well as conspiracy theories regarding their secret power, were at the peak of their influence and most of the leading figures of the age belonged to one order or another. Arising as they did as antimonarchical and generally democratic movements against increasingly absolutist monarchies, these groups sometimes claimed for themselves a moral position beyond good and evil in order to achieve their goals. It was inevitable that their momentum should communicate itself to the literature of the day.

Apart from all questions of literary merit, the *Bundesroman* had a pronounced form, or formula, that was absorbed by many leading writers of the day. Central to the genre is the idea of a secret society that somehow guides—or seeks to control—the life of the hero and enlist him in its cause. This produces a constant tension between the central figure and the order, which traditionally represents an ideal to which the hero is being educated. In almost every case the secret society is described according to established patterns that are based, in turn, on the familiar hierarchy of actual orders—most particularly orders of strict observance such as the Rosicrucians. At the head of the order is a High Tribunal of Elders, whose Superior represents the incarnation of its spiritual principle. The order has its seat in a mysterious building, often a castle, which encompasses various secret chambers along with an extensive archive. Before the novice is accepted, he must submit to an examination and swear an oath of loyalty. He is given a Letter of Apprenticeship and the appropriate insignia, is entitled to participate in the festivals of the lodge, and must sometimes undertake secret journeys in the service of the order. The novice is accompanied or guided on his wanderings by an emissary or "genius," who represents the human incarnation of the order, in contrast to the Superior, who exemplifies its spiritual principle. The emissary is traditionally characterized by various set features, among which the most salient are omnipotence, omnipresence, a timeless appearance, a sparkling glance, foreign origin, and the quality of mutability. Although the lodge novel, and the orders themselves, gloried in mystery and secrecy, the writers of the eighteenth century were not able to be absolutely consistent in their response: they almost always supply a rational solution to the various mysteries at the end.

Earlier works in France and Germany had responded to the general interest in secret societies and the lure of the arcane with fictions set in earlier periods.[18] Jean Terrasson, for instance, located his popular historical novel *Séthos* (1730) in ancient Egypt and depicted the hero's initiation into the cult of Isis. The novel was later studied assiduously by Freemasons, especially in Germany, in their effort to trace Masonic rituals back to ancient Egyptian mysteries as depicted there. Karl Friedrich Bahrdt, in his rationalizing *Explanation of the Plans and Aim of Jesus* (*Ausführung des Plans und Zwecks Jesu* [1784–92]), introduced Jesus as a member of the secret order of Essenes, with whose assistance he manufactured his "miracles" and managed to survive the crucifixion and live in secrecy for many more years.[19]

Wilhelm Friedrich Meyern's (1762–1829) anonymously published *Dya-Na-Sore* (1787–91), the first volume of which Schiller reviewed, is purportedly translated "from the Sam-skritt" and tells the story of four brothers who, after thirty pages of fatherly advice, leave home in ancient Tibet to experience the world and to become the saviors of freedom and avengers of injustice in "the ruins of their fatherland."[20] Taken in hand by a secret society displaying many of the rituals familiar from European secret societies, two of the brothers, Tibar and Altai, are educated with a high-flown rhetoric that sounds suspiciously like the elitist propaganda of Meyern's youthful conservatives: namely, that even in a "democracy," security should rest in the hands of an oligarchy. Driven into exile for their conspiratorial activities, they later return and, aided by their brother Dya, overthrow the tyrannical ruler. But the people, not yet worthy of their "freedom" in the new military state, return to their former tyranny through a counterrevolution in which Tibar and Dya are both killed. Their graves become a gathering point for patriots, and their lives are recorded in some sixteen hundred pages by their brother Altai. (The novel is best known today at secondhand from its treatment in Arno Schmidt's satirical "conversations in a library" concerning works from the age of German literary classicism. In a chapter subtitled "The Blondest of Beasts" it is characterized as a "prophetic description of a Super Third Reich" and as "the ideal SS-Handbook.")[21]

During these same years Christoph Martin Wieland published his *Peregrinus Proteus* (1791), whose hero (based on Lucian's second-century satirical depiction of his contemporary, the Greek Cynic Peregrinus) is driven by a rapturous desire to enter into community with higher beings. Like Apuleius's Lucius, he moves with blind naiveté through the world of late antiquity, experiencing initiations into various cults—of Venus Urania, of early Christianity, of Gnosis—and is finally driven into Cynicism and, ultimately, death by the realization that he, and his family's fortune, have been exploited in each case for the various goals of the secret societies. In all these novels the arcane amounts to the depiction of historical cults, rationalization of alleged miracles, and imposition of modern political views on purportedly ancient societies.

Schiller's *The Ghost-Seer*

Paradoxically, the work that provided the principal impetus for the wave of lodge novels during the 1790s was a fragmentary fiction by one of the few major literary figures of the age who, though frequently approached and surrounded by friends who belonged, never sought or accepted membership in the secret orders: Friedrich Schiller's *The Ghost-Seer* (*Der Geisterseher* [1789]).[22]

The Ghost-Seer—sometimes, with reference to the term as used by Kant in his critique of Emanuel Swedenborg's theosophical speculations, translated as *The*

Spiritualist[23]—in contrast to the earlier works, was the first important lodge novel actually set in the European present and modeled after such contemporary societies as the Freemasons and Illuminati. Written during a pause in the composition of his *Don Carlos,* the novel parallels the plot of the drama: in each case a weak and impressionable hero is manipulated by a shrewder and stronger companion. But in contrast to the drama's Marquis Posa, a revolutionary apostle of liberty, the novel's mysterious "Armenian" is the emissary of a secret society seeking to convert the future ruler of a German Protestant land to Catholicism and thereby to spread its power and influence. This work, Schiller's greatest popular success during his lifetime, was undertaken initially to fill space in the fourth volume of his journal *Thalia,* where it appeared in five installments from 1787 to 1789, when the still fragmentary work was published as a book. But it turned out to be an unexpectedly profitable enterprise. "This much is certain," he confided to his friend Christian Gottfried Körner while writing a later installment (May 15, 1788), "that I shall exploit this public taste and make as much money from it as I possibly can." What, beyond the general lure of the arcane, was the public taste that he was hastening to exploit?

In the summer of 1786, when Schiller began writing, several sensational events fascinated the public mind. First, Frederick the Great, who died on August 17 of that year, was succeeded on the Prussian throne by his nephew Friedrich Wilhelm II (1744–97), who was notorious for his conspicuous interest in the occult and for attending séances at which he believed he was communicating with the spirits of the deceased. An initiate since 1781 in the Order of the Gold and Rosy Cross, he was followed into the palace by two leading members of the order: Johann Christoph Wöllner, as his chief minister, and Hans Rudolf Bischoffswerder, who functioned as his most intimate privy counselor and significantly affected the direction of his reign. This development led many people to worry that the affairs of the powerful Prussian state would be guided by a Catholic conspiracy.[24]

Second, only a year earlier the notorious charlatan Giuseppe Balsamo, who, calling himself Cagliostro, had captivated the European aristocracy with his frauds and illusions, was arrested in Paris in connection with the infamous Affair of the Diamond Necklace. Although acquitted of that charge and others, which he sought to refute in his *Mémoire* (1786), he was subsequently imprisoned for life in Rome on grounds of Freemasonry. The exposé of Cagliostro's swindles was led in Germany by Elise von der Recke (1756–1833), a German-Baltic baroness, who in 1779 as a young woman had met him in Mitau (Jelgava, in present-day

Latvia) and, made susceptible by the recent sudden death of her favorite brother, succumbed temporarily to his influence. (Like many other contemporaries, Goethe was fascinated by Cagliostro's adventures and, during his Italian journey, interviewed his family near Palermo.) But her good sense soon saw through his behavior and tricks, and in 1787 she published a widely acclaimed "Report on the Famous Cagliostro's Stay in Mitau in the Year 1779 and His Magical Operations" *(Nachricht von des berühmten Cagliostro Aufenthalt in Mitau im Jahre 1779 und dessen magischen Operationen).* Before her book appeared, the author published a poem in the leading intellectual journal *Berlinische Monatsschrift* (May 1786), which was introduced by a seven-page essay recounting Cagliostro's shameful deceptions and praising Von der Recke for her courageous exposure. The poem itself, composed in praise of a portrait of her recently deceased father, begins with a censure of those who pretend to recall the deceased in a different manner:

Die Wunderkunst: nach ächter Schwärmer Sinn,
Abwesende, ja Todte darzustellen,
Lokt' einst zu einer Zauberinn
Selbst einen stolzen König hin.
Wie leicht verführt in hundert Fällen
Das Herz den Kopf!—Auch läßt sich gern
Die liebe Phantasie von schlauen Mystikern
Durch süße Täuschungen bethören.
Dann schwingen sie sich zu den Sphären
der Geisterwelt, und spiegeln Wunder vor:
Daß über all das Sehen und das Hören
Schon mancher den Verstand verlor.[25]
[The magic art—in the sense of genuine visionaries
to represent distant ones, even the dead—
once enticed to an enchantress
even a proud king.
How easily in a hundred cases
the heart seduces the head!—Even
dear fantasy lets itself be bewitched
by the sweet deceptions of clever mystifiers.
Then they vault up to the spheres
of the spirit-world, and pretend miracles:

so that all the sights and sounds
cause many a one to lose his common sense.)

The author appended a brief note saying that she was persuaded to publish her poem by "the danger of the increasingly mindless enthusiasm, the spirit-seeing, and all secret arts" and that she was qualified by the circumstance that she, too, "with the best intentions in the world and only a few years ago, was in danger of succumbing to raptures and dark superstition."[26]

Von der Recke's poem with its afterword elicited two months later a response by Friedrich Eugen, Prince of Württemberg, who thanked "the noble Elisa" for her attack on superstition, rapture, and foolishness and against the deceivers and phantasts who exploit it.[27] But he went on to surmise that "the sublime Elisa" would not disagree with his belief that conjurations and communication with "the purer higher spirit" are possible within the framework of religion—a statement that immediately led contemporaries to suspect the influence of the Catholic Church, which had already succeeded in converting other members of the royal family in Protestant Württemberg. That same July issue contained a long article offering "something more about secret societies in Protestant Germany" ("Noch etwas über Geheime Gesellschaften im protestantischen Deutschland"), which begins by thanking the *Berlinische Monatsschrift* for its repeated warnings to every patriotic German, and especially every Protestant, against the widespread secret societies, and then goes on to hint at the growing influence of the Jesuits in Germany.

This, then, was the public interest to which Schiller was referring and appealing: the widespread obsession with secret societies and their conspiracies, especially those with a Catholic-Rosicrucian-Jesuitical cast, and with accomplished charlatans in the mold of Cagliostro. And not least: his own fascination with the phenomenon of lesser and impressionable spirits being manipulated by more sophisticated and determined minds. So despite his lack of interest in the project that (in a letter of Feb. 12, 1789) he labeled "a farce," he continued work on it for two years.[28] "Right down to the present hour I can't win any interest from this accursed Ghost-Seer," he confessed to Körner on March 3, 1788. "What demon inspired me to it!" Two weeks later (March 17) he complained about the time he was wasting on his "scribbling" *(Schmiererei)*. But his readers demanded installment after installment.

When the story begins, the thirty-five-year-old (unnamed) Protestant prince from an unspecified German land, still (like Friedrich Eugen of Württemberg) third in line for the throne, is whiling away his time in Venice, incognito and accompanied only by a few trusted servants.[29] Because his neglected education was interrupted by early military service, he has no sound intellectual basis for his unexamined beliefs and is easily susceptible to outside influence. Shortly after the narrator, the Count of O**, encounters him and begins his account, they are accosted on St. Mark's Plaza by a masked man in Armenian garb who congratulates the prince on his good fortune because, "At nine o'clock he died." They learn a week later that the prince's cousin passed away at that exact hour. Since only an elderly and childless uncle now stands between him and the throne, the prince is immediately hailed by the nobles of the republic as the presumptive successor to the throne of his land.

The next evening, following a contretemps in a café where he is threatened by a group of Venetians, he is rescued by guards of the Inquisition, who accompany him to a hearing, where he sees his attacker beheaded. A week later, in the course of an expedition to a village outside the city, the company is regaled by various seemingly magical tricks: despite his incognito he is recognized by the crowd, a lost key is mysteriously returned, and a Sicilian conjurer summons up the spirit of a deceased friend. Suddenly the Armenian appears, now in the guise of a Russian officer, and exposes the conjurer, who is arrested. When the prince and the count visit the Sicilian in prison, he explains how he accomplished his various hoaxes and tells them legendary stories about the Armenian, who is reputed to be a timeless being (and whose figure, along with that of the Sicilian, is clearly based on accounts of Cagliostro). The prince reasons that the Armenian, seeking to exploit him in some manner, had arranged all the earlier mystifications—from the announcement of his cousin's death and the intervention of the Inquisition to the tricks and conjurations of the Sicilian. (In seeming confirmation of this theory, the Sicilian disappears from prison.)

Now overconfident of his powers of reason and insight, the prince rejects as irrational and even hateful the religious views that he had hitherto unquestioningly accepted. "An exposed deception made even the truth suspicious to him" (106), and his reading matter in the course of the next year fills his head with further doubts. "He had entered this labyrinth as a credulous enthusiast, and he departed from it as a doubter and ultimately as a complete free-spirit" (108). At this point he is initiated into a secret society known as the Bucento: a group preaching universal equality but in fact proclaiming sophistries that the prince's reason, "supported by so little basic knowledge," is incapable of seeing through (109). Soon, manipulated by "an invisible hand" (112), his closest friends, who might have saved him, are required on various grounds to leave Venice.

The prince's character, hitherto modest and considerate, takes a sharp turn for the worse. When another German prince arrives whose brilliance overshadows him, the prince consumes all his funds in the effort to compensate. Having rescued a wealthy young Venetian, the Marchese of Civitella, from attackers during this period, he is befriended by the young man and his uncle, a cardinal. When the marchese realizes that the prince has resorted to borrowing money from a Jewish moneylender, he generously puts his own fortune at his disposal until the prince's funds should be transferred from home. Rather than returning to Germany as expected, the prince remains in Venice, having fallen in love with a young woman whom he sees praying in a Catholic church and takes to be Greek. Meanwhile, he falls ever more heavily into debt through gambling.

At this point the prince is abruptly summoned home, where reports have been received of his womanizing and gambling, of his consorting with visionaries and conjurers, of his suspicious relationships with Catholic prelates, and of his inappropriately extravagant lifestyle. "It was even rumored that he was on the point of completing this objectionable behavior by an apostasy to the Roman Church" (155). Offended by these remarks and demands, the prince breaks with the court at home and becomes wholly dependent financially upon the Marchese of Civitella. When the narrator receives the next report three months later, the marchese has been mortally wounded—apparently by the prince because the cardinal has sent out assassins in search of the prince, who has taken refuge in a monastery. Meanwhile, his Greek beloved has died from poisoning. But by the time the narrator arrives in Venice to help, he learns that all has turned out well: the prince's debts have been settled, the cardinal reconciled, the marchese restored to health. The prince himself has just heard his first mass in the arms of his new best friend, the Armenian. The narrator, the Count of O**, is turned away from his friend's door by his new acquaintances.

Schiller's novel remained a fragment at this point. In the early months of 1789 he managed to revive his interest in the project temporarily by writing many pages of a philosophical dialogue between the prince and one of his remaining friends. "Chance gave me an opportunity to introduce a philosophical conversation that I needed in any case in order to present to the reader the free-spirit epoch that I had the prince experience," Schiller confided to Körner (Jan. 26, 1789). But the interest did not last; Schiller soon discontinued all work on his novel; and, realizing that the philosophical discussion constituted an unacceptable break in the narrative, he removed it from the text proper and placed it in an appendix in the published work. So the novel remained a fragment, albeit an enormously popular and influential one.

We realize in retrospect that *all* the action, and not simply the magical tricks and conjurations of the early pages, is manipulated by the Armenian and the secret Jesuitical society that he represents. The initial deception—the announcement that the prince's cousin was about to die—was in effect the triggering action. Having learned (before the prince) that the successor was ill with a fatal disease—or having poisoned him—and realizing that the prince would soon be in line for the throne, the cabal set its sights on him with the goal of converting him so that a Catholic would succeed to the throne of the Protestant land. (The analogy to contemporary circumstances in Württemberg and Prussia is instantly obvious.) From that point on all the major events—the disappearance of a trusted servant and his replacement by Biondello, a creature of the Armenian; the chance "rescue" of the marchese from his attackers; the interference with the prince's financial transfers, making him dependent on his Italian friends, as well as suppression of letters from his German friends; the forced departures of his German friends; his membership in the Bucento, where he met leading Catholics of Venice; the murder of the beloved "Greek" woman, whose love might have interfered with their plot; even, no doubt, the pretended mortal wounding of the marchese and the anger of the cardinal—all of these events occurred in order to enmesh the prince more deeply in the conspiracy of the secret order and to make him more dependent upon the support of the mysterious Armenian.

All these devices in various modifications were rapidly appropriated by other writers in Germany of the 1790s, which was beset with rumors of conspiracies surrounding the revolution in France. We also note that, while Schiller provides hints at the maneuvers and tactics of the secret society, we are offered no insight whatsoever into their beliefs—apart from the general desire to spread the reach of their power. The attraction lies wholly in the occult machinations of the group and in the subtlety of Schiller's psychological insights into the mind of a naive quester deluded by the false appeal of mystery and vague ideals.

Schiller's Successors: The Continuations

The Ghost-Seer, as popular in its day as Dan Brown's thrillers are today, left its fans with such a sense of unfulfilled expectations that it was soon completed by another writer. In 1796 Ernst Friedrich Wilhelm Follenius (1773–1809), in his anonymously published *Friedrich Schillers Geisterseher,* took up the story where

Schiller's fragment had discontinued.[30] After clarifying certain details of Schiller's text—for example, the prince attacks and wounds Civitella because he catches him "in an amorous situation" with the Greek woman (1:164)—Schiller's narrator, the Count of O**, enlists two English friends, Lord Seymour and Johnson, "the noble conjurer," in his battle against the Armenian and his fellow-conspirators. (Volumes 2 and 3 of Follenius's continuation are entitled "Johnson der edle Taschenspieler"; the clever Johnson, who becomes the prince's servant and confidant, functions as the antagonist to the Armenian's henchman Biondello.) Further mystifications take place with conjurations, apparitions, and masquerades, and the Armenian gains the prince's consent for the assassination of the ruler. In the end, however, the Armenian is unmasked and imprisoned beneath the notorious lead roofs of Venice. There he clarifies with rationalizations all the remaining mysteries: the initial report of the cousin's death was realized by poisoning; the Inquisition beheaded a puppet rather than the actual Venetian; the apparitions were created by his assistant; and so forth. After the Armenian's grotesque death—he pounds his head on the floor until it shatters and is infected by maggots that devour his "malice-filled" brain—the prince is rescued by his friends and taken back to Germany, where he retreats to an isolated castle. Ashamed of his earlier behavior, he succumbs to a profound melancholy and is killed by lightning after reading a posthumous letter from his beloved "Greek" (actually a German noblewoman), who tells him that she was blackmailed by the Armenian into assisting him in his machinations and that she truly loved the prince. The details of the conspiracy itself, we learn in the final pages, remain covered by a "dark veil."

Other continuations followed, such as a twentieth-century rendition by Hanns Heinz Ewers, undertaken in 1922, as the author relates in his afterword, despite the indignation of critics, who accused him from the anti-Semitic right of being "a perverse Jewboy [Judenjungen] to whose repulsive desire for publicity nothing is sacred" and, from the socialist left, of being an "incapable pornographer."[31] Ewers—who was already well known as the scriptwriter for the 1913 film classic *Der Student von Prag*—begins by recapitulating Schiller's own work, somewhat modernizing the language, identifying the Sicilian conjurer as Count Cagliostro, and giving names to the places and characters: the hero becomes Prince Alexander and his friends Count Osten (who is identified as a cousin of Elisa von der Recke!) and Baron Zedtwitz. The Greek beloved, whom the prince calls Veronika, has not died but gone away in secret. Civitella becomes one of the prince's most loyal friends, warning him repeatedly against the machinations of Biondello and the Armenian. Nevertheless, following his conversion, which he undertakes for purely political reasons—to gain the support of the Catholic rulers in Vienna, Munich, Dresden, and elsewhere—the prince returns to his country in central Germany, angered and frustrated to learn that the deceased heir to the throne has actually through a secret marriage left behind an infant child who now, with his mother, stands in line to succeed the ruling duke. The Armenian shows up in various guises: as a French abbé, a Turkish magnate, and as Dr. Teufelsdröck (a name familiar to English readers from Thomas Carlyle's *Sartor Resartus*), who is capable through hypnotism of turning even strong men to his will. Various adventures take place: the infant heir is kidnapped; Zedtwitz is misled by the Armenian into attempting to murder the ruling duke; the prince is fed laudanum, which alters his personality; and he is arrested on suspicion of conspiring in the murder of the duke. Finally, Lord Seymour (from Follenius's sequel)— again through the clandestine influence of the Armenian—offers the prince the service of the English Hessian troops to overthrow the duke and seize power. The prince, on the advice of his beloved Veronika, who reappears mysteriously from time to time, is on the point of ordering the attack when he learns that she is in reality another tool of, and perhaps the lover of, the Armenian-Teufelsdröck, as well as the mother of the young heir to the throne. Utterly dismayed at the deceptions to which he has been subjected, he calls off the attack and retires to his room, where presumably he commits suicide. At this point the account ends, and we learn that it is allegedly the work of a German student named Ewald Recke, who obtained the lost papers of Count Osten and, after using them for his dissertation, sold them to Ewers.

Of a wholly different nature is Kai Meyer's "The Ghost-Seers" (*Die Geisterseher* [1995]), which amounts to a skillful modern imitation of a traditional lodge novel. The action takes place in 1805 with historical figures—Goethe, Schiller, E. T. A. Hoffmann, the brothers Grimm, Elise von der Recke, and others—who are involved in an utterly fictitious plot: a chase across Europe, from Weimar to Warsaw and back to Burg Stolpen near Dresden, to recover Schiller's manuscript with the conclusion of *The Ghost-Seer*. The manuscript, which is thought to reveal the secret of the Philosopher's Stone, is also being sought by a sinister conspiracy of Rosicrucians led by the Armenian from Schiller's novel. It turns out that the entire matter is a deception: the belief in the Philosopher's Stone was a delusion of the dying Schiller (who was poisoned by Goethe to prevent him from sharing the fatal information with the public), as well as the conspiracy.[32] As the rationalizing Jacob Grimm puts it: "We *wanted* to believe in all these things—the stone, the Armenian—and for that reason we saw everything linked together, suspected behind every person a conspirator, believed finally in the magical masquerades of the Armenian. What fools we were . . . !"[33] Schiller's manuscript is burned and, accordingly, never read. Meyer's novel turns out to be an attack on the all-too-ready belief in conspiracy theories in Germany both of the early nineteenth century and of the late twentieth.

Schiller's Successors: The Imitations

One of the most popular contemporary imitations was Carl Grosse's four-volume *The Genius* (*Der Genius* [1791–95]), which captivated German youth of the Romantic fin de siècle, including Ludwig Tieck and E. T. A. Hoffmann. The work was informed in no small measure by the adventures—as fantastic as those of any novel—of its author, who was born in 1768 in Magdeburg as Carl Friedrich August Grosse and died almost eighty years later (1847) in Copenhagen as Count Edouard Romeo Vargas Bedemar.[34] The son of a successful doctor, he enrolled in 1786 as a student of medicine at the University of Göttingen, where he also began his prolific literary career with essays on the sublime and on transmigration of the soul and with a translation of the works of the Scottish poet and moral philosopher James Beattie. In late 1788 he moved to the University of Halle, where he seems to have been involved with several secret societies. Soon, however, he undertook a journey to Switzerland and Italy, from which he returned to Göttingen in an elegant green uniform, sporting the cross of the Knights of Malta and announcing himself as the Marquis Grosse von Vargas, a title he claimed to have inherited from a deceased Italian aristocratic wife. His claim was soon exposed as a fraud, and in 1791 Grosse was compelled to leave Göttingen. He spent the next two years in Spain, writing along with his novel a volume of malicious memoirs attacking Göttingen's academic society, which had ridiculed and rejected him. In 1793 he showed up in Italy as Edouard Romeo Count of Vargas, a title to which in 1795 he added the honorific Baron Bedemar. His hitherto enormously productive literary activity ceased almost completely, and following service as an officer in the Austrian military, he spent much of his remaining life in Denmark, where he attained a certain reputation as a mineralogist and mining expert.

Der Genius may be regarded as the exemplary conspiracy fiction or *Bundesroman* of the 1790s.[35] The utterly improbable "plot" of this loosely episodic novel is almost totally irrelevant.[36] Moving across prerevolutionary Europe from Spain through France to Germany and ending almost predictably in Venice, the scene shifts from elegant country estates to palaces in Madrid and Paris, from peasant festivals to student groups at the University of Toledo, from masked balls in Paris to the Carnival of Venice. The literally dozens of characters, whether disguised as peasants or hermits, are almost invariably from the nobility of various lands. The first-person narrative, which begins *in mediis rebus* and then continues under the fiction of a simultaneous contemporaneous account, provides no organizational help for the reader through chapter divisions or headings. The action involves murders, kidnappings, mysterious apparitions, mistaken identities, betrayals, and the deaths of beloved wives and children; the love interest usually involves sexual threesomes, in which the man betrays his best friend with the friend's wife, or the wife falls in love with the husband's best friend. Lengthy philosophical discussions take place in elaborately described interior and natural settings. The denouement, involving shifts in narrative standpoint and numerous interpolated and frequently interrupted stories, which often repeat or double other episodes, is so confusing that the author himself apologizes in his preliminary remarks to the fourth volume for its bewilderment, explaining that when he wrote the first parts, he had an entirely different plan in mind than the one that "the ill mood of the public" (537) forced upon him, causing him to lose sight of the "ideal of harmony."[37]

All the action, to the extent that it affects the first-person narrator, the Marquis C* of G**, is controlled by a mysterious society. In the first paragraph, and with an implicit allusion to the "invisible hand" of Schiller's novel, the narrator tells of the path through life "that I followed or was *led* [down]" (7). "From all the complications stemming from apparent accidents there emerges an invisible hand, which perhaps hovers over many a one of us, controls him in the darkness, and may have woven long in advance the thread that he believes he himself is weaving in careless freedom" (7). He claims that every act of his life, even the seemingly most arbitrary ones, must have been calculated before his birth in their terrible archives and that they sought to make him their tool for horrid crimes. Karlos first hears of this mysterious group at home in Spain, where it seeks to turn his beloved Elmire against him and arranges for her early death. The order, as such, appears only twice in the course of the lengthy novel. In the first part Karlos is persuaded by a friend to join the group, which is presented to him as a society of superior men determined to obtain from the creator "the fabric of nature and human development" (89). He is conducted by a mysterious old man through a rocky landscape and forest to a building with long corridors and spacious halls, where he is finally led into a room illuminated by chandeliers and mirror-walls. There he is greeted in silence by an assembly of masked people clad in white and sitting before a table covered with books, a cross, a dagger, a goblet, and several other symbolic instruments. Their leader's countenance, "a perfect painting of loftiest humanity," seems to reveal "the quiet plan of a new arrangement of the world ["Weltbau"]" (109). When the assemblage unmasks, Karlos is astonished to see "a society of faces full of apostolic humanity" (110). He tells them that he wishes to join their group, insofar as it is consistent with his responsibilities as a human being: "to love people, to do well to everyone he encounters, to forgive everyone who hates him, to love everyone who wishes him well" (110). But the Superior informs him that he must cast off all human bonds if he wishes to join their society. They will take him in even if the world turns him away, but "our Lodge rejects the tears of humanity" (111). When Karlos wavers, they tell him that he will not be compelled to join them. But they ask him to listen to their reasons, saying that he too must surely be disappointed in their homeland. "All the social estates are in disarray, or rather they have been extinguished in a single estate: that of the despots. The populace is a miserable slave. Desperation led this group together" (114). They now constitute the midpoint for the collective strengths of the world, and the happiness of the world under their guidance is their goal. Hence the symbols on the table: belief (the cross), otherwise the dagger or goblet of poison! Karlos finally agrees to accept membership, swearing to doubt nothing, to trust their decisions, to obey their orders, and to play his assigned role. Dagger and poison, the leader concludes, are humanity's consolation. When the happiness of mankind demands it, let the individual fall, even if it be the monarch. At this threat against the king of Spain, with its implication that Karlos is to be its tool, he hesitates again, but the Superior explains that their forefathers gave them monarchs; they are simply demanding back their rights and judging the monarchs by a higher standard. Overwhelmed by the promises of happiness to come, Karlos finally accedes, laying his hand on the cross and drinking from the goblet. The dagger is used to puncture his arm for blood, which his new brothers drink from a chalice.

For hundreds of pages following this initiation, the secret order, though mentioned frequently as catalyst for various occurrences, does not again appear as a group. But it is represented by its "genius," named Amanuel, who suddenly emerges to protect Karlos when danger threatens during his various adventures or to turn him back when he tries to evade the group. (It later turns out that Amanuel is none other than Karlos's faithful servant, Alfonso, who in turn when dying reveals his identity as Karlos's maternal uncle and the leader of the Order.) Other figures, such as the sinister Don Bernhard, represent the group's hierarchical policies. "If everyone fulfilled his proper place, then the world would be perfect. But that everyone recognize his proper place—that's the difficulty, and that's why we're there" (577). In book 4, finally, Karlos with his wife, Adelheid, again attends a meeting of the order featuring a celebration of the Eleusinian Mysteries (583). A procession of priests and priestesses dressed in long white garments and long locks garlanded with flowers greets them as they pass by with their torches. Recognizing them from the first encounter years before, Karlos exclaims that "they were my brothers, who celebrated my return with delight." When Don Bernhard and Adelheid take the oath, "immortal words, never before heard, were spoken!" A great curtain is raised, and "we saw things, incomprehensible and inexpressible; sounds swirled over to us from a different world; heavenly visions swayed past in ordered rows, all our premonitions were fulfilled, and the boldest hopes of reality were stilled" (583–84). Yet in the midst of the rhapsodic tumult Karlos is overcome by jealousy because he sees Adelheid alienated from him by Don Bernhard. Following this short scene at the end of the first part of book 4, the secret society virtually disappears from the novel. In the final episode, which takes place in Venice, Karlos and his friend the Count of S** are miraculously rescued from an ambush by their estranged wives—and live happily ever after.

Essentially, then, Karlos's life, like that of Schiller's prince, is guided and controlled by a secret society whose tenets he mistrusts. For all its high-flown rhetoric the society amounts to an oligarchic cabal, which seeks to overthrow the monarchy and at the same time control the nonnoble classes, assigning each person to what it regards as his or her own proper place. This political aspect of the society is underscored when Karlos, at the university in Toledo, tries with a group of friends to found a political group to defend the monarchy: "We were not for revolutions; we felt that the monarchical form of government was always the best for the whole. Glowing in our hearts with a noble freedom, we felt that we would always be able to escape its [monarchy's] pressure, without rebellion against divine and human laws, by means of the simple laws of intelligence and strength; and without sacrificing any privileges resulting from those laws proclaimed for the coherence of the whole by the commands of a single individual" (334). But no sooner did they seek to put their theories into action than the entire enterprise was frustrated as their funds and papers mysteriously disappeared and the members were variously led away. "Suddenly all our plans were thrown into an incomprehensible disarray in the strangest manner by invisible hands" (336). Clearly, the students' democratic and nonviolent theories were at odds with the explicit goals of the society. We recognize the lodge with its "genius" and symbols, as well as the unsuccessful antilodge. Oddly, however, the secret society disappears without explanation in the final section.

Had Karlos's account concluded with the radiant celebration of the order at the end of the first part of book 4, it would have left us with no doubts. But an unexpectedly added second part leaves many questions open. The beauty of the celebration is marred in retrospect by the account of Adelheid's estrangement from Karlos through the seductive attentions of lodge member Don Bernhard, whom the jealous Karlos murders and secretly buries. He then puts Adelheid into a convent in the hope of effecting her recovery. Although they are ultimately reconciled, the fact that the order is not mentioned again leaves open the question of its continued relevance and role in their lives. The depiction of the lodge itself and its festivities is hardly original, depending as it does on the Eleusinian Mysteries, and beyond its general goals we learn none of the inexpressible "secrets" into which Karlos claims to have been initiated.

Other writers sought to capitalize on the excitement generated by Schiller's novel and by the public fascination with secret societies. Jean Paul's (Jean Paul Friedrich Richter [1763–1825]) choice of a title for his first novel is illuminating: *The Invisible Lodge* (*Die unsichtbare Loge* [1793]). "With this title I basically have nothing in mind although, by the time I write the preface, it may occur to me what I have in mind," he confided to a friend while writing his work, "but I won't rest until others believe that they find more in it. I'll state in the preface: I'm half ashamed that I was constrained by an unavoidable title-oddity to appear similar to those authors who attach colorful titles to their works simply for the sake of the purchasers and the publisher. But since it was important to me to win the attention of those few students of nature [Naturforscher] who properly understand this title: may the reviewers allow me this little Masonic apron."[38]

In fact, secret societies play virtually no role in the novel, which like Schiller's *The Ghost-Seer* remained fragmentary. Knigge expressed his disappointment in an otherwise encouraging review, stating that "one seeks vainly in the entire work for anything that would clarify the book's title."[39] The novel—as whimsical as all of Jean Paul's fiction, half satire and half idyll—is part bildungsroman and part political-social critique. The hero, Gustav, spends the first eight years of his life underground, where at the request of his mother's family he is educated by a young Moravian known simply as "the genius." Following this experience, which is intended to provide him with a transcendent perspective that will protect him from the seductions of the real world, he is taught in the idyllic setting of his paternal palace by a tutor named Jean Paul. But his subsequent training as a military cadet exposes him to courtly life, where, despite his love for the lovely Beata, he soon succumbs to the seductive intrigues of the duchess-regent. As a friend of the illegitimate princely son Ottomar, he becomes involved in Ottomar's plot to overthrow his tyrannical brother. When at this point the novel ends, we are told simply that Gustav is in prison, apparently accused of being a member of a conspiracy. But the informant tells us that he is bound by his oath to reveal nothing. In his preface to the second edition of the novel (1822) Jean Paul tried to explain what he meant by the title, which was supposed to express "something that refers to a hidden society, which however remains hidden until I expose the third or final volume to the light of day or to the world."[40] In sum, in Jean Paul's *Die unsichtbare Loge*, at least in what we have of it, the lodge or order remains wholly invisible.[41]

Another first novel by a young writer is routinely cited among the leading lodge novels of the period: *William Lovell* (*Geschichte des Herrn William Lovell* [1795–96]) by the early Romantic Ludwig Tieck (1773–1853). The plot of the epistolary novel depends heavily on family feuds that took place before the birth of the present generation of sons and daughters. William Lovell's love for Amalie Wilmont and his friendship with Eduard Burton are undermined because Lovell Sr. was betrayed by the grasping Burton Sr. when they were both young men. As for Amalia, Lovell has already betrayed her love with a French seductress when his father rejects their alliance on the grounds that she is an unsatisfactory match. In the course of his Grand Tour through France and Italy Lovell encounters a charming young Italian, Rosa, who arranges his liaison in Paris and then, in Rome, introduces him to Andrea, the head of a secret group. Lovell is initially suspicious because he has heard "that our age is possessed by the rage of appearing strange and secretive in that manner" (185).[42] But when he attends a meeting, he is surprised and pleased to learn that it is simply a society of impressive men who meet without rituals to discuss matters of import. "I have never stood in a temple with such reverence, never found in a book the thoughts that here penetrated me" (186). When after the death of his father Lovell learns that he has been stripped of his inheritance through the machinations of Burton Sr., he returns to England in disguise and tries unsuccessfully to poison his former friend and, more effectively, to seduce and then abandon his friend's sister. Back in Paris, he ekes out a living by gambling but then, on his way back to Rome, is stripped of all his earnings by robbers.

Pinning all his hopes on the mysterious Andrea, he is first turned away from the house and later admitted and ridiculed by the old man who, dying, hands him an explanatory manuscript. Andrea, it turns out, is in reality an Englishman named Waterloo, who has long hated Lovell's family because the father cheated him of his beloved, who then died in childbirth with young William. Motivated by a "burning hatred against Lovell, I would have been willing to dedicate my entire life in order to embitter his" (307). Inventing his own secret society, which he created as a sort of Ponzi scheme, rewarding some members with the dues of others, he managed to control young Lovell's entire life. He sends Rosa to Paris as his emissary who, under the guise of friendship, corrupts Lovell's morals and thus alienates the son from his virtuous father. He commissions Lovell to go to England with assignments—the murder of Eduard Burton—that Lovell manages to spoil "as unskillfully as an ignorant boy" (315). But even his attempts to turn Lovell into "a weird monstrosity" (315) fail, he points out sarcastically, because Lovell is incapable of change. Utterly dismayed by these revelations and by the evil he has brought about, wittingly and unwittingly, Lovell is prepared to spend the remainder of his days quietly in isolation with Rosa, who has also become disenchanted with Andrea's schemes. But before he can do so, he is killed in a duel by Wilmont, who has long been searching him out for the desertion of his sister Amalie and the seduction of Burton's sister Emilie. The novel, written when the author had not yet completed his twenty-first year, shows no firsthand knowledge of secret societies or insight into their rituals and beliefs. Indeed, Andrea's cabal is unusual to the extent that it is created expressly for the purpose of carrying out one man's plots and not for the sake of any general religious, social, or political goals. But with his novel the young author skillfully exploited the lure of the arcane that entranced the public of the 1790s.

Secret societies make their way, though often peripherally, into many other fictions of the decade. In the ethereally lovely prose of Friedrich Hölderlin's (1770–1843) epistolary novel *Hyperion, or the Hermit in Greece* (*Hyperion, oder der Eremit in Griechenland* [1797–99]) it is not the hero himself who is involved with the "Order of Nemesis" ("der Bund der Nemesis") but his friend Alabanda. When Alabanda introduces Hyperion to members of the order in Smyrna, he is immediately offended by their rhetoric and, convinced that "they're swindlers," has nothing further to do with them.[43] He later learns that they have guided Alabanda's life for years. When the eighteen-year-old Alabanda was a shipwrecked sailor in Spain, a stranger came to his assistance. The man, whom he recognized as his benefactor, approached him again later in Trieste and introduced him into a group of men known as the Order of Nemesis. "Intoxicated by the great sphere of influence that was exposed to me, I ceremoniously bequeathed my blood and my soul to these men" (144); but, he adds, he actually witnessed little of the activities of the group. Later, out of his attachment to Hyperion, he broke his vow and must now fear the consequences. What those consequences are we never learn: Alabanda suspects that it may be his death ("What can they take besides my blood?" [145]), but Hyperion imagines that the "rascals" will take him in hand again: "he has certain good friends . . . who are skilled in helping those upon whom life lies too heavily" (159). In any case the Order of Nemesis has no function in the larger plot of the novel, which deals with Hyperion's love for the muse-like Diotima and his involvement in the 1770 war against the Turks: first with a Greek revolutionary group that, degenerating into a band of looters, is defeated; and then with the Russian fleet, where he is seriously wounded. The novel amounts to the autobiographical account that Hyperion, having lost his best friend and his beloved through death and having forsaken his grandiose dreams, writes to his German acquaintance Bellarmin years later from his isolation in the mountains of Greece.

Perhaps the most enduringly famous of the genre designated in German as *Trivialroman* (popular fiction) was *Rinaldo Rinaldini* (1799–1801), by Christian August Vulpius (1762–1827), Goethe's brother-in-law, which was translated into many languages and continues to lead a lively life in movies and TV programs in various European countries and languages. The multivolume work, more of a "robber novel" *(Räuberroman)* than lodge novel, relates the tale of a Sicilian bandit who is recruited by the mysterious "Old Man of Fronteja," who proclaims a "temple of wisdom," to join the revolutionary forces seeking to liberate Corsica from the French. The old man, who turns out to have been his former tutor, has secretly guided his life; but Rinaldo, who might have been a hero but remained a bandit, refuses to join the revolutionary movement and is killed. The secret society, while present in the background, is not central to the action. Here again, as in Hölderlin's *Hyperion*, we find the fashionable combination of lodge novel and revolutionary conspiracies.

Sublimated Lodges: Mozart's *The Magic Flute*

In two cases, however, the premises of the lodge novel shaped cultural works of the highest order to a significant extent. It is well known to all opera lovers from their program notes that Mozart's *The Magic Flute* (*Die Zauberflöte* [1791]) is a

"Masonic opera."[44] Mozart (1756–91), who was initiated in 1784 and became a Master Mason in the Viennese Lodge "Charity" (Wohlthätigkeit), was an enthusiastic participant in lodge activities and had already composed a number of Masonic songs and cantatas in addition to his major orchestral work, *Maurerische Trauermusik*.[45] In 1791 he was approached by an acquaintance, the writer and theater director Emanuel Schikaneder (1751–1812), himself a Mason (albeit at the time suspended from his lodge in Regensburg), to compose the music for a Singspiel that he proposed to write for his Theater auf der Wieden in the Viennese outskirts. According to the borrowing practices prevalent at the time in the popular genre of "magic opera" (Zauberoper) or "fairy-tale opera" (Märchenoper),[46] he planned to base his libretto on a fairy tale by August A. Liebeskind, "Lulu or the Magic Flute" ("Lulu, oder die Zauberflöte"), which had recently been published in the third volume of *Dschinnistan* (1789), a collection of Oriental tales edited and partially written by Christoph Martin Wieland.

In Liebeskind's tale, which relies heavily on familiar mythological motifs, the Radiant Fairy's daughter has been kidnapped by an evil sorcerer (see Demeter and Persephone) along with her talisman, a fiery golden sword that all the spirits and elements obey. When the young Prince Lulu ventures into the Radiant Fairy's land, she commissions him to regain her possession, promising him in return the hand of her daughter. She gives him a flute that subdues all who hear it (see Orpheus) and a ring that enables its bearer to change his own shape. Lulu, transforming himself into an old man, goes to the magician's castle, where he succeeds in winning the love of the Radiant Fairy's daughter, subduing the sorcerer and his henchmen, and seizing the sword. The sorcerer flees in the form of an owl (see Apuleius's sorceress), the Radiant Fairy destroys his castle, and the prince is united with the fairy daughter. We immediately recognize the parallels between the premises of Liebeskind's fairy tale and act 1 of *The Magic Flute*. But how did Mozart and Schikaneder, in a manner reminiscent of the shifting images of Dionysus and Pentheus in *The Bacchae*, make the leap from the good fairy and evil magician of the fairy tale to the wicked Queen of Night and the noble Sarastro of act 2? And why has Monostatos (the evil henchman in the fairy tale) remained in Sarastro's kingdom of light?

It was long assumed that a radical break occurred in the composition between acts 1 and 2, occasioned by the production of another Singspiel based on the same fairy tale and presented that summer at the theater of Schikaneder's competition.[47] According to that theory the composer and librettist decided to change act 2 by employing material from Terrasson's popular novel *Séthos,* which had already been translated twice into German (immediately in 1732 and then again in 1778). As already noted, the novel was much admired in Masonic circles, and the Egyptian mysteries had been further analyzed as the basis for Masonic ritual in an authoritative article "Über die Mysterien der Ägypter" (in the *Journal für Freymäurer,* 1784) by Baron Ignaz von Born (1742–91), secretary general of the Grand Lodge of Vienna, who was rumored to have provided the model for the figure of Sarastro. The novel provided both a suitable background to gratify the Egyptomania currently prevailing in Europe and an elaborate description of initiation rites for the cult of Isis and Osiris, which were taken by many Masons (as well as Cagliostro) as the source of their own rituals. In the process, the argument goes, Schikaneder neglected to make all the necessary changes in the first act, leaving the "star-flaming queen" (as she is repeatedly called there) as a wholly sympathetic figure, so that the break is still apparent.

Recently, a wholly different explanation has been advanced, most persuasively by the eminent Egyptologist Jan Assmann, who contends that Mozart and Schikaneder collaborated closely on the libretto from the outset and already had Terrasson's novel in mind as a source. Any apparent breaks or discontinuities in the text—notably the shift from the heartbroken mother in act 1 to the vengeful Queen of Night in act 2 and from the description of Sarastro in act 1 as a villain (Bösewicht) to his appearance in act 2 as the noble priest of the cult of Isis—are intentional. The Masonic collaborators set out to realize in operatic form a Masonic mystery play: that is, to render, and to cause the audience along with Tamino to experience, the major shift of consciousness—from superstition to truth, from dark to light, from wilderness to civilization, and fundamentally from illusion to disillusionment—in an "Enlightenment mystery" (Aufklärungsmysterium).[48]

Whatever position one takes in the critical controversy, and regarding the literary merits of the libretto, it is clear that act 2 of *The Magic Flute* depicts essentially a ritual of initiation. As we learn there (scene 8), under Pamina's father the realms of day and night, of sun and stars, were originally undivided. The king at his death freely handed over the "sevenfold solar circle" to the capable hands of Sarastro and the initiates, leaving the realm of night to his wife.[49] It is the goal of the opera to portray the reunification of those opposed realms—day and night, sun and stars, male and female—through the union of Tamino and Pamina: a development parodied at every stage on a comic level by Papageno and Papagena.

The ritual of initiation is prepared in act 1, when Tamino is led by the Three Boys into the temple realm, where he sees the Temple of Wisdom flanked by the Temple of Reason and the Temple of Nature (symbolizing the Masonic and Enlightenment goal of synthesizing reason and nature in a higher wisdom). (Meanwhile, Pamina undergoes different but analogous rituals of feminine initiation practiced in the so-called Masonry of Adoption.)[50] There he is greeted by a priest who informs him that the defamations he has heard about Sarastro are false. But when Tamino asks where he can find Pamina, the priest tells him that "oath and duty bind [his] tongue" until "the hand of friendship leads you into the sanctuary for an eternal union" (1.15).[51] As act 1 ends, Sarastro instructs his priests to conduct Tamino and Pamina, with their heads covered (in Masonic fashion), into the "temple of trial" (Prüfungstempel).

As the second act opens with the stately procession of the priests, Sarastro tells them that Prince Tamino is wandering around the northern gate of the temple ("northern" because the sunlight of Enlightenment never reaches it), seeking to rid himself of the "veil of night" that obscures his insight and to gaze into the sanctuary of light. He assures his fellows, who according to Masonic ritual interrogate him about the candidate's qualities, that Tamino, possesses virtue *(Tugend)*, discretion *(Verschwiegenheit)*, and charity (*Wohlthätigkeit*—the name, we recall, of Mozart's lodge). On the basis of these assurances the priests agree to admit him to the next stage: the more difficult trials that await him. The first trial, Tamino learns (2.3), is the test of silence (the standard requirement, we now recognize, of all cults): he will see Pamina but may not speak to her. (Papageno, of course, fails the test of silence, chattering at every opportunity to his priest-guide, to the Three Ladies, to Papagena.) After Tamino passes the test, eliciting from the ignored Pamina one of the loveliest arias in the operatic repertoire (2.18), he is led into the assembly of priests (whose specified arrangement in three triangular groups of six each reflects Masonic number and space symbolism) and is permitted to greet Pamina before he is taken away again to face "deathly dangers." (In the comic parallel Papagena is taken away from Papageno when, through his chatter, he shows himself still unworthy of her.)

In the next scene Tamino is led in by two men in black armor and fiery helmets and placed before a great pyramid bearing an inscription taken almost verbatim from the novel *Séthos* that the men recite:

Der, welcher wandert diese Straße voll Beschwerden,
Wird rein durch Feuer, Wasser, Luft und Erden;

Wenn er des Todes Schrecken überwinden kann,
Schwingt er sich aus der Erde himmelan.
Erleuchtet wird er dann imstande sein,
Sich den Mysterien der Isis ganz zu weihn.
[Whoever wanders this road full of tribulation
will become pure through fire, water, air, and earth;
if he can overcome the terrors of death,
he will raise himself heavenward from the earth.
Inspired, he will then be able
to dedicate himself wholly to the mysteries of Isis.]

At this point Pamina is permitted to join him and, hand in hand, they undergo the tests of fire and water, as Tamino plays the magic flute given to him earlier by the Three Ladies of the Queen of Night and that, he now learns, Pamina's father carved from the wood of a thousand-year-old oak. When they pass these initiatory tests, they are led off in triumph to the spiritual temple (while Papageno and Papagena go off to enjoy their purely earthly paradise). The Queen of Night, along with her Three Ladies and Monostatos, who has gone over to their side, is plunged by thunder and lightning into eternal night, her power forever destroyed. Tamino and Pamina, in the priestly garb of the cult of Isis, are welcomed by Sarastro and the assembled priests to herald the new era unifying male and female, sun and stars, day and night, spirit and nature.

The opera contains various other musical elements and visual symbols from Masonic ritual and lore (e.g., the three chords that routinely occur to introduce significant moments: the three knocks that proclaim the Apprentice degree in Masonic ritual); or borrowed from *Séthos* (e.g., the serpent that frightens Tamino in the opening scene).[52] For our purposes, however, it suffices to have noted the extent to which this glorious opera—a great success in its own day and, to the present, one of the most enduring and celebrated works on operatic stages across the world—exemplifies the lure of the arcane in late eighteenth-century Europe. The music still pulls us into a wondrous acceptance of all the action, as unlikely as it may sometimes seem. Unlike the novelists, Mozart and Schikaneder actually presented the rituals and symbols of Freemasonry, in all their Egyptian pomp and splendor, visually on the stage. In the last analysis, however, the opera uses the trappings of the society not for any secret doctrines—after all, the realm of light overcomes the realm of darkness—but for its espousal of the Enlightenment ideals of virtue, charity, and humanity.[53]

Sublimated Lodges: Goethe's *Wilhelm Meister's Apprenticeship*

One of the greatest contemporary admirers of *The Magic Flute* was Johann Wolf-gang Goethe (1749–1832). Having become acquainted with the opera early in 1794—when it was first performed in Weimar and while he was director of the Weimar theater—he scheduled its performance eighty-nine times. Its popularity almost immediately inspired him with the idea for a continuation, which he began writing in 1795. In his fragmentary libretto Sarastro embarks on a holy pilgrimage while the Queen of Night broods over plans for revenge with her ac-complice Monostatos.[54] They enclose the infant son of Tamino and Pamina in a golden sarcophagus, which later is transported to the underworld realm where earlier the two lovers had undergone the trials of fire and water. (The casket is reminiscent of one in a scene in Andreae's *Chymical Wedding*, which Goethe knew well.) The grieving parents confront the elements once again to rescue their son, who, now transformed into a winged "Genius," emerges from his im-prisoning box and flies away. At this point Goethe's text breaks off, but in the following scenes the "genius," following his capture by Monostatos, is supposed to be recovered by Tamino with the help of Papageno.[55]

Like Mozart, Goethe had direct experience with Freemasonry, having at his own request been admitted to the Weimar lodge "Anna Amalia" in June 1780.[56] During the next two years he advanced through Journeyman to Master and, in 1782, was receiving instruction in the fourth or "Scottish" degree when the Wei-mar lodge, along with many others in Germany, was suspended. But Goethe's secret-society activities did not stop: in early 1783 he was initiated into the local order of Illuminati. (He became active in the Freemasons again in 1808, when the Weimar lodge was reopened.) His utterances from these years make it clear that Goethe was less interested in the ritual and mystifications of the various orders—which he regarded as ridiculous, counterproductive, and even harmful—than in their social, political, philanthropic, and generally Enlightenment goals. One of his most illuminating poetic fragments from these years, "The Mysteries" ("Die Geheimnisse" [1785–86]), which is based loosely on the Rosicrucian *Fama*, depicts a secluded mountain retreat occupied by twelve brethren presided over by their leader Humanus.[57] As Goethe's remarks regarding the project reveal, the brothers represent the twelve historical religions of the world, whose stories and histories he proposed to relate in the following episodes. His unsuccessful "comedy" *Der Gross-Cophta* (1792), centering on a figure resembling Cagliostro and a plot based on the notorious Diamond Necklace Affair, involves secret societies only peripherally: the Conte di Rostro attracts adherents by promising to introduce them to the secrets of his "Egyptian Lodge."[58] Essentially, however, the work was intended as an exposé of the currently fashionable charlatans and their various frauds. (Goethe sent part of his royalties to Cagliostro's family in Palermo, which had been shamed and impoverished by his exposure and imprisonment.)

Goethe's greatest contribution to the lure of the arcane was his novel *Wilhelm Meister's Apprenticeship (Wilhelm Meisters Lehrjahre)*, which appeared in four volumes in 1795 and 1796. The work is in no sense a lodge novel of the sort represented by Schiller's *The Ghost-Seer* or Grosse's *The Genius*. It is, rather, a panorama of prerevolutionary European society—indeed, probably the most representative European novel of those decades. The secretive Tower Society (Turm-Gesellschaft) constitutes only one among the various typical social groups that the hero experiences in the course of his *Bildung* (a key word in the novel: spiritual-intellectual development).

Goethe began writing a novel entitled "Wilhelm Meister's Theatrical Mission" *(Wilhelm Meisters theatralische Sendung)* in 1777, a youthful project that he discontinued in 1786, having completed only six books. The novel amounted to Goethe's contribution to an ongoing debate in Germany regarding the potential role of the theater in the cultural life of the nation and the ethical development of the individual: a debate punctuated by such key works as G. E. Lessing's *Hamburgische Dramaturgie* (1767–68) and Schiller's essay "The Theater Considered as a Moral Institution" (1784). The fragmentary work is in the tradition of the *Künstlerroman* or artist's novel, in which the hero, an aspiring writer, forsakes the petit-bourgeois security of his family to experience and express himself in the world of the theater, which he encounters in its manifold aspects, ranging from the puppet plays of his childhood and the tightrope walkers of local festivities to the traveling players and established stage of the day, along with accompanying scandals, long arguments about Shakespeare, and discussions about a national theater.

When the composition was interrupted by Goethe's trip to Italy and as his horizons were broadened by his practical experiences at the court of Weimar and the reality of the French Revolution, his views changed. When he took up his novel again in 1794, the "theatrical mission" was reduced simply to the initial episode in Wilhelm's personal development, culminating in a performance of *Hamlet*, in which Wilhelm assumes the role of the prince. Otherwise, the world of the novel was considerably expanded to embrace other elements, including a religious dimension encompassing the "beautiful soul" of the Pietist community and the Catholic devotion of Wilhelm's adoptive daughter, Mignon. His conversations with his friend and brother-in-law, Werner, inform him about the increasingly important realm of business and commerce. And his contact with the nobility in all its moral ambivalence exposes him to the intellectual world of the Enlightenment, to world affairs in the political turmoil of the 1780s, to a lifestyle that he regards as the only reliable vehicle of social culture—and to the secretive Tower Society on the estate of his new acquaintance, the nobleman Lothario. In this rejection of art (the theater) as the exclusive means to personal development, Goethe transformed what had been a *Künstlerroman* into the true prototype of the bildungsroman.[59]

The secret society is introduced in a single short chapter (bk. 7, chap. 9). One morning before dawn Wilhelm is escorted by his friend Jarno through unfamiliar rooms and galleries to an iron-braced door in the tower. After knocking—we are not told whether he gives the Masonic three knocks—Jarno leaves Wilhelm alone in a small dark room. Summoned by an unfamiliar voice to enter, he raises the curtain and finds a room that resembles a chapel, but instead of the altar he sees an elevated table and behind it a curtain covering what appears to be a painting. Along the walls stand lovely cases covered with protective grates of the sort one sees in libraries; but instead of books they hold many manuscript rolls. He is ordered to sit down, but the rising sun casting its rays through the stained-glass windows so blinds Wilhelm that he must hold a hand before his eyes. Now in brief succession four figures appear whom he had encountered previously in his life: a man with whom he discussed his grandfather's art collection (bk. 1, chap. 17); a country parson with whom he debated the role of destiny and chance in human development (bk. 2, chap. 9); an officer who raised doubts about the intentions of his friend Jarno (bk. 3, chap. 11); and the figure who in the performance of *Hamlet* appeared mysteriously as the ghost of the prince's father (bk. 5, chap. 11). Following this procession the abbé appears and, summoning Wilhelm for the third time, hands him his Letter of Apprenticeship, informing him that his years of apprenticeship have now been accomplished.

The symbolism of the scene is evident. Using devices familiar from rituals of the secret societies—standing alone in a dark room, being summoned three times, being blinded by an illumination so bright that one needs to cover the eyes (Illuminati)—the scene recapitulates in dramatic form the principal elements and episodes of Wilhelm's education.[60] The décor itself—the altar-like table, the curtain that seems to conceal a painting, the bookcases—symbolizes the realms of religion, art, and intellect that have contributed to his spiritual and intellectual development. The four figures remind him respectively of the worlds represented in each of four earlier books: his prosperous bourgeois home, the troupe of traveling players, the count's palace where the players performed, and the professional theatrical group that performed *Hamlet*. The Letter of Apprenticeship that he is handed—and of which the reader is given only the opening lines— consists essentially of maxims derived from Wilhelm's own experience: "Art is long, life is short, judgment difficult, opportunity fleeting," and so forth.

This scene has been variously criticized, notably by leading British scholars. Eric Blackall, in an incisive chapter on the novel, speaks of "the hocus-pocus of the Society of the Tower."[61] And in his masterful biography Nicholas Boyle characterizes the scene as a "breathtaking farrago" and "a parody of Freemasonry," of lodge novels in general, and even of his own novel.[62] German critics have been kinder, calling the scene an "aestheticizing appropriation" and "aesthetic functionalization" of secret-society material.[63] The debate can be traced back to Schiller, who read the novel carefully in manuscript, book by book, and wrote a detailed critical evaluation for his friend. In a long letter of July 8, 1796, Schiller observes that the novel in some respects resembles the ancient epic inasmuch as it has "machines" that represent the gods or a ruling destiny.[64] In Goethe's novel this "higher reason" working in secret is represented by the "powers of the tower" (die Mächte des Turms), which guide Wilhelm without his knowledge and are necessary to achieve Goethe's poetic aim. However, Schiller objects, the novel does not explain clearly enough the significance of the "machinery" and its essential relationship to the inner workings of the plot: "Many readers, I fear, will believe that they detect in that secret influence only a theatrical play and an artistic trick in order to increase the complications, to arouse surprises, and so forth." The eighth book, he concedes, provides the "historical" explanation for everything but fails to satisfy the poetic necessity for those devices.

It is certainly true that the Tower scene is inserted without adequate preparation. The "Theatrical Mission" contained no hint of the lodge theme, and Goethe introduced those four anticipatory figures—or gave them retrospectively their significance—only after he began revising and writing the later books in such a manner as to suggest that Wilhelm's life is guided or at least monitored at critical junctures by a mysterious agency. However, Schiller also provides the clue for the justification of the scene, apart from its ironic appeal to the popular lure of the arcane. Namely, in a novel that spends so much time in the world of theater (five of eight books) and whose hero is so long obsessed by theater, it seems absolutely appropriate at this stage to recapitulate the formative influences of Wilhelm's development theatrically. That is the mode to which he (and the reader) responds, more than to the maxims of the Letter of Apprenticeship. Moreover, to highlight the purely playful, theatrical nature of the scene, we should note that none of the four figures who appear there has any further role in the novel: they are truly bit players introduced for the sake of the skit performed in the Tower room. It is a conscious attempt to exploit what Jarno calls "the inclination of youth to secrets, to ceremonies, and great sayings" (548).[65]

As Wilhelm subsequently learns, the members of the group—Jarno, Lothario, and their friends—came together as young men under the guidance of the abbé, who as a former member of an unspecified secret society—possibly Jesuits?—appreciated the educational value of secrecy and organizational form. So they constituted a group with the customary three levels and an archive with accounts of each member's years of apprenticeship. These accounts, along with Wilhelm's Letter of Apprenticeship, suggest that what is commonly called "destiny" or "fate" is actually simply the sum of the accidents that shape the individual's life. Candidates who proved unable to understand the process of development and to mature morally and physically were put off with "mystifications and other hocus pocus" (549). At this point, Wilhelm learns, the group of friends, which began as a loose lodge *(Turm)* is transforming itself into a "society" *(Sozietät)* (564). Their cultivation-education-development *(Bildung)* has reached a level at which they are all eager to move beyond their hitherto self-restricted and essentially local limits into the world at large.[66] "Man needs to be only slightly acquainted with world affairs to notice that great changes stand before us and that property is no longer secure anywhere" (563). Lothario is going to America, the abbé to Russia, and Wilhelm is offered the chance to accompany either of them. As it turns out, he decides to marry Lothario's sister, the baroness Natalie, and travel with her to Italy—a move that prompted the Romantic poet Novalis, recovering from his initial admiration, to ridicule the novel as "pretentious and precious" and to scoff at Wilhelm's apprenticeship as "the pilgrimage to a patent of nobility."[67]

In any case we can now see the "Tower" chapter of the novel as a sublimation of the lodge novel as introduced by his friend Schiller only seven years earlier and as practiced in a succession of trivial novels of the decade.[68] Even though Goethe regards the Tower lodge and the succeeding Society with a recognizable degree of irony, he used the trappings of secret societies—with which, as we have seen, he was personally acquainted—in a justifiably consistent manner to signal the completion of his hero's "apprenticeship," which, after all, began with an obsession with the theater. It is the very process of his development from a naive and clueless youth filled with unrealistically idealistic notions, and utterly insensible to the motivations and feelings of others, to a mature adult with realistic views and aims, that has culminated in the ironic attitude with which he is now able to review his past life as represented theatrically in the little pageant presented for his sole benefit in the Tower and to take his place—with or without patent of nobility—in the group of friends who have transcended personal goals in the hope of benefiting society at large. (It is symptomatic of this process that Wilhelm, when he leaves home for a career in theater, gives up his family name, Meister, to which he is entitled again only when he has concluded his apprenticeship.)

Irony inevitably suggests a high degree of recognition and insight: Goethe's ironic insight into the lure of the arcane for the late eighteenth-century reading public. But, as his late Masonic poem "Symbolum" (1815) states, for all his earlier reservations he recognized the symbolism of the Masonic way:

Des Maurers Wandeln
Es gleicht dem Leben,
Und sein Bestreben
Es gleicht dem Handeln
Der Menschen auf Erden.[69]
[The Mason's journey
resembles life,
and his endeavors
resemble the actions
of people on earth.]

For Goethe, in the final analysis, the secret society was not simply a literary tool; it was a constitutive element of the culture of his age and provided recognizable symbols for the process of *Bildung* that he treasured.

From the many German lodge novels we can safely conclude that secret societies of various sorts—Rosicrucians, Freemasons, Illuminati, Jesuits, and others—were a familiar fact of life in the Germany of the prerevolutionary period. Schiller's justification for writing his *Ghost-Seer* and Mozart's and Schikaneder's appropriation of the genre make it clear, moreover, that the public was eager to be entertained by works featuring such societies with their lure of the arcane: from the Armenian's subtle deceptions in Schiller's work to the trials and ceremonies of *The Magic Flute*. In the sublimations of the opera and Goethe's *Wilhelm*

Meister the society is presented as having a higher humanizing and philosophical purpose, much as was the case in the early Rosicrucian manifestos. In the lodge novels, in contrast, which were explicitly written for a more popular readership, we note a pronounced turn to conspiracy: in Schiller's novel and its continuations, as well as Grosse's *Der Genius* and even in Hölderlin's *Hyperion*. In all of them, moreover, and in contrast to the undirected wanderings of Lucius, Parzival, and Christian Rosencreutz, the secret society actively engages the hero from the start and leads him in his quest toward its own goals, whether good or evil. With the lodge novel, then, we note a further stage in the progression from cult to conspiracy.

CHAPTER FIVE

Secret Societies of Romantic Socialism

Romantic Socialism

The two decades from the July revolution of 1830 in France to the years preceding and following the more general European revolutions of 1848 witnessed enormous intellectual ferment and social turmoil. Although society and culture in France and Germany displayed on the surface the bourgeois tranquility known respectively as the July Monarchy and the Biedermeier Period, the stability was misleading. "We sleep now that we are on top of a volcano," Alexis de Tocqueville warned the Chamber of Deputies shortly before the uprisings of March 1848.[1]

Essentially the turmoil stemmed from a widespread sense that the French Revolution had destroyed the traditional values and order that had long governed European society without replacing them with a valid new system or fulfilling its own promise. The rapid industrialization of Western Europe with the concomitant urbanization of the populace had created a tense new relationship between work and capital that generated a proletariat ruthlessly exploited by the newly wealthy—a development that led to dissatisfactions not just among the abused workers but also among the landed aristocracy, whose authority was challenged by the factory owners; the older bourgeoisie, whose status was threatened; and the peasantry, whose welfare was undermined. These developments produced a spectrum of political views ranging from conservatives demanding a reestablishment of the monarchy to more liberal thinkers convinced that change of some sort was necessary. These attitudes on the left, which embraced moderate republicanism by way of liberal democracy to socialism, can be collectively designated as utopian or romantic socialism—a socialism that must be distinguished rigorously, as did Friedrich Engels in his *Socialism: Utopian and Scientific* (1878), from the more radical and materialistic Marxist version proclaimed in the *Communist Manifesto* of 1848.[2]

Romantic socialism, while not a coherent theory but rather an amalgam of sometimes conflicting ideologies, was essentially based on two ideas that can be traced back at least to early German Romanticism: an organically unified society motivated by pristine Christian values. The poet and thinker Friedrich von Hardenberg, for instance, who is better known under his pen name, Novalis, wrote in 1799 a fundamental essay entitled *Christendom or Europe (Die Christenheit oder Europa)*, in which he praised "the glorious radiant times when Europe was a Christian land, when *One* Christendom inhabited this humanly formed part of the world, when *One* great common interest unified the most remote provinces of the wide spiritual realm."[3] Although the work was known and influential among his younger Romantic contemporaries, it was not published for broader public impact until 1826—just in time to affect the new social thought developing in Germany among such thinkers as Ludwig Feuerbach in his *Essence of Christianity (Das Wesen des Christentums* [1841]). Similar ideas were promulgated in France by Claude-Henri de Saint-Simon in his battle against industrialized capitalism, notably in his book *Le nouveau Christianisme* (1825), in which like Novalis he argued for a socially organic society based on the underlying Christian concept of fraternity.

Neither Novalis nor Saint-Simon knew the word *socialism,* which was coined and gained currency in the 1830s, notably in the writings of George Sand's friend and intellectual mentor Pierre Leroux, who used it as a contrast to egotism and individualism.[4] His best-known work, *De l'humanité* (1840), combined, as did Feuerbach, an almost Hegelian belief in a humanity progressing through history with an equality based on eternal Christian moral values. This idealizing view of Christianity was reinforced by the most recent developments in biblical criticism: notably David Friedrich Strauss's *Life of Jesus (Das Leben Jesu* [1835]), which by differentiating carefully between the "mythic" and the "historical" Jesus presented the image of a very human social prophet who regarded all humankind as God's children and hence as brothers to one another. "And from this there results for their behavior among one another an equality that obliges us to behave toward others no differently than toward ourselves—not to judge them severely but ourselves leniently; and generally to treat them as we wish to be treated by them."[5] Strauss calls this precept "the fundamental moral principle of Christianity" and "the basic idea of humanity: the subordination of all individuals under the common idea of the humanity that lives in all and that should be recognized and respected by each in every other" (207).

This early and still romantic socialism, informed by the aforementioned sense of social and moral disintegration stemming from the French Revolution, was conceived as "a remedy for the collapse of community rather than for any specifically economic problem."[6] It reached its apogee in the 1840s with such thinkers in France as the utopianists Etienne Cabet and François Fourier, the religious socialist Pierre Leroux, the journalist Victor Considerant, and the early feminist Flora Tristan. Its German counterpart is represented by a group of writers from the period known as *Vormärz* (Pre-March, or preceding the revolution of March 1848)—for example, the poet Heinrich Heine, the theologian Ludwig Feuerbach, the publicist and novelist Karl Gutzkow, and others—whose catchwords included *humanism, socialism,* and *democratic activism.*[7] It is no accident that one of the most widely read and discussed works of the period was Alexis de Tocqueville's *Democracy in America* (1835–40).

As mild, idealistic, and nonrevolutionary as these views usually were, they were viewed with suspicion and sometimes outlawed by the conservative and often corrupt and scandal-ridden governments in France, Germany, and other countries. As a result, their adherents frequently found themselves together in secret societies, which thrived during these years despite their prohibition: in addition to such older societies as the Freemasons, Rosicrucians, Templars, or the German *Tugendbund* (League of Virtue), new republican groups like the *Carbonari* in Italy and France, the *Société des Droits de l'Homme* and *Société des Familles* in France, or the *Bund der Geächteten* (League of Outlaws: German foreign workers in France) emerged. It is symptomatic of the great surge of interest in secret societies during these years that the first major bibliography of "Freemasonry and the secret societies associated with it" was published in Germany in 1844 and, among its fifty-four hundred items, cites some sixty works published from 1814 to 1841 in the "battle against secret societies."[8]

It was no doubt this widespread interest that prompted Thomas De Quincey a few years later and with a certain exasperation to write his essay on "Secret Societies" (1847).[9] His cynical exposé, stemming from his curiosity about *what* they do and what they do it *for* (2:276), focuses first on "the great and illustrious

humbug of ancient history, THE ELEUSINIAN MYSTERIES" (2:297). He then asks
if the modern world has no hoax of its own corresponding to the Eleusinian mysteries, confessing that, given his poor opinion of the ancient world, "it would
grieve me if such a world could be shown to have beaten us even in the quality of
our hoaxes" (2:307) and that "a man must be a poor creature that can't invent a
hoax." But not to worry: "For two centuries we have had a first-rate one; and its
name is *Freemasonry*." In the same tone he goes on to ridicule the procedures of
Masonic conclaves. George Sand had a much more positive view. When she
wrote that "Europe (principally Germany and France) is filled with secret societies, subterranean laboratories where a great revolution is being prepared whose
crater will be Germany or France" (3:372),[10] she was referring to the 1750s, but she
had in mind by implication her own period of the 1840s. The combination in the
1840s of romantic socialism and secret societies informed several of the finest,
most representative, and most popular works of the decade.

George Sand's Socialist Utopia

Consuelo and its sequel, *La Comtesse de Rudolstadt,* George Sand's longest and
finest novels, together constitute what has been called the French *Wilhelm
Meister*[11]—an analogy that, given the author's admiration of Goethe, is by no
means far-fetched.[12] But the works, appearing serially from February 1842 to March
1843 and then from June 1843 to February 1844 in the *Révue Indépendente,* may
be regarded not only as a feminine, even feminist, bildungsroman. Set as they are
in Venice, Bohemia, the Vienna of Maria Theresa, and the Berlin of Frederick
the Great with a corresponding cast of historical figures—in addition to the two
rulers such actual persons as Wenzel Anton Graf Kaunitz, Albert Joseph von
Hoditz, and the cousins Friedrich and Franz von Trenck—they offer at the same
time a fascinating historical panorama of central European society in the mid-
eighteenth century. (Most of the action takes place in the decade following the
Wars of Austrian Succession, 1740–48.) Even though the author herself disclaimed
the intention of writing a historical novel—"It is our duty as novelist to pass rapidly over the historical details" (2:455)—she consulted for authenticity a wide variety
of primary sources, including histories of music, geographical works, and mem-
oires of contemporaries.[13]

The *Wilhelm Meister* analogy, which is routinely albeit loosely adduced in Sand
studies, needs to be more specifically defined. Like the first five books of Goethe's

novel, *Consuelo* provides a rich and knowledgeable depiction of contemporary theater, represented here as operatic performance in Venice and Vienna rather than dramatic stage.[14] The historical composers Nicola Porpora and Joseph Haydn play major roles in the fiction, along with numerous secondary historical figures such as the famous castrato Cafferelli (Gaetano Majorano) and the Viennese impresario Ignaz Holzbauer. In its depiction of the musical world of the period—the competing styles of Italian and German opera, the techniques of operatic production, the new infusion of Slavonic music (expedited by Sand's lover, Chopin), the petty intrigues of the singers and patrons (informed by the experiences of Sand's close friend, the mezzo-soprano Pauline Viardot), the response of the audiences (which the author knew at firsthand from her own frequent attendance)—the work easily holds its own in the distinguished sequence of musical novels leading by way of Romain Rolland's *Jean Christophe* to Thomas Mann's *Doktor Faustus*. In *La Comtesse de Rudolstadt,* in contrast, the musical-theatrical aspect soon gives way to the *Bundesroman* or lodge novel, known in French as the *roman initiatique.*[15]

Since I will focus here on *La Comtesse de Rudolstadt,* we can pass rapidly over the longer (nine-hundred-page) and equally fascinating *Consuelo,* whose principal characters appear again in the sequel. Consuelo—her name is actually an Italian nickname derived from her baptism as Marie de Consolation (2:53)—is the daughter of an itinerant Spanish songstress. When she is orphaned at a young age in Venice, her outstanding voice wins her the support and affection of the teacher-composer-conductor Porpora, who mentors her despite the jealousy and envy of her more favored competitors to a spectacular success on the operatic stage. Dismayed when her young betrothed, Anzoleto, betrays her with a seductive rival, she leaves Venice and, under the name Porporina, goes to the gloomy "Castle of Giants"—Sand uses the French term "Château des Géants" and the German "Riesenburg" interchangeably—in the forests of Bohemia, where she becomes the companion and musical tutor of Amelie, a young scion of the noble family von Rudolstadt. There she falls in love with Albert, the heir of the family, who is gifted with second sight and afflicted by a kind of genealogical madness: he feels himself to be identical by metempsychosis with his ancestors and guilty of the crimes they committed in past religious wars. Her affection and commitment—she braves the terrors of dark staircases and crypts to rescue him from the three-chambered underground sanctuary where he is tended by his servant Zdenko, who is equally subject to mad ecstasies—restore him to his

senses and to his worried family (father Christian, uncle Friedrich, aunt Wences-
slawa) as he falls in love with Consuelo and with her father's approval offers her
his hand in marriage.

Unable to decide between love and career, she runs away and makes her way
through various picaresque adventures back to Vienna in the company of the
young Joseph Haydn. There her vocal virtuosity and stage success impress the
empress Maria Theresa, who wishes to recruit her for the court opera on the condition that she make herself respectable by marrying Haydn. However, since they
are both in love with others, she leaves Vienna with Porpora, who has signed a
contract to conduct at Frederick the Great's theater at Sanssouci. On the way they
are persuaded to detour to the castle of Count Hoditz, where they encounter
Frederick the Great in disguise, who is greatly taken by her personality and views
of music. Later, at Prague, she learns that Albert is dying and longs to see her
before his death. She arrives back at the Riesenburg just in time to give him the
consolation of her hand in marriage. When Albert dies a few hours later, Consuelo renounces her title and privileges as Countess of Rudolstadt, as well as all
claims on the family fortune, and sets out with Porpora to honor his contract in
Germany and to reclaim her musical career.

Consuelo revolves largely around music and the heroine's personal development, or *Bildung*. This is not to say that Sand's social ideas are absent here. As
Consuelo and Haydn are making their way to Vienna, for instance, her sympa-
thies are aroused by the peasants—"victims of hunger and necessity" (2:132)—
who share their food with the two wanderers. "The men are chained to the soil,
subject to the plow and their cattle; the women chained to their masters, that is,
to the men, cloistered at home in eternal servitude and condemned to work without relief in the midst of the sufferings and anxieties of maternity." But the views
that become thematically central in *La Comtesse de Rudolstadt* remain largely
peripheral and incidental here. Similarly, elements of mystery cults, Orphic as
well as Egyptian, are evident when Consuelo, like Orpheus a singer, descends to
the underground sanctuary to rescue Albert and restore him to his family in the
world above—elements with which Sand was familiar from the English Gothic
novel (notably Ann Radcliffe's *The Mysteries of Udolpho*)[16]—as well as her wide
reading in such works as Claude Robin's *Recherches sur les initiations anciennes
et modernes* (1779) and Antoine Bailleul's *L'initiation aux anciens mystères des
prêtres d'Egypte* (1821: actually the French translation of a 1770 German compila-
tion of Egyptian texts by C. F. Köppen and J. W. B. von Hymnen entitled *Crata
Repoa*).[17] But in the first volume we find as yet no trace whatsoever of any secret

society. Sand's appropriation of a secret society as the vehicle for her social-utopian views awaits *La Comtesse de Rudolstadt*.

George Sand (1804–76, pen name of Aurore Dupin Dudevant) had been obsessed with such phenomena as the occult, the supernatural, hypnotism, metempsychosis, and ecstatic states of consciousness since childhood, an obsession furthered by her dedicated reading of such writers as Ann Radcliffe and E. T. A. Hoffmann.[18] These interests led, in turn, to her fascination with secret societies, notably during the 1840s, which from the start was tied to the social and socialist views that she shared with most of her friends. The preface to her novel *Le Compagnon du Tour de France* (1841)—the title refers to the organization of craftsmen and artisans whose origins reach back historically into the Middle Ages and legendarily to the temple of Solomon—opens with the statement: "To write the history of secret societies from antiquity to our own time would be a highly useful and interesting task but one that surpasses our powers."[19] She goes on to relate secret societies to social concerns, arguing that "since inequality reigns in empires, equality has necessarily needed to seek the shadows and mystery in order to work toward its divine goal" (35). Sand is realistic enough to realize that secret societies often react to intolerance with intolerance, to the egotism of the ruling society with a contrary egotism, and to blind fanaticism with an equally blind fanaticism, citing as example the "double character" of the Knights Templar. "Such is the evil inherent in secret societies" (36). In this novel, which deals with the conflict between social classes and with such looser organizations as craftsmen's guilds, Sand does not yet depict secret societies as such. Everyone knows, she writes, "that a large segment of the working class constitutes itself into diverse secret societies, not acknowledged by law but tolerated by the police" (38)—societies defined by their obligations.

But her correspondence in the following years demonstrates how thoroughly she immersed herself in works dealing with the history of secret societies. We have already noted her reading in books dealing with the Egyptian mysteries. Occupied in the winter of 1842–43 with the study of heresies, she wrote to her friend, associate, and informant Pierre Leroux that what is really needed is "a great work on the *occult* history of humanity"[20]—a work merely hinted at in the official histories of the world. She comes to the realization that "the history of these mysteries, I believe, can never be carried out except in the form of a novel"— the task that she set for herself in *La Comtesse de Rudolstadt*. "I shall invent the important personages of my secret society, but it is necessary for me to attach them to certain *historical* names in their German manifestations."[21] To this end she asks her friends, several of whom were Freemasons, for books and for "a personnel of Freemasons as precursors of the Illuminati, imbued with the same revolutionary principles, and preparing the way for Illuminism just as Illuminism (which was not born until 1776) prepared the way for Jacobinism."[22] (Her own novel, she stresses, is set in the years 1730 to 1760.) One of these sources, which she read that summer, was F.-T. Bégue Clavel's *Histoire pittoresque de la franc-maçonnerie et des sociétés secrètes anciennes et modernes* (Paris, 1843).[23] As she wrote to Pierre Leroux, her spiritual mentor: "You don't know what a labyrinth you've gotten me into with your Freemasons and your secret societies. It's a sea of uncertainties, an abyss of shadows." And that same month (June 3, 1843) she confided to her son Maurice: "I am up to my ears in Freemasonry."[24] The secret society that she invented for the purposes of the novel, *les Invisibles*—a name that presumably goes back to the invisible "deputies of the Rosy Cross" who announced their presence in Paris in 1622 (see chap. 4) and were henceforth known as the Invisibles—was put in the service of the social goals and the search for social justice that occupied her during these same years leading up to the revolutions of 1848: the ideas of romantic socialism combining social egalitarianism and a kind of Christian mysticism with a passionate feminism.

Sand's model for the fictional rendition of a secret society in a contemporary setting—in contrast, say, to the ancient setting of Terrasson's *Séthos*—was Goethe's *Wilhelm Meister's Apprenticeship,* which had by then been translated three times into French (1802, 1829, and 1843). Goethe—his life, not his novel—provided another essential detail for the novel. During the years 1782 to 1808, when the Masonic lodge "Amalia" in Weimar, to which Goethe belonged, was suspended, he and other members from Weimar frequently attended meetings of the fellow-lodge in the nearby town of Rudolstadt, the lodge to which the philosopher Fichte was admitted in 1794. (It is perhaps worth noting that in the 1802 translation of Goethe's novel many alterations were made, including the hero's name, which was changed from Wilhelm Meister to Alfred—a name suspiciously close to that of Sand's Albert.)

The first half of *The Countess of Rudolstadt,* which begins in Berlin a year after her departure from Albert's deathbed, amounts to a continuation in plot and style of *Consuelo.* Consuelo, while continuing her brilliant singing career, becomes involved in various court intrigues involving such historical figures as Frederick the Great; the king's sister Amalia and her forbidden affair with Friedrich von Trenck; the king's brother Prince Heinrich, an adherent of the Rosicrucians (Sand apparently conflates Heinrich with his nephew Friedrich Wilhelm

II); the notorious Count of Saint-Germain, who reputedly had enjoyed numerous reincarnations; Cagliostro (who, born in 1743, could not have been in Berlin in the early 1750s); and others. Consuelo is startled on several occasions when she sees figures who eerily resemble her dead husband, Albert: in the first scene she faints onstage when she believes that she spots Albert in the audience; a short time later she sees him again in what is purportedly a conjuration by Cagliostro; and he wanders the corridors of the palace as Trismegistus, the "sorcerer" of the mystically inclined Princess Amalia. For her participation in the palace intrigues—she bears secret letters to the princess from her lover, Baron von Trenck—she is imprisoned by the king in the fortress of Spandau. There she encounters Gottlieb, the jailer's seemingly deranged son and a disciple of Jacob Böhme's teachings, who first tells her about the Invisibles, a secret society that gives aid to poor workingmen, and then bears messages to her. After three months the Invisibles rescue Consuelo from Spandau and convey her to an estate several days' journey from Berlin, protected by a masked figure named Liverani, to whom she feels a strange and irresistible attraction and whom she regards as "an archangel bearing under his wing a young seraphim annihilated and consumed by the brilliance of the divinity" (3:267).

There, in a house decorated with maxims and dressed in the white gown of a neophyte, she undergoes what turns out to be the first stage in a long (two-hundred-page) process of initiation. Several days after her arrival (chap. 26) she is conducted through subterranean passages to a great Gothic hall, where she is interviewed by a council of eight figures in red cloaks and white masks. Claiming to be above human law and such human circumstances as fortune, birth, and title, they know of her marriage to Albert von Rudolstadt and ask if she wishes to join their ranks and share their idealistic belief in human perfectibility. She is given a week's time for deliberation. Then (chap. 28), because she expresses reluctance at baring her soul to a group of men, she is brought before another single masked figure, who introduces himself as her confessor and tells her that Albert is still alive: his "death" was a hereditary cataleptic seizure from which he was secretly rescued. The news casts Consuelo into the terrible dilemma of loyalty to the husband she admired but never unreservedly loved and her new passion for Liverani, who, still masked and against all rules of the order, approaches her from time to time on the estate. She is given the order's handwritten history of the mysteries of antiquity, Christianity, and the ensuing secret societies to study.

When she has successfully emerged from the various trials of initiation—confession, a period of silence, no questions, study, and so forth—she is again brought before the council (chap. 31), welcomed into the Temple of the Order, and introduced into its doctrine. The religions of antiquity, she is reminded, had two faces: the secret one of the spirit and the public one of form or the letter. Through her reading she now understands the esoteric mysteries of the past. "The Christian idea, enveloped in the words of its revealer in more transparent and purer symbols, came into the world to bring the knowledge of truth and the light of faith into the souls of the people" (3:362). But theocracy, the inevitable and abusive by-product of religions constituted in times of trouble and peril, soon veiled and altered the original dogma, and the temple was no longer, as in the past, the sanctuary of truth. Yet the truth descended into the lower classes: poor monks, obscure doctors, humble penitents, virtuous apostles of primitive Christianity. "The time is near when the veil of the temple will be rent forever, and when the mob will assault the sanctuaries of the holy ark" (3:363). That time is not yet present, she learns; it is still an age of secret religion. The Invisibles are still inside the temple, warding off those who interpose themselves between them and the people.

This is the temple into which Consuelo is now initiated and welcomed: a sort of übersociety embracing fanatics, mystics, philosophers, poets, and others, as well as members of other sects, ranging from the Knights Templar to Quakers and Moravians. It is their goal not simply to found a universal empire based on a New Order but "to reconstitute a religion" (3:368). "The mysterious and profound formula for the work of the Invisibles" is *liberté, fraternité, égalité* (3:371). Europe, she is told, is currently teeming with secret societies, "subterranean laboratories where a great revolution is being prepared" (3:372):

> You will learn the secret of the Freemasons, a grand fraternity which, under the most varied forms and with the most diverse ideas, works to organize the practice and to speak the idea of equality, although women are admitted only by virtue of adoption and may not participate in all the secrets of the doctrine. We will treat you like a man; we will give you all the insignia, all the titles, all the formulas necessary for the connections that we will have you establish with the lodges and for the negotiations with which we shall charge you. (3:373)

Consuelo firmly declares herself now prepared to suffer the martyrdom of persecution in the service of the Order even though such rulers as Frederick the Great, himself a Freemason, distrust and persecute other societies, such as the Rosicrucians to which his brother Heinrich and sister Amalia belong, albeit only at the second level.

In the next five chapters (32–36) Consuelo's confessor reveals herself to be a woman: none other than Wanda von Prachalitz, Albert's mother. Like him, she suffered a cataleptic seizure that was taken for death; buried alive, she was rescued and brought to the estate and care of the Invisibles by her loving friend and physician Marcus, a senior member of the order. She tells Consuelo about Albert's earlier life under her watchful albeit unrecognized eye: his seven years of travel and study, his initiation into the rituals and superior ranks of Freemasonry, a "preparatory society" (3:410) for the Invisibles. And she exposes the charlatanry of Cagliostro, whom Consuelo had encountered in Berlin: his conjuration of Albert was actually a stealthy view of Albert conducting a meeting of Rosicrucians in the Berlin palace. She concludes with an account of Albert's false death through catalepsy and his resurrection by the same Marcus who had saved her.

At this point (chap. 37) Consuelo is ready for her final initiation into the order, which takes up the remaining chapters of the lengthy novel. Dressed in a wedding gown, she is taken from her house on the estate by gondola along with the still-masked Chevalier Liverani—past the main palace, where she hears her former lover Anzoleto, now fat and singing badly, entertaining the company—to a landing in the gardens. There (chap. 38) she is borne in an enclosed sedan chair to a ruined chapel, where she witnesses a Masonic initiation ceremony. When asked her opinion, she says that it is cruel and barbarous, brought from the East by the Knights Templar, "who wanted to subject society to a sort of monastic despotism" (3:454). Her response reveals to the Invisibles the true feelings of her heart, which are beyond the superficialities of the Freemasons and Templars, who retain traces of a barbarism required in an age when spirits are still imbued with the principle of inequality. Having passed this test, she is now ready to enter "the universal temple which receives all men mingled in the same cult, the same love" (3:456). She is sent alone (chap. 39) through subterranean chambers and dungeons where—a vivid reminiscence of Sand's own visit to the ruins of the palace of the Inquisition in Barcelona—she treads on the bones and ashes of generations of victims and sees torture tools that give evidence of humanity's past crimes and afflictions in the name of religion. "We have spoken to your mind by the solitude to which we condemned you and through the books that we put into your hands; we have spoken to your heart through paternal words and exhortations alternately severe and tender; we have spoken to your eyes through ordeals more painful and profoundly meaningful than those of the ancient mysteries" (3:472), she is told.[25] Now her fatherly judges can either crown her or set her free forever. When the judges ask who she is, she proudly proclaims herself the Countess of Rudolstadt, still faithful to her husband although she loves Liverani. The dilemma is resolved when Liverani is unmasked and turns out to be Albert.

In the course of a splendid ceremony, accompanied by the mysterious sounds of a glass harp, the Invisibles contemplate the "immense logogriph" (3:481)—that is, the puzzle or riddle—of their self-contradictory century, where cowardice is paired with grandeur, knowledge with ignorance, barbarism with civilization, enlightenment with error, unbelief with faith, and other contrasts. They pledge themselves again to the challenge of healing it in expectation of the "evangelical republic" (3:482) that is soon to come. The novel ends à la *The Magic Flute* with the festive consecration of the marriage of Albert and Consuelo and her definitive initiation into the Order of the Invisibles.

In a brief epilogue—which introduces a surprising new association with Wolfram's *Parzival*[26]—we are told that the temple where Consuelo was initiated and married was known poetically as the Holy Grail and the members of the tribunal as Guardians of the Temple—a hint regarding the prehistory of the Invisibles—and that Albert had attained the highest degrees of Freemasonry, as well as the Invisibles. The couple is then sent out into the world to proselytize for the Invisibles. While Albert goes about his assignment, Consuelo sings for ten more years at courts all over Europe. Then Albert, who has gone to Prague to see his dying aunt Wenceslawa, is imprisoned on the charge that he falsely claimed to be Albert von Rudolstadt simply in an attempt to gain an inheritance. Five years of court trials exhaust their savings, and Consuelo, in despair, loses her voice. The Invisibles, having been hounded and dispersed, are unable to help them. They wander off, poor and persecuted, and disappear from history.

Then, to our surprise, a long (wholly fictitious) letter from none other than Baron von Knigge is appended, in which Knigge reports to a friend about a walking tour he made in 1774 with his companion Adam Weishaupt in the Bohemian Forest. There they encounter Albert (his mind now deranged), his protective wife Consuelo, and three of their children. (Two others are in the care and tutelage of Haydn in Vienna.) Albert first enchants them with his violin music and then, in a moment of inspired lucidity, urges Weishaupt to act on the mission to which he feels called: to liberate humankind. In an ecstatic vision Albert reveals to them, corresponding to the Divine Tetrad—Father, Son, Holy Spirit, who are unified in a higher fourth being—the Human Tetrad of sensation, feeling, and knowledge, which reveal themselves in society, religion, and politics as materialism, mysticism, and atheism. The New Age envisioned by the Invisibles will ar-

rive when the three aspects, long divided, are once again brought in the fourth
and higher unity of the Human Tetrad. At that moment the great republic will
arise, proclaiming liberty, fraternity, and equality. With that message Albert, re-
lapsing again into his serene madness, wanders off into the forests with his family. But the appended letter, combined with the earlier allusions to the Holy Grail
and the Knights Templar, provides a complete intellectual and historical geneal-
ogy of the Illuminati, which according to George Sand can look back by way of
the Invisibles, the Freemasons and Rosicrucians, and the Knights Templar and
the Holy Grail to the mystery of primitive Christianity itself—and, presumably,
beyond its own brief history to the secret societies of the 1840s.

Other Lodge Novels of Romantic Socialism

The Countess of Rudolstadt is without question the finest among the French
lodge novels of romantic socialism, combining as it does George Sand's dream of
a social utopia with Christian idealism and integrating that vision into a history
of secret societies from antiquity to the present. It was innovative, moreover, to
the extent that it depicted a woman's initiation into the otherwise almost all-
male society[27]—not wholly so since Wanda von Prachalitz is also a member. But
it was by no means the only one.

A decade earlier George Sand's onetime lover Charles Didier published his
popular novel *Rome souterraine* (1833), which was welcomed by the republican
press in the early years of the July Monarchy and at the same time, in 1835, led the
list of French works condemned by the Catholic Index.[28] (Sand paid indirect
tribute to Didier's novel when Albert's mother, in her account of her son's life,
tells Consuelo how she and Marcus first initiated him into the Invisibles' project
for universal regeneration "in Rome, in the subterranean chambers dedicated to
our mysteries" [3:407].) Unlike Sand's novel this conspiracy thriller, albeit based
on the historical circumstances of 1823 in Rome and the spirit of the *risorgimento,*
is pure fiction with no historical figures. But it is set in the city that Didier knew
intimately from his sojourn there in 1827–28, shortly after the period described
in the novel. The Carbonari, outlawed in 1821 by Pope Pius VII,[29] have for their
security occupied underground chambers in Rome (although not precisely the
catacombs of the early Christians). From there they hope to take advantage of
the papal conclave—Pope Pius VII died that year—to incite a revolution in
Rome and to create what their charismatic and heroic leader, Anselme, calls an
"Ausonian Republic" (183): a political utopia unifying all of Italy (named after

the Ausones, the original prehistoric inhabitants of central and southern Italy). Italian unity is also the goal pursued by another secret society, the aristocratic society of the "Sanfédistes" (followers of the sacred faith), who aspire to an Italy of princes joined under the authority of a pope who favors their cause. "Like the carbonari, the consistory had its statutes, its degrees, its emblems. Each initiate on penetrating the sanctuary received a brass medallion whose mystical symbol was intended to recall to him incessantly the goals of the association" (268). They have placed their hopes in the second major figure of the novel: the Grand Penitent, the cardinal of Pétralia. The cardinal, a grand and noble figure known as "the bastard of Sicily" and whose character was highly acclaimed by George Sand and other contemporary readers,[30] has his own agenda: to restore the papacy to its former power and glory in a unified Italy. When Anselm infiltrates the Sanfédistes to learn their plans, the cardinal confides in him his own secret hopes. The two men form an alliance, but the Austrian secret police check the projects of the Grand Penitent, who soon dies, and then, led by their Captain Orlandini in a battle at the Forum, defeat the insurrection of the Carbonari, almost all of whom are killed or executed along with Anselme. The novel ends with the hope of the sole elderly survivor that he may be "perhaps destined to unite to the generation of martyrs the generation of avengers. The future will tell" (693).

Almost simultaneously with *Consuelo* another *roman feuilleton* appeared in the *Journal des Débats* from 1842 to 1843, Eugene Sue's phenomenally popular *Les mystères de Paris*. Sue, born the same year as George Sand (1804), was an unexpected propagandist for romantic socialism. The son of a prosperous physician and Chevalier de l'Empire, he studied medicine and then tried his hand as a painter before in the 1830s turning to writing—first with a series of sea novels— and leading the gay life of a fashionable man-about-town. Then in 1841 he experienced a sudden and unanticipated conversion to socialism and began the course of writing and activities that led in 1850 to his election as the socialist candidate to the seat of deputy: a career interrupted a year later by his arrest and subsequent exile to Savoy. Although *Les mystères de Paris* takes place largely among the criminal gangs of the Paris underworld, it has nothing to do with secret societies. Dealing as it does with corrupt bankers, magistrates, and intriguing nobility, it offers rich material for Sue's socialist agenda. But the hero, paradoxically, is neither a man of the people nor French but, rather, a German prince, Rodolphe, from the (fictional) grand-duchy of Gerolstein, who, under pseudonyms, helps the poor and rescues the downtrodden before returning to his position at home. And the focus is purely sociopolitical, with no religious dimension.

In contrast, Sue's next and equally celebrated novel, *The Wandering Jew (Le Juif errant,* which appeared serially in 1844 and 1845 in *Le Constitutionnel),* revolved around a secret society: not an imaginary one, like the Invisibles of *La Comtesse de Rudolstadt,* but the Order of Jesuits, which, suppressed since 1767, had been restored by papal order in 1814 and, with all the faults and vices of what Sue regarded as its "collective egoism,"[31] was regaining strength and influence in Europe.[32] The Jesuits as depicted by Sue and exemplified in the figure of the diabolical Rodin—a reptilian and seemingly servile figure who is actually a powerful senior in the order—easily match or surpass in their sinister evildoing the most heinous villains of the 2009 thrillers. Using quotations from contemporary pamphlets, as well as such Jesuit documents as their *Constitution,* Sue portrays a society of black-robed, wicked, and designing priests who in their rapacious quest for power and wealth have totally forsaken the basic principles of Christianity. Sue attacks many other targets of romantic socialism: antifeminism, anti-Semitism, the defective regulations of lunatic asylums and other institutions, a legal and economic system that penalizes the poor—for instance, with unreasonable demands for bail, with low wages, with exorbitant interest rates—and rewards the wealthy and powerful. But the principal object of his polemics is the secretive Order of Jesuits, which corrupts its members to a corpselike obedience through its educational policies; recruits outsiders as compliant lay Jesuits of the "short robe"—including a number of scheming aristocrats whose intrigues progress from the amorous through the political to the religious—through partnership in criminal activities; involves by shrewd calculation many unwitting collaborators—notably simple devout believers—in their machinations; and regards secular law as nothing more than an inconvenience to their goals.

Sue's novel is at once more realistically plausible and exciting—in accordance with the demands of the *roman feuilleton*—than most modern thrillers. The plot of the immensely long work revolves around the descendants of a French Protestant, Marius de Rennepont, who, persecuted and largely dispossessed by the Jesuits, died in 1682 and left as his inheritance his remaining hidden wealth, stating that it should be reinvested over the years and distributed among his surviving descendants 150 years later. For each branch of the family he left a medal inscribed with the date and place of the future meeting on February 13, 1832; and he entrusted the management of his estate to the family of a devoted Jew, Samuel, whom he had saved from the Inquisition. It was his hope that his descendants would be "charitable souls, passionate with commiseration for those who suffer," and that they would assemble around their new fortune, which, "concentrated by this association and wisely managed, may render practicable the most admirable Utopian schemes" (506–7)—in sum, the romantic socialist agenda.

The Jesuits, having become aware of the testament and inheritance, which in the meantime has swollen to the vast sum of 212 million francs, have sought through all possible means to lay their hands on it. Of the seven surviving descendants, whose lives this "C.I.A. *avant la lettre*"[33] has stealthily observed—not just in France but in places as remote as Siberia, India, and the United States— they enlisted one unwittingly in their own ranks, requiring him, Gabriel, to assign all his future property to the order. They dispose of the others or prevent them from being present on the assigned day by various surreptitious and illegal means: by drugging one (the Indian prince, Djalma), by sequestering two young twin girls (Rose and Blanche Simon) forcibly in a convent, by committing another (Mademoiselle Adrienne de Cardoville) under false pretenses to a madhouse, by sending one out of town on a wild-goose chase (the factory owner François Hardy), and by imprisoning another for nonpayment of alleged debts (the factory worker Jacques Rennepont). By the middle of the novel the plot seems to have succeeded: only the angelic Gabriel shows up at the assigned place and time and, faithful to his vows despite his distrust of the order's non-Christian goals, reassigns to the Jesuits his share in the inheritance—which, in the absence of the others—amounts to the entire fortune. At the last minute a mysterious figure emerges and points out to the lawyer a codicil to the will requiring a three-month postponement of the final disposition.

This figure turns out to be Herodias, cursed to wander the earth eternally for demanding the decapitation of John the Baptist, and the spiritual sister of the Wandering Jew of the title. These two, who appear only rarely and mystically in the novel to bring aid to the descendants, serve as the tutelary spirits of the family: the Wandering Jew specifically because, himself originally an artisan, he is the patron of working men, "a race always suffering, always disinherited, always enslaved" (764). In addition, the Wandering Jew is cursed because his presence is often the herald of the dreaded plague or cholera.

It looks at first as though the Jesuits have failed. Several of the descendants and their friends, having become aware of their plot to keep them away from the initial meeting, are now on their guard. But Rodin, eschewing the cruder and illegal methods of his former superior, works more stealthily on the emotions of his victims. In addition, he is powerfully motivated by his secret ambition to use the Rennepont fortune to become general of his order and then pope. By pretending hypocritically but persuasively to have been innocently exploited by his former masters, he manages to worm his way into their confidence and then, by truly diabolical manipulations, succeeds in using their emotions to destroy them all: the workingman, Jacques Rennepont, is given the means to drink himself to death; the factory owner, M. Hardy, is so distraught by the treachery of his best friend, the abandonment by his lover, and the destruction of his utopian factory that he enters a Jesuit retreat, signs over his rights to the inheritance, and then dies; the twin girls are tricked into visiting a plague hospital, where they quickly succumb to cholera; and the young lovers—the Indian prince Djalma and the Parisian aristocrat Adrienne—are maneuvered into a double suicide. Yet Rodin himself is cheated of his victory: at the moment when he receives the announcement of his succession to generalship of the order he dies of poison by order of Vatican leaders, who have become aware of his overweening ambitions. The order itself loses the unethically won inheritance: the relevant deeds are destroyed by their faithful Jewish caretaker, Samuel.

In an epilogue we learn that Gabriel, having been expelled from the order, has bought a farm with a small endowment from Adrienne and lives there with the remaining close friends of the descendants. The narrative ends with the deaths of the Wandering Jew and his sister, Herodias, who have been released from their eighteen centuries of cruel trial by the new dawn arising in the east. "Soon the sun of a new emancipation will arise, which will spread upon the world its clarity, its vivifying warmth like that of the star that will soon be resplendent in the heavens" (1105). In his brief conclusion the author reminds us that he has been attacking not all individual Jesuits but "the abominable spirit of their *Constitution*" and the books of their classic theologians (1107). To answer the criticism that he has set the poor against the rich, he points to the figure of Adrienne, who personifies the noble and generous impulses of the aristocracy, and to M. Hardy, who exemplifies the social achievements of the worthiest employers. Rather than arousing social discord, he has sought to create "a work of union, of reconciliation, between the two classes placed at the two extremes of the social ladder" (1107). In sum, Sue has brought together two principal themes of the decade: romantic socialism and secret societies. He does not focus, as did George Sand, on the process of initiation but exposes, rather, the arcane machinations by which the Order strives to achieve its unholy goals and to combat social progress. To this extent *The Wandering Jew* is a direct predecessor of many contemporary conspiracy-thrillers.

The Resurrection of the Rosicrucians

It is fascinating to note the parallels between two novels where any reciprocal influence is highly unlikely: George Sand's *Consuelo / Countess of Rudolstadt* and Edward Bulwer-Lytton's *Zanoni* (1842).[34] Both works are historical novels set in the eighteenth century of the Enlightenment and in the exotic distance of countries other than those of the authors. Both show the influence of *Wilhelm Meister's Apprenticeship* as a lodge novel of initiation by the German writer both enormously admired. In both we encounter lovely young Italian opera stars—one in Venice, the other in Naples—attracted and married to mysterious heroes from abroad who represent secret societies. These heroes seek to introduce their beloveds to the arcane lore of their societies and must rescue them from captivity: respectively, Frederick the Great's Spandau fortress and Robespierre's dungeons. Finally, both works end with the disappointing frustration of all the glorious goals pursued therein.

While these and other similarities are no doubt due to the expectations of the genre—notably the German lodge novel—conspicuous differences between the works of the two generational contemporaries reflect their different intellectual and political views. Sand's Invisibles, as we saw, proclaimed a sodality uniting and transcending such earlier societies as the Freemasons and Illuminati. Bulwer-Lytton's mystical brotherhood, in contrast, is an ancient order antedating not only the Rosicrucians and other modern societies but even the Pythagoreans and Platonists. "In ages far remote,—of a civilization far different from that which now merges the individual in the state,—there existed men of ardent minds, and an intense desire of knowledge" (474).[35] Their works "constitute the initiatory learning, not only of the Rosicrucians, but of the nobler brotherhoods I have referred to" (xvii).

Whereas the Invisibles sought to recover the ideals of the French Revolution and to create a romantic social utopia based on human equality, Zanoni's brotherhood strives to form "a mighty and numerous race with a force and power sufficient to permit them to acknowledge to mankind their majestic conquests and dominion, to become the true lords of this planet, invaders, perchance, of others, masters of the inimical and malignant tribes by which at this moment we are surrounded" (225)—in short, a master race of the sort envisaged in Bulwer-Lytton's later novel *The Coming Race* (1871), which anticipates Nietzsche's *Übermensch* and later found admirers among the Nazis. The author calls the French Revolution with the utmost cynicism "that hideous mockery of human aspirations." He disdains the "fanaticism of unbelief" (53) and ridicules "the fancy which ran riot amidst the hopes of a social Utopia" (77), leading to the horrors depicted devastatingly in the later chapters.

Bulwer-Lytton's Viola, like Sand's Consuelo, is the orphaned daughter of a musician and a gifted singer; and Zanoni, like Albert, is a brilliant and learned visionary who speaks many languages. But unlike Albert, linked by birth to the reality of his time, Zanoni is reputedly an ageless Chaldean, an immortal who, having forsaken the pleasures of life for those of the mind, for many centuries has lived and studied the secrets of the universe. He and his master-magus Mejnour are the only two survivors of the primal secret order, the forerunner of all subsequent cults and societies. But there are vast differences between the two. "Wisdom contemplating mankind leads but to the two results,—compassion or disdain" (35). Mejnour's passionless visage has none of "the lofty yet touching sadness that darkens the glorious countenance of Zanoni." It is their understanding that the universe consists of "two essences of what is imperishable": art and science, the ideal and the real, intuition and empiricism (478). According to the allegorical structure of the novel,[36] Mejnour, who has aged through the centuries, has dedicated himself to science, the contemplation of the actual, and has no interest in beauty or human emotions. Zanoni, whose love of beauty has kept him eternally youthful, contemplates the ideal as the interpreter of the real through art. Many former members of the order, including the forefathers of several other figures in the novel, gave up their eternity for the sake of temporal satisfactions.

Zanoni meets Viola in Naples in the years immediately before the French Revolution. Although they are powerfully attracted to each other, he is reluctant to sacrifice his search for knowledge for mere earthly gratifications. So he selflessly urges Viola for the sake of her own happiness to marry the English artist Glyndon, who also loves her and can offer worldly security. Zanoni keeps a watchful eye on Glyndon because the laws of his brotherhood require him "to guide even the remotest descendants of men who have toiled, though vainly, like your ancestor, in the mysteries of the Order" (163). (The figure of Glyndon, as a young man whose life is guided by the Genius of a secret society, shows the influence of Goethe's novel.)[37] Glyndon is so greatly impressed by Zanoni's wisdom that he gives up marriage to Viola to pursue arcane knowledge under the tutelage of Mejnour. At that point Zanoni, to Mejnour's dismay, succumbs to an all-too-human love of Viola. "Either must I be drawn down to the nature of the beloved, or hers must be lifted to my own" (322). Since Viola in her pure instinctive humanity— and unlike Consuelo—is incapable of rising to Zanoni's heights of mind, she cannot be brought into the order; Zanoni gives up his immortality and loses much of his mystical power. While Glyndon goes to the Castle of the Mountain for his initiation into the order with Mejnour, Zanoni and Viola retreat for months of bliss on a Greek island. But Glyndon, like Viola, proves too humanly weak to survive the initial trial of patience (which Consuelo, we recall, easily passed): he is seduced by a sensual peasant girl and, in a premature search for secret knowledge, enters Mejnour's forbidden chamber, where he experiences the horrid Dweller of the Threshold, who separates the ideal and the real and protects arcane wisdom from the noninitiated; as a result Mejnour rejects his apprenticeship. Meanwhile, Zanoni and the pregnant Viola must leave their island when it is threatened by plague.

Glyndon, having given up art along with his quest for scientific knowledge—in other words, the approaches of both Zanoni and Mejnour—returns for a time to London, where he becomes a wealthy speculator. But, dissatisfied with his life and excited by the spirit and professed ideals of the Revolution, he goes to Marseilles to join the movement. Meanwhile, in Venice, in 1793, Zanoni fears that his presence—now that he is surrounded by human evil and unprotected by his former powers—will bring harm to his wife and child and so leaves them. The superstitious Viola, falsely warned against Zanoni by Glyndon and by her priest, leaves Venice and accompanies Glyndon to Paris, where Robespierre's Reign of Terror—the earthly political manifestation of the Dweller on the Threshold—has reached its height. Zanoni, fearing for her safety, follows her there, where Viola, as a result of various jealousies and conspiracies, has been betrayed as a counterrevolutionary to Robespierre and his henchmen. Zanoni obtains Viola's release by volunteering to take her place on the scaffold, where he is guillotined, "renouncing earthly immortality for spiritual eternity."[38] But he has succeeded in stirring up the opposition so that, on the same day, Robespierre and his followers are overthrown. Viola dies in the dungeon before her release. As the novel ends, their orphaned child, representing the union of idealism and human instinct, "smiled fearlessly on the crowd" (534); but as the child of the real and the ideal and without a guide, it is destined to lapse into an ordinary human existence.

Like Sand's novel *Zanoni* combines politics and mysticism in a typically mid-nineteenth-century manner. But the two authors' depictions of the mystical side differ as radically as their sociopolitical views. Sand takes great pleasure in depicting the Invisibles as a very human society with its ranks, rituals, emblems, and all the accoutrements of secret societies along with political goals. Bulwer-Lytton, in contrast, has little to say about the structure of his eternal order, which at the time depicted in the novel has been reduced to no more than two members. (This circumstance no doubt reflects the fact that secret societies were so often forbidden both in prerevolutionary Europe and again in pre-1848 Europe.) But at far greater length and in much more detail than Sand he discusses its beliefs, going so far as to introduce supernatural visions to represent allegorically its various aspects: for instance, the fearsome Dweller of the Threshold, who bars the way to true understanding for those incapable of surrendering their mortality and accepting the rules of the order and pursues those who forsake true belief; and Adon-Ai, the splendor of Faith, which imparts its marvels and fortitude to those capable of believing.

Like his contemporary George Sand, Bulwer-Lytton had been attracted since his early youth by mysticism and the occult,[39] themes that show up beyond *Zanoni*, notably in his tale *The Haunted and the Haunters* (1859) and his novel *A Strange Story* (1862). Many of his ideas stem from a serious study of mysticism and Neoplatonism, as attested in *Zanoni* by the quotations that introduce each chapter and by the many footnotes.[40] Moreover, internal evidence demonstrates Bulwer-Lytton's familiarity with at least one of the major original Rosicrucian manifestos. Mejnour asks Glyndon during his initiation: "Do you imagine that there were no mystic and solemn unions of men seeking the same end through the same means before the Arabians of Damus, in 1378, taught to a wandering German the secrets which founded the Institution of the Rosicrucians?" (271)—a clear allusion to the *Fama*.

As the author makes clear in his (fictional) introduction, the entire novel resulted from the narrator's "desire to make myself acquainted with the true origin and tenets of the singular sect known by the name of Rosicrucians" (xii). At the specialty bookshop where he sought further information, he encountered an elderly customer with a profound knowledge of "this august fraternity, whose doctrines, hinted at by the earliest philosophers, are still a mystery to the latest" (xiii). (Although his name is never mentioned, several hints suggest that the gentleman is none other than the aged Glyndon.)[41] When asked for further information, the old gentleman informed him that only a Rosicrucian could explain their mysteries. "And can you imagine that any members of that sect, the most jealous of all secret societies, would themselves lift the veil that hides the Isis of their wisdom from the world?" When they later met again, the same gentleman "condescended to enter into a very interesting, and, as it seemed to me, a very erudite relation, of the tenets of the Rosicrucians, some of whom he asserted, still existed, and still prosecuted, in august secrecy, their profound researches into natural science and occult philosophy" (xvi). But the Rosicrucians, he continued, are "but a branch of others yet more transcendent in the powers they have obtained, and yet more illustrious in their origin." It was this same old gentleman who, upon his death, left to the author a manuscript in ciphers containing the account of Zanoni that constitutes the novel we go on to read: "a truth for those who can comprehend it, and an extravagance for those who cannot" (xx).

Even though Bulwer-Lytton was elected (without his consent) Honorary Grand Patron of the English Rosicrucians and has often been claimed as a member,[42] the evidence for his membership is scanty at best. It is certainly an oversimplification to characterize *Zanoni* as a Rosicrucian novel.[43] Formally, certainly, its pattern is based on lodge novels after the model of the eighteenth-century German works and featuring Glyndon as the neophyte, Viola as a combination of Mignon and Natalie, Zanoni as the Genius, Mejnour as the Superior. And its allegedly "Rosicrucian" spiritual content belongs to a long historical tradition of which Rosicrucianism constitutes no more than a significant part. A more immediate intellectual source can be found in the German Romantic writers and thinkers whom Bulwer-Lytton admired and who, from Schelling with his "duality philosophy" down to Hegel, regarded as their principal goal to reconcile and synthesize the real and the ideal. As for its alleged supernatural elements, in retrospect we recognize that Bulwer-Lytton's ideas to a great extent constituted "an attempt to work out in literature what many contemporary scientists were actively engaged in exploring"[44]—magnetism, electricity, hypnotism, telecommunication, and other obsessions of Victorian science.

Bulwer-Lytton's literary reputation in England during his lifetime careened wildly between popularity and contempt. *Zanoni,* which the author regarded as his finest novel, while acclaimed by Thomas Carlyle and a few others, was overwhelmingly criticized. His mystical works, profoundly influenced by such German writers as Goethe, Schiller, and Novalis and highly speculative in their thought, were felt to be too foreign, too spiritual, and, accordingly, were received much more enthusiastically by readers abroad and especially in Germany, where the popularity of lodge novels continued unabated.[45]

Romantic Socialism Etherealized

The logical and probably longest (at four thousand pages) successor to the novels considered up to this point was Karl Gutzkow's commercially and critically acclaimed *Knights of the Spirit* (*Die Ritter vom Geist* [1850–51]), which appeared as a *roman feuilleton* in the *Deutsche Allgemeine Zeitung.*[46] As he confided to his friend, the journalist and novelist Levin Schücking, Gutzkow set out to write "a political Wilhelm Meister, simple, natural, true to life."[47] But the novel also contains numerous references to the works of such contemporaries as George Sand, Eugene Sue, and Bulwer-Lytton;[48] indeed, the basic plot device—the attempt of one of the heroes to win back a contested inheritance, which is ultimately destroyed by fire—suggests specific parallels to *The Wandering Jew*. Gutzkow was so keenly aware of the similarities that in the preface to the first edition he explicitly asked the readers not to assume that he was simply imitating the French (1:39). We also recognize many other devices familiar from nineteenth-century melodramatic fiction: orphaned children searching for their fathers, fathers returning from America with new identities, seemingly impossible love affairs, confused identities, wily intrigues of sinister schemers, and so forth.

But in contrast to the traditional sequential narrative *(Roman des Nacheinander)* Gutzkow invented what in the preface to the first edition (1:41–42) he termed the new novel of simultaneity *(Roman des Nebeneinander)*: all the action is compressed into the two years from June 1849 to September 1851 in and around an unnamed royal capital that clearly resembles Berlin; and the novel turns out to be in some respects a roman à clef, featuring several clearly recognizable figures from the Berlin of that day. The mostly brief chapters enable the author to juxtapose scenes from the most heterogeneous settings—urban palaces and squalid tenements, splendid villas and wretched hovels, country inns and city restaurants, elegant boudoirs and artists' ateliers, which are described in vivid detail. "Throne and cottage, marketplace and forest are thrown together in conflict" (1:42). The roughly twenty well-defined central figures, accompanied by a two-score cast of secondary characters, constitute a full spectrum of examples from every level of society, from the king and queen through the aristocracy, the upper and lower middle classes, artists and artisans, down to the urban proletariat and the rural peasants, all of whom are vividly characterized through the extensive dialogues that constitute the principal tool of the narrative.[49] Through this treatment, Gutzkow believed, "humanity can once again seize faith and confidence from poetry—that the earth is ruled by one and the same spirit" (1:42). In any case the novel provides an unparalleled panorama of cultural, social, and political life in mid-nineteenth-century Prussia, which has been suggestively compared to the fashionable panoramic paintings of the period.[50] In another connection Gutzkow speaks of "a concert, where the author hears all the instruments and voices at the same time within and next to one another."[51] Gutzkow was well aware of his novel's shortcomings—what in the preface to the third edition he called the "clattering mechanism" (1:48) of its often sensationalizing melodramatic plot. But what it lacks in literary originality is more than adequately offset by its unparalleled documentary value.[52]

The action comprises many interrelated plots, of which two are principally relevant here. A young legal intern, Dankmar Wildungen, while visiting his mother, a parson's widow, in the village of Angerode, discovers an old chest containing documents proving that many valuable properties now claimed by both city and state rightfully belong to him and his brother, the artist Siegbert. As the chest is being brought back to the city, however, it mysteriously disappears and ends up in the hands of the unscrupulous legal representative of the municipality. Much of the succeeding action involves the efforts to recover the chest and the papers it contains, and the lengthy court case that ultimately reaches the supreme court for adjudication.

In the course of their search the brothers encounter a young journeyman-carpenter who turns out to be Prince Egon von Hohenberg, who upon his mother's death has returned in disguise from travels and adventures abroad to claim his heavily indebted inheritance. As a parallel to Dankmar's search, the prince seeks to find among the scattered possessions from the family castle a portrait of his mother with a hidden panel containing a secret message for him. Their seemingly similar democratic hopes for a better future—similar because of the prince's working-class experiences abroad—lead initially to a close friendship among the three young men, in the course of which Dankmar's physical resemblance to the prince also results in various complications. When Egon learns from the portrait-message that he is actually the child of his mother's brief extramarital affair with a nonaristocrat and, as it turns out, a cousin of the two brothers, he is suddenly and for the first time overcome by the urgent desire to be the prince he had long and with a certain indifference believed himself to be. His very name turns out to be symbolic of his self-serving ambition since his friends regard him as "the prototype of the egoist" (3:540). Suddenly asserting reactionary royalist views, he becomes minister-in-chief of the kingdom and in his quest for power turns against his former friends and their allies, whom he accuses of conspiracy and seeks to imprison. After many twists and turns of plot his true identity is exposed in a confrontation with his father (who has returned from America). He resigns his high office and, following a reconciliation with his former friends, retires with his wife to Nice. The brothers win their case and marry the girls they seemed long destined to lose, but the vast wealth they are awarded through the restitution is lost in an accidental fire. Siegbert and his wife emigrate to Switzerland while other friends, under political suspicion, go to Paris and elsewhere. At the melancholy conclusion of the novel only Dankmar remains in his native kingdom to work for the future.

The novel owes its place in our literary progression to the fact that the brothers plan to use their inheritance not for personal aggrandizement but to support the secret society they establish, the Knights of the Spirit, for the betterment of society. The first element of the name is based on the fact that the inheritance goes back to the Knights Templar. The documents that Dankmar discovers include the archive covering the Knights of St. John from 1320 to 1636, who inherited the charge and wealth of the outlawed Templars and later converted to Protestantism (1:93). In his testament their sixteenth-century ancestor, Hugo von Wildungen, left his properties to *propinquis equitibus.* The city has maintained in its argument for three centuries that the Latin phrase refers to those knights who stood closest to Wildungen in rank and, hence, to their descendants: that is, the modern municipality. The high court to which the case is eventually referred, however, discovers two commas obscured in the original text and embracing the word *equitibus,* suggesting that the passage should properly be read "to my relatives, themselves knights" (3:464). Accordingly they restore the inheritance, which includes many properties marked with the symbol of the Knights of St. John, a four-leafed clover, to the brothers. The Templars and Knights of St. John constitute a leitmotif threading throughout the entire narrative.

When the novel opens, we find the artist Siegbert at Tempelheide, a village just outside the royal city and formerly owned by the Templars, where he is sketching the simple church, which is adorned by a cross whose arms end in four-leafed clovers (1:61). (Tempelheide clearly refers to the Berlin neighborhood of Tempelhof, which historically was originally owned by the Knights Templar.) From this point, where we are given a brief initial sketch of the Templars and Knights of St. John, allusions to those orders recur constantly.[53] The brothers, sons of a village pastor, grew up in a house attached to a Templar house in another village owned by the order, "one of the most lovely remnants of the Middle Ages" (1:82). In that connection Dankmar reminds his brother of the history of the Templars and the fiery death of Jacques de Molay before informing him of the archives of the order that he discovered in their village. Later the scheming city counselor who misappropriated the relevant documents tells a confidant how the wealth of the knightly monastic orders was scattered during the religious wars and the succeeding secularization and how, in the process, the city "fished up seventeen houses, . . . the basic property of Tempelheide and a number of other properties that all once belonged to the Johannite order of Angerode" (1:414). Many other passages refer to the Jesuits, the Freemasons, and in particular to a recently formed social group, the "Reubund" ("order of remorse"—Gutzkow's parodistic allusion to the "Treubund" or royalist "order of loyalty," which actually existed in the Berlin of King Friedrich Wilhelm IV). Given this context—the frequent allusions to secret societies and specifically to the Templars and Knights of St. John—it is hardly surprising that the friends—Dankmar, Siegbert, Egon, and Egon's friend, the French carpenter Louis Armand—when the idea of a secret society first occurs to them, imagine their own new order in knightly terms: Knights of the Spirit. They see themselves as the legitimate successors of the original knights, and the notion of historical continuity is frequently stressed. But what sort of order do they have in mind?

The March revolution of 1848 in Prussia was a tragicomedy of errors. In response to demands generated by the revolutionary agitation and the politically oriented literature of the 1840s King Friedrich Wilhelm IV, the humane but politically inept "Romantic king," issued a proclamation in which he promised to accede to several key demands of the democrats, including a constitution and freedom of the press. When crowds gathered before the Berlin palace to express their thanks, the military guard mistakenly feared violence and, in their efforts to clear the area, killed several civilians, an action that in turn precipitated street fighting. Fearing civil war, the king ordered the withdrawal of the troops and paid public homage to the bodies of the victims, which were displayed in the palace courtyard. However, his gesture of solidarity with the people and the ensuing formation of a liberal government were deeply resented by the conservative monarchists, the Junkers, who regarded it as a defeat and concession of power to the democrats. When the new Diet threatened to move too radically to the left, the king dismissed the liberal ministers and appointed a group of conservatives in their stead. Although a constitution was ratified in January 1850, the king retained all essential powers, both civil and military. The sociopolitical result was a period wrought by inner turmoil and dissension, where individuals and parties without consensus pursued their special interests and where all the grand hopes and ideas of Young Germany had collapsed.

During these years, a period known in German literature as "poetic realism," the political orientation that had characterized Young Germany of the 1840s yielded to a generally unpretentious and essentially conservative literature with no ambition for political activism. Typically Friedrich Hebbel (1813–63), the great-

est dramatist of these years, turned from the social-critical orientation of his earlier works to historical dramas with religious and artistic themes or to topics
such as those in *Gyges und sein Ring* (1856) or his "German tragedy" *Die Nibelun-
gen* (1862), in which he sought to find ancient analogies for modern political and
ethical ideas. Similarly Gustav Freytag's great social novel *Debit and Credit* (*Soll
und Haben* [1855]) amounts to a hymn in praise of the German merchant class
and its solid bourgeois values. The public, disenchanted by the failure of the revolution, turned its attention either inward or toward lighter forms of entertainment, and whatever political discussion still took place was so fragmented that
no unified opposition could emerge. Schopenhauer's pessimism was the appropriate philosophy for this disillusioned age. In contrast to the pre-1848 novels in
France, which expressed a certain hope for the future, these later works are characterized by a sense of resignation and sobriety, as well as "hatred and persecution," as Gutzkow put it in the preface to the third edition (1:47).

Karl Gutzkow (1811–78), born in Berlin as the son of an employee in the service of a Prussian royal prince, was educated at a leading Gymnasium and later,
as a student of theology and philosophy at the University of Berlin, attended lectures by such luminaries as Friedrich Schleiermacher and G. W. F. Hegel.[54] As a
political journalist with radical views, he wrote for various publications, but the
twenty-four-year-old achieved true notoriety for his attacks on ethical norms
and religious faith with his novel *Wally the Skeptic* (*Wally die Zweiflerin* [1835]),
which portrayed a liberated woman pursuing free love and ultimately committing suicide out of religious despair. Sentenced to a month's imprisonment for
contempt of Christianity, he was identified in a denunciation by the Federal Diet
as a leader in a loose circle of young liberal political-religious-ethical critics and
writers, who for all their differences came to be known collectively as Young
Germany *(Junges Deutschland)*. For the next ten years, while editing his journal
Der Telegraph für Deutschland, Gutzkow achieved considerable success with his
dramas, culminating in his tragedy of religious intolerance, *Uriel Acosta* (1846).
Although he was in Berlin at the time of the March revolution, he did not participate actively in the events. But the failure of the revolution, which he attributed
to the lack of any common goal among the various constituencies, produced the
sense of disenchantment defined above and a conviction that social progress
could be achieved in Germany only by a commonality of spirit among the various groups and parties transcending the various special political interests. It is
this sense that underlies the secret society of "Knights of the Spirit" that Dankmar Wildungen and his friends hope to organize.

The secret society, while mentioned repeatedly in passing, is depicted in three principal scenes, of which the first occurs midway through the novel (book 5) and after the theme of secret societies has been well established through historical references.[55] In their discussion of early Christianity and previous forms of spiritual community the four friends reveal a spectrum of democratic and oppositional views, ranging from Dankmar's liberal monarchism (1:148) and Siegbert's "half socialist" notions (1:76) to the communism of Louis Armand, who had formerly belonged to a French craftsmen's guild of the sort portrayed in George Sand's novels.[56] Dankmar, expressing his admiration for the organizational skills of the Jesuits, believes that a similar order with a nobler mission could redeem the world. All the historical examples reveal "a profound and ancient need of humankind to liberate itself from the tangential exigencies of existence" (2:268). In words that seem to anticipate the existentialism of Heidegger and Sartre, he remarks that "we are cast into this world without protection, without guides. We must struggle alone to win our share of, I shall not say happiness and joy of life, but only of the possibility to exist" (2:269). Our humanity is the sole bond that connects us. "The state is no league of humanity, society is cruel and loveless, the princes treat the peoples as inherited property. . . . Life has become a great danger." Arguing that some means must be found to shorten the process of development of the age, he proposes that man should "found a society of the general human spirit against the misuse of physical force" (2:271). Within fifty years, he believes, such a league of the free human spirit could clarify all the contested issues permeating and confusing the present. Over Egon's objections he insists that the society must initially be secret, like early Christianity itself, with its own rituals of initiation. "The nature of every polemical thought, which must strengthen itself through like-thinkers, requires secret preservation" (2:273). The conversation continues for some time, but at this point—the autumn of 1849—the conception of the Knights of the Spirit remains no more than an idea.

Some weeks later—Egon has already turned away from his friends and embarked on his parliamentary career—Dankmar and a few others meet secretly in a basement room of the Ratskeller, where Dankmar repeats more fully and forcefully his earlier arguments. "Humanity is split apart—not only in its interests but also in its spirit" (2:483). A superficial Christianity no longer holds people together. The state unites its citizens only in war. The true misery of the age is "a result of the total non-organization of the battles of the spirit" (2:283). To combat this situation, he says, "I want to found a secret [geheimen] order—not a clandestine [heimlich] one." Conspiracies emerge from clandestine orders, he continues. The Jesuits and Freemasons, in contrast, are orders with secret rituals and symbols; but they are simply secret and not inaccessibly clandestine. Every secret society needs three things: a motivating idea, symbols, and adequate means. "The Knights of the Spirit are the new Templars. It is their charge to guard and protect the temple that humankind must build on earth in honor of God" (2:483). Their mission is a crusade against the enemies of this temple of the spirit. Dankmar continues for some pages to outline his dream of the new secret order, but in contrast to the secret societies of romantic socialism this one has no clearly defined social or political goals. It remains on the abstract level of "spirit," which should transcend more mundane goals in its effort gradually and eventually to unite humankind as a whole.

In the following months the group recruits more members: its method of assuring independent thought rather than enlisting an obedient mob is the requirement that new members must be recruited from a social level higher than that of the recruiting member. By this time, however, Egon has become minister-in-chief and has set his minions to persecute and prosecute the society, whose democratic hopes he regards as a threat to the reactionary policies of the post-revolutionary monarchy. Yet Dankmar hopes within the course of a year to be able to go public with a dedicatory meeting at which the group and its new representatives will determine the suitable form for its development. "It is the spirit that continues to have an effect. The hour will come when its works, which are now still being prepared in silence, shall step into the light of day" (3:335).[57] That hour arrives when a wealthy new member purchases and restores a former Templar castle, Tempelstein, near the French border of the kingdom. On September 15, 1851, a hundred members from different lands gather at Tempelstein for what turns out to be a solemn though ultimately melancholy ceremony. "They reveal plans, drawings, parchments with seals" (3:518) and admire the new "Book of the Spirit" that represents the symbolism of the order. But at that same meeting the newly restituted funds meant to sustain the order accidentally catch fire and are burned up. A much-aged Egon, who has resigned his ministership, appears and celebrates a reconciliation with his friends. But at the end almost all the members, still under suspicion of conspiracy by the reactionary government, emigrate with the promise that they will come together again in one year's time.

In Gutzkow's novel we witness something altogether new: the conception and organization of a secret society from its first idea and gradual elaboration in a single mind through its theoretical acceptance by a small group to its founding dedication by a large company of new members—a society whose benevolent goal is regarded by the authorities as a threatening conspiracy. In its detailed portrayal of a contemporary secret society linked historically to the Templars and Knights of St. John and structurally to the Jesuits and Freemasons, the novel fulfills the expectations associated with the lure of the arcane. At the same time, the goals of these Knights of the Spirit have become so ethereal that they have nothing in common with the more practical goals of French romantic socialism or any of the earlier secret societies. In fact, the only practical result of the democratic goals is evident in the various marriages, which unite various social classes: Siegbert marries the daughter of aristocracy, Dankmar a daughter of the prosperous middle class, Prince Egon the daughter of a disgraced bureaucrat, and the carpenter Louis a daughter of the peasantry.

The novel reflects Gutzkow's own attitude—more theoretically intellectual than practically political—and his disillusionment following the March revolution of 1848, in which all the glorious if unrealistic ideals of Young Germany were deflated. Gutzkow's contemporary, the prominent critic Julian Schmidt, took the author to task in a leading journal for his visionary view that fuzzy-minded secret societies of "intelligent but confused people" were a more effective means of political change than actual political parties.[58] In comparison with Gutzkow's secret society, he remarks elsewhere, "the conspirators of 1848 appear as pure wisemen of the world."[59] Yet it is easy to agree with Arno Schmidt's appreciation in dialogue-form of Gutzkow's life and works that the novel deserves reading today for three reasons: its theme that salvation will come neither from above by imposition nor below by revolution but by gradual evolution through the organization of the elite; such snapshots or transparencies (Dias) of contemporary social life as grape-harvesting, popular dance balls, and the first literary depiction of Berlin tenements;[60] and the advance in prose form represented by the novel of simultaneity, which reached its high point with James Joyce.[61]

Disillusionment

Gutzkow's Austro-Hungarian (originally Croatian) contemporary Eduard Breier (1811–86), a journalist and prolific author of popular and often anticlerical novels, had a more cynical view of secret societies. His *Rosicrucians in Vienna* (*Die Rosenkreuzer in Wien: Sittengemälde aus der Zeit Kaiser Joseph's II* [1852]), set like Sand's and Bulwer-Lytton's novels in prerevolutionary Europe, offers a panoramic view of the Vienna of 1786. Like Sand's two novels, it has a strong historical

basis with a cast involving a number of actual figures, including Emperor Joseph
II, Haydn, Mozart and his two librettists (Da Ponte and Schikaneder), known
bookdealers and writers, and even a now older Baron Friedrich von Trenck,
whom we know from *The Countess of Rudolstadt.* The catalytic moment of the
action, on March 10, 1786, is the public execution of the notorious murderer
Franz Zahlheim. Another scene portrays the aftermath of the premiere of *The
Marriage of Figaro* and the dispute between Mozart's friends and Salieri's admirers (bk. 4, chap. 1). A major figure is Cagliostro. (We learn only in the final pages
of volume 4 that he is actually an impersonator of the real Cagliostro, who is
awaiting trial in Paris for the Diamond Necklace Affair; but he plays his part so
convincingly that we, along with all the characters in the novel, assume that he is
truly the famous magician and soothsayer.)

The intricate and melodramatic plot, which after four volumes of twists and
turns results happily in the marriage of the two young couples and the appropriate punishment of the scoundrels, amounts less to a romantic-socialist vision
than to an exposure of the corruption of the Rosicrucians, the scheming charlatanry of Cagliostro and his kind, and the blind idealism of the Illuminati. The
Viennese Rosicrucians—prohibited in Austria since 1766 by imperial edict—are
depicted as a bungling group whose schemes invariably fail.[62] We are given, to
be sure, an elaborate depiction of an initiation test and rituals of induction into
the lodge "Of the Seven Planets" (bk. 1, chap. 10), as well as a brief history of the
order. But their principal scheme goes awry: to gain wealth by obtaining from a
legitimate Prussian chemist currently operating in Vienna his secret formula
for "philosophical gold-salt" (*philosophisches Goldsalz,* an actual aurotherapeu-
tic elixir made from gold dust and aqua regia and formerly sold for considerable
sums). (In Austria the eighteenth-century craze for alchemy was so great that
Empress Maria Theresa promulgated an explicit policy against it.)[63] They succeed in part, but the various members of the order involved in the plot suffer as
a consequence: Wendelin—one of the two young heroes—is required to seduce
the wife of the chemist's assistant and in the process almost loses his true beloved; an older member, a trusted officer who misappropriates funds from
the state treasury in order to purchase the formula from the assistant and his
wife, is sentenced to the pillory and to four years imprisonment; the chemist's
assistant is left jobless and penniless when his wife runs away with another man
and with their money. Yet another member of the order is sentenced to the galleys for forging money to win the affections of Cagliostro's beautiful seductress, Seraphina.

Meanwhile, the various wonders performed by the false Cagliostro are eventually exposed rationally. He almost succeeds in seducing the beautiful sister of the executed criminal by claiming to conjure up the spirit of her dead brother; we subsequently learn that the role was played by his assistant, who resembled the brother. He manipulates the second young hero, Lohberg, the illegitimate son of a deserted mother, by claiming mysteriously to know his family secrets and by offering to reveal them if the young man will obey his wishes. It turns out that he, the false Cagliostro, is himself the young man's father who cruelly deserted his mother before his birth.

The only positive role played by a secret society is that of the Illuminati, who at the time were illegal in Vienna. The false Cagliostro, it turns out, was sent to Vienna many years earlier, with money and authority, to represent the interests of the order: "to plant the banner of light, of freedom and of fraternity in all lands at once" (4:156).[64] In one scene (bk. 2, chap. 21) Cagliostro receives and reads reports sent "in the Name of Light, Freedom, and Fraternity" by representatives in Bohemia, Hungary, Transylvania, Brussels, Innsbruck, and elsewhere. And apparently in the service of the order he writes and publishes pamphlets—defending both the murderer Zahlheim and the embezzling officer—intended to stir up the people against the monarchy. But as his ambitions and passions overcome him, he assumes the role of Cagliostro and uses his position in the order for personal goals. At the end, accordingly, the order, having learned of his misbehavior from other agents in Vienna, sends a jury of three masked members who try him and sentence him to death according to their law: "An Illuminatus must kill himself rather than betray the Order" (4:161). As an act of redemption he sends his son a letter with documentation condemning the evil guardian who had earlier exploited his grandmother and mother, forcing the latter, in order to obtain her inheritance, into a marriage with the false Cagliostro that never took place and left him illegitimate.

The Illuminati have no functional role in the novel, however, appearing only at the last moment as *dei ex machina* to punish the villain. In general, Breier's frequently repeated theme concerns the paradoxical circumstance that such chicanery as that practiced by the Rosicrucians and Cagliostro could actually have succeeded in the Age of Reason. He cites a statement by Catherine the Great of Russia attacking her century's belief in alchemy, conjury, and charlatanry of every sort (4:16–17). Elsewhere he expresses his own consternation: "Our readers will perhaps find it incomprehensible that, in an epoch claiming 'Enlightenment' as its password, men of reason and education could concern themselves with alchemy and ghost-seeing. They will be astonished—and rightfully so—to meet in the so-called philosophical century, at a time when the press was already exerting its powers, when the encyclopedists were displaying their full activity, when science gradually began to become a common property—in such an age to meet people who seek the Stone of the Wise, produce elixirs, and conjure spirits" (1:109–10). People of the Josephine age, he concludes with his customary cynicism, dealt with Enlightenment just as his own contemporaries were dealing with freedom: "everybody talked about it and only a few understood it" (1:111). In other words even the social and political ideals proclaimed a century earlier by the Illuminati have failed to be realized in post-1848 Europe—a view akin to De Quincey's skepticism and one that deflates the hopes expressed by his French romantic-socialist contemporaries only a decade earlier. Yet those very hopes and ideals, he implies, were sustained by the same lure of the arcane that made people susceptible to the humbug of Cagliostro and the Rosicrucians.

The novels of romantic socialism mark a further step forward in the progression from pagan cults to conspiracy fiction. All of them are informed by a keen awareness of the history of secret societies going back by way of the Knights Templar to the Egyptian orders, and they depict various aspects of occult orders: for instance, the elaborate initiation ceremonies (Sand), the evanescence of an ancient order (Bulwer-Lytton), the creation of a new society (Gutzkow). Although most of them are set in the Europe of immediate prerevolutionary decades, they all reflect directly (notably *The Knights of the Spirit*) or by analogy the euphoria of the years preceding and the disenchantment of the years following the revolutions of 1848. Implying as they do that societies, given the unworthiness of the existing aristocracy, require a specially qualified and secret elite to govern them properly, they betray increasingly a disillusionment with the proclaimed ideals of liberal democracy. In the last analysis, these novels represent both the positive and negative views of secret societies: from the evil machinations of Sue's Jesuits and the incompetence of Breier's Rosicrucians to the political activism of Didier's Carbonari and the idealizing visions of Sand's Invisibles, Bulwer-Lytton's master race, and Gutzkow's Knights of the Spirit. In sum, virtually every device of the contemporary conspiracy thrillers can be found in these page-turners of the mid-nineteenth century.

CHAPTER SIX

Modern Variations

The Madness of Occultism

"What a bizarre epoch," marvels Durtal, the hero of J.-K. Huysmans's novel *Là-bas* (1891: translated variously as *The Damned, Lower Depths,* and *Journey into the Self*). "Just at the moment when positivism is at its height, mysticism awakens and all the madness of occultism commences."[1] Durtal, who is writing a biography of the sadistic pedophile and heretic Gilles de Rais, believes that he needs to experience a Black Mass in order to comprehend fully the Satanism of his subject. Learning that Black Masses are still celebrated secretly in fin-de-siècle Paris, he is on the point of being taken to one by his sinister mistress. His friend des Hermies advises him that "it's always been like that"—that all centuries resemble one another as they end. "Magic flourishes when materialism is raging." He reminds Durtal of what happened as the eighteenth century was coming to a close, when (as we saw in chapter 5) charlatans and secret societies flourished at the peak of the Enlightenment. Looking back, we can see that more or less the same thing occurred at the beginning of the seventeenth century, which produced the initial Rosicrucian hoax at a moment when both rationalism and alchemy were thriving; at the end of the so-called twelfth-century Enlightenment, when the Knights Templar were transformed into the Knights of the Holy Grail; in the late Roman Empire, when a host of foreign cults, such as that of Isis, invaded Rome; and even at the end of the fifth century BCE, when the disintegration of Greek rationalism opened the way for such mystery cults as those of Demeter and Dionysus.

The early twentieth century, whose remarkable scientific and technological advances were matched by the social, political, and diplomatic turmoil that resulted in World War I, witnessed an equally spectacular resurgence of secret societies, as well as occult and mystical movements of various sorts. It is no accident that Georg Simmel was prompted during these years to write his major study "Secrets and Secret Societies."[2] The phenomenon is due in significant measure to the pronounced loss of religious faith produced by such nineteenth-century theological and scientific developments as the Higher Criticism and Darwinism, both of which undermined the authority of the Bible and unquestioning belief in theological authority. Many thinking individuals, cut loose from the faith of their childhood and not content with the mindless consolations of fundamentalism, sought substitutes in such surrogates as art; others took flight to the East in hope of finding a still unspoiled paradise; still others succumbed to the political promises of communism and to myth of the sort that underlay National Socialism.[3] The resurgence of the occult can be understood in one sense as simply another of such surrogates for lost religious faith.

It is symptomatic that William James's renowned lectures on the psychology of religion, *The Varieties of Religious Experience* (1902), contain two (nos. 16 and 17) that deal with mysticism and are illuminated by a number of examples drawn from his own era. In addition to the Satanism depicted in Huysmans's novel, the period also witnessed a remarkable resurgence of Rosicrucianism,[4] along with the establishment of such mystical movements as Madame Blavatsky's Theosophy (1875), William Wescott's Hermetic Order of the Golden Dawn (1887), and a quarter-century later the Anthroposophy of Rudolf Steiner (1913). Various other associations of those years, especially in Germany, while not secret societies per se, shared features linking them to such movements: for instance, the German Youth Movement, founded in 1897, and soon developing into the *Wandervögel*, and even the select group surrounding the poet Stefan George.[5]

Huysmans, who was personally acquainted with various figures from the occult scene in Paris, had attended séances and claimed to have been present at a Black Mass. In any case his novel amounts to a veritable catalog of fin-de-siècle occultism: it not only describes the contemporary conflict between orthodox Catholicism and various deviant cults—kabbalists, Hermeticists, Rosicrucians, Spiritualists—and provides an extended biography of Gilles de Rais; it also alludes in the course of the narrative to many figures and ideas from the history of religion, religious mysticism and occultism, heresies, and demonology: Anna Katharina Emmerich, Michael Psellus, Jakob Sprenger, Albertus Magnus, Raymond Lully, Eliphas Lévi, Martin Del Rio, Sinistrari d'Ameno, among others. Moreover, the plot loosely adheres to the pattern we have repeatedly observed, most conspicuously in *The Bacchae*. Durtal is obsessed by the lure of Satanism and Black Masses, to which he is ultimately admitted through the offices of a female emissary. But, unlike many other works, the background cult plays no role in directing his life; in fact, appalled by what he witnesses, he rushes out of the Black Mass before its conclusion with no intention of any further participation. Indeed, in the sequels to this first volume Durtal undergoes a conversion to devout Catholicism. *Là-bas* cannot be regarded as a lodge novel in the same sense as the works considered in earlier chapters. However, it anticipates the development of the genre in the following decades as it is classicized and the secret society is collectivized, criminalized, and sophisticated. During those same decades in France the Ligue France-Catholique was publishing a journal entitled *Revue Internationale des Sociétés Secrètes* (1912–39), which featured articles attacking various "conspiratorial" groups ranging from the Freemasons to the Rotarians and contributions promulgating the anti-Semitic *Protocols of the Elders of Zion*.

The Classicization of the Lodge Novel

No one regretted the disintegration of traditional European society, which was being undermined and destroyed by modern technological and political developments,[6] more than Hugo von Hofmannsthal (1874–1929), whose forty-year-old Count Hans Karl Buhl (in his play *Der Schwierige,* 1922) heartily dislikes such modern contrivances as the telephone, "this indiscreet machine" (act 1, sc. 12). "Formerly," he wrote in his moving document of the modern crisis of language— his fictitious letter of 1603 from Lord Chandos to his friend Francis Bacon ("Ein Brief," 1902)—"in a kind of enduring intoxication all being appeared to me as a great unity: spiritual and physical world seemed to constitute no opposition, nor did courtly and animal being, art and non-art, solitude and society."[7] At present, in contrast, his spirit has so completely forsaken any sense of meaning or any divine providence that "I have even lost the ability to think or to talk coherently about anything" (48). As his sense of impending crisis deepened, Hofmannsthal essentially gave up the lyrical plays and poems of self-expression upon which his youthful fame had been based and turned in compensation to works based either on the classical antiquity he admired—for instance, the *Elektra* (1904) and

Ariadne auf Naxos (1912), upon which Richard Strauss based his operas—or the historical Austro-Hungarian Empire in which he felt spiritually at home and portrayed in *Der Rosenkavalier* (1911).

The novel *Andreas,* on which Hofmannsthal worked from 1907 until his death in 1929 and whose only completed chapters resulted in a substantial fragment of 1912–13 (first published in 1930), may well be regarded in one sense as a fictional counterpart to *Der Rosenkavalier.*[8] Like that opera it is set in the prerevolutionary Austro-Hungarian Empire. Like the opera's Octavian, who is torn between his love for the Marschallin and Sophie, the young Viennese nobleman Andreas von Ferschengelder falls in love with the lovely daughter of a prosperous family—in the opera newly ennobled and here of ancient knightly descent—and is distracted for a time by his affection for an older woman from the nobility but finally returns to his true love. There is even a scandalous scene caused by servants in the home of the beloved's family, although here it is Andreas's servant and not the coarse attendants attached in the opera to Baron Ochs. To be sure, the novel is a fragment, and we know the dénouement in part only from the many pages of notes that Hofmannsthal maintained over the course of some twenty years.[9]

Andreas has set out in 1778 for Venice on a traditional *Bildungsreise,* but while en route in the Carinthian mountains, he meets the Finazzers, a family of wealthy country landowners, and quickly falls in love with the daughter, Romana. His idyllic stay is rudely interrupted, however, by a violent episode: the criminal servant Gotthilff, whom Andreas in his blind innocence and youthful inexperience has employed, assaults a servant girl, sets fire to her room, and makes off with Andreas's horse and half his funds, which are sewn into the saddle. Andreas makes his embarrassed apologies to the family and travels on to Venice, unable to bid for Romana's hand until he has himself sufficiently matured to be worthy of her. In Venice he encounters two noteworthy persons, who contribute to his development through what Hofmannsthal (in his essay *Ad me ipsum*) called "the allomatic principle" of mutual transformation ("gegenseitige Verwandlung") between individuals: the mysterious Knight of Malta, Sacramozo, whose character, appearance, and influence are based on Stefan George, Hofmannsthal's friend and mentor before their break in 1906;[10] and a woman whose severe dissociation of personality causes her to appear as two wholly different characters, the saintly Maria and the coquettish Mariquita.[11] (Hofmannsthal borrowed the notion of the allomatic from another lodge novel, Ferdinand Maack's *Twice Dead: The Story of a Rosicrucian from the Eighteenth Century* [1912]).[12] Just at this point the fragment ends, and we must rely on the extensive notes to understand Hofmannsthal's shifting plan for the remainder of the novel.

From what little we have, however, we quickly realize that the novel is a fictional counterpart not only to *Der Rosenkavalier* but also to Schiller's *Ghost-Seer* and to the lodge novel generally.[13] Like Schiller's work, *Andreas* is set mainly in Venice but includes frequent references to developments back at home: the entire episode at the Finazzer estate, for instance, is presented as Andreas's recollection following his arrival in Venice. Andreas is mentored by a figure like Schiller's Armenian: Sacramozo, who wears the black robe of his Maltese Order but without the required cross and who is reputed by some to be in the service of the Jesuits and by others to be a Freemason (83). Like Schiller's prince, Andreas first encounters the mysterious woman with whom he becomes infatuated while she is praying in a church. That Hofmannsthal knew Schiller's work is more than speculation: he included it in the anthology of German tales that he published in 1912, the very year in which he was writing the existing chapters of *Andreas*. Of Schiller's work he observed that "grand circumstances are represented there, broadly conceived state intrigues, many individuals connected in a single grand destiny."[14]

Hofmannsthal did not share the interest in the political that he attributes to Schiller; but his notes make it clear that the discussions between Andreas and Sacramozo touch on a wide variety of philosophical issues, and certainly the destinies of the various figures are meant to be "allomatically" connected. "In the company of the Maltese, indeed simply through the association with him, Andreas's existence refines and collects itself. . . . In the Maltese he has a presentiment of mastery in the playing of his own role" (31–32). Although Sacramozo appears only as an individual—and as one who suggests his disaffection with his order by his refusal to wear its cross—Andreas wonders (in one of the notes) if he belongs to a secret society such as the Jesuits or the Freemasons, or an even more secretive order: Templars or Rosicrucians (160). Another note mentions "the celebration: a ceremoniously symbolic affair. Andreas's initiation. It remains unknown in which figure Sacramozo himself took part in the celebration" (146). In short, Sacramozo represents a secret society, but the role this order was to play in the novel remains unclear. It is obvious, however, that Sacramozo exercises an enormous influence in Andreas's spiritual education: by exemplifying for him the meaning of form and discipline in life (160). In a curious variation from the normal pattern the forty-year-old Sacramozo commits suicide when his mission has been fulfilled: that is, when Andreas has reached sufficient maturity to manage his own life and future. "He can no longer expect that further enlightenment, redeeming revelations, will come—he cannot suspect among his elders resources that have been kept back from him—he may not approach anyone with pleas, like a trusting student—he is himself the highest authority; in life he no longer stands with curiosity" (146). He regards suicide as "the genuine philosophical act" and "the most sublime act of self enjoyment, the most truthful disposition of the spirit over the body" (113).

We also learn that Maria-Mariquita succeeds in resolving her dissociated personality and, as the saintly Maria, presumably continues her spiritual quest while Andreas, having achieved maturity allomatically through his love of Maria and his friendship with Sacramozo, returns to claim Romana. (Some critics assume that Maria remains in society to assert her rightful place as a noblewoman and that Andreas never returns to Romana.)[15]

In sum, with his *Andreas* Hofmannsthal set out to attempt what might well be termed the classicization of the lodge novel, just as he had achieved a classicization of the traditional rococo comedy in *Der Rosenkavalier:* through a sublimating adaptation of its form to install the minor genre in the pantheon of literary models. Here, rather than the political goals customary in the lodge novel in its original German Romantic or its romantic socialist manifestations, the secret society as symbolized by the Maltese Knight is concerned with loftier philosophical issues that contribute to the development of the individual. As David Miles observes, "Andreas' development does not press ever outward toward a Goethean fulfillment of the total personality, but rather inward . . . to an ultimate renewal and reassertion of the self."[16] To this extent one can agree with Richard Alewyn's assessment that *Andreas,* despite the fragmentary form in which we have it, "may be counted among the complete creations of world literature."[17]

The Collectivization of the Order

Novels written by various hands, known as "Doppelromane" or "Kollektivromane," have appealed to German writers at least since Romanticism. In 1808 four friends calling themselves the Order of the North Star ("Nordsternbund") published an amusing parody of Goethe's *Wilhelm Meister* entitled "The Trials and Tribulations of Karl" *(Die Versuche und Hindernisse Karls).* A few years later another quartet of Romantic authors, styling themselves the Order of Serapion ("Serapionbund"), undertook "the Novel of the Baron of Four" *(Der Roman des Freiherrn von Vieren),* but most of the manuscript was destroyed in a fire, and only a few remaining chapters were later published.[18] The same Romantic spirit of collaboration produced one of the wittiest satires of the age, "The Strange Story of the Clockmaker BOGS" (*Die wundersame Geschichte von BOGS dem Uhrmacher* [1807]), by the poet Clemens Brentano and the myth-scholar Joseph Görres.

The appeal of such collaboration was not limited to Romanticism. At century's end one of the founding works of German naturalism was the collection of three stories entitled *Papa Hamlet* (1889) and allegedly translated from the Norwegian of Bjarne P. Holmsen: actually the pseudonym of the joint authors Arno Holz and Johannes Schlaf. Between the wars Marxist writers found in the form an appropriate exemplification for the ideals of proletarian-revolutionary literature, as in *The Last Days of . . .*, published in 1931 serially in *Die Rote Fahne,* by "K. Olektiv" (pseudonym for Mani Bruck and Jürgen Kuczynski).[19] The following year, in an effort to capitalize on the new popularity of the genre, a group of eight well-known writers brought out a collective detective story under the title "The Locked Door" *(Die verschlossene Tür)* in the journal *Literarische Welt* (1932). More recently a collective of fifteen writers in residence at the Literarisches Colloquium in Berlin was inspired by Walter Höllerer with specific reference to the Romantic "Doppelroman" to produce a novel called "The Guest House" (*Das Gästehaus* [1965]). The phenomenon has not been limited to Germany: the collective form has also been popular in Scandinavia, as well as in other literatures.

It is hardly surprising, then, to ascertain that the motif of the secret society worked its way into at least one well-known version of the collective novel written during the tumultuous prewar years: *The Novel of the Twelve (Der Roman der XII* [1909]). To undertake this work the Berlin publisher Konrad W. Mecklenburg persuaded twelve prominent writers of the period, with no underlying preliminary plan or outline, to write successive chapters of a narrative, each based simply upon the material received from the preceding contributors.[20] (One of the authors was Hanns Heinz Ewers, whom we have already encountered as a continuator of Schiller's *The Ghost-Seer.*) There is no need to recapitulate in any detail the "plot" of the work, which shifts unpredictably from chapter to chapter. Basically, it is the story, taking place mostly in Berlin, of a successful young man, Dr. Gaston von Dülfert, who entertains the fancifully utopian plan of founding a "Glass City" on the Lüneburg Heath, and his love for the Norwegian beauty Karen Holmsen. In the course of the first eleven chapters we learn about the prior lives and adventures of the two central figures. At one point it is hinted that they are actually brother and sister; later various disclosures suggest other possibilities for Gaston's parentage. There are amusing depictions of a meeting of a German feminist society ("Allgemeiner deutscher Frauenbund") that Karen attends; of an airplane crash that almost costs Gaston his life; of a string quartet that the two lovers form with the intention of undertaking a concert tour; of a séance conducted by an Italian charlatan; and so forth, depending on the ingenuity and proclivities of the individual contributors. By the end of chapter 11 the situation has become so confused and complex—complicated by the fact that Karen, dismayed by circumstances, has left Berlin for Munich, while Gaston's detested first wife has absconded with their children to a secret location—that it can be resolved by the final contributor only through the machinations of a secret society.

At the beginning of chapter 12 Gaston awakens from the drunken stupor into which he has been driven by his despair and receives two mysterious letters delivered mistakenly to his house—the house in Berlin occupied decades earlier by his deceased father. One, written in a fanciful Latinate language similar to that of the seventeenth-century Rosicrucian manifestos, is addressed in the present to Gaston's allegedly dead father by a lodge brother, announcing the delivery to "the Grand Master of our ancient Order" (373) of their favorite wine, the Red Lion *(leo ruber)*. Included in this epistle is a second letter from the elder Dülfert's former housemaid and crudely penned in a lively Berlin dialect. It appears that she and others have been commissioned by Dülfert and his order to keep an eye on Gaston and inform his still-living father about his activities. Here, she reports that Gaston is a wastrel (Hallodri), that his first wife, Anna—whom the father has long detested—neglects the children, and that the children are in danger of being completely ruined if something is not quickly done. Long aware that Dülfert belongs to a secret society—she has seen his black gown and suspects the Freemasons—she implores him to take his symbolic Carpenter's Square ("Winkeleisen," which in her Berlin dialect she calls a "Winggeleise"), which even the police respect, and rescue the children, informing him where they are to be found every day in the Berlin Tiergarten. Astonished, Gaston remembers that his father's library included volumes of alchemy and mysticism extending from the Bible by way of Christian Rosencreutz down to "the great theosopher Dr. Rudolf Chatterer" ("Schwätzer"—a not so hidden allusion to the prolific Rudolf Steiner, renowned for his lectures) and now understands the references to his secret society.

When his wife comes screaming to his door and demands to know where the children are, he surmises that his father must still be alive and, with the assistance of his lodge brothers, has somehow rescued his children from their vengeful and neglectful mother, who was holding them simply in order to blackmail Gaston. He rushes to Munich and, in a grand recognition scene, father and son are reunited. The father, we learn, had decades earlier fallen into despondency over the death of his beloved, Gaston's true mother, and depression because of his unloved wife, whom Gaston had long taken to be his mother. He was rescued from this drunken despair (like Gaston's own) by his friend Pistorius, who arranged his acceptance into the (unspecified) secret order, where he was saved from his alcoholism by the marvelous "Red Lion" wine favored by the order. Subsequently he arranged to falsify his death in Vienna, sending a stone-filled coffin back for burial, and settled down to a new life in Munich. Although his father tries to make light of matters, it is clear to Gaston that in "the secret compartment of his soul" he believed in mysteries that he would never reveal (391). The children, whom he did indeed rescue with the assistance of his lodge brethren, are brought in, as well as Karen.

In a finale we learn that Gaston and Karen are married six months later. Their wedding reception is attended by twelve unexpected guests: the twelve authors of the preceding chapters. In an ingenious twist they are introduced virtually as members of a secret order that has kept watch over Gaston and Karen: "Each of them stands in a more or less close connection with one of you and has taken a lively interest in your destiny" (402).

In sum, we find again the traditional pattern of a hero on a quest—first for his visionary Glass City on the Heath and then for his beloved and his children—who is helped to his goal by a secret society. Here, however, the secret society shows up at the last minute and, with no earlier hints regarding its existence, as virtually the only device through which the complicated plot can be resolved. And its treatment—the comical language of the letter, the fetishizing of the Red Lion wine, the far-fetched intrigue involving the father's alleged death and the kidnapping of the children, and the introduction of the authors themselves as lodge brethren—gives a new humorous twist to a device that had hitherto appeared in literature largely as a serious theme, whether political or more generally philosophical and ethical.

The Criminalization of the Order

André Gide's (1869–1951) tale *Les caves du Vatican* (1914; translated as *Lafcadio's Adventures*) is best known for the notorious *acte gratuit* in which Lafcadio spontaneously kills a complete stranger by shoving him out the door of a speeding train. (Gide called his work a *sotie:* that is, a farce or burlesque, and Lafcadio's act has accordingly been called a caricature and parody of the true gratuitous act.)[21] Lafcadio Wluiki is the illegitimate son of a Romanian *demimondaine* and Juste-Agénor de Baraglioul, one of her lovers during his term as a French diplomat in Bucharest. Brought up by his mother and a succession of "uncles," Lafcadio has developed into a cynical and utterly amoral young man when his father, at the time of his death in 1893 and without acknowledging any rights of family, bestows on him a sizable annuity that will enable him to live comfortably and undertake a journey away from Europe to a new life in the East. The dying father charges his son Julius, a novelist aspiring to the Académie française, with arranging matters. Julius is related through marriage to the husbands of his wife's two sisters: the atheistic scientist and Freemason Anthime and the impecunious but devout businessman Amédée. It turns out to be Amédée whom the now elegantly clad Lafcadio, regarding him as a filthy and grotesque figure (825: "ce sale magot"), pushes out of the train: "A motiveless crime," he thinks, "what an embarrassment for the police" (829).

In one of the many ironies of the work, the theory of the *acte gratuit* is first elaborated on the very day of the murder in a conversation between Julius and that same Amédée about their brother-in-law Anthime, who three years earlier converted to Catholicism as the result of a seemingly miraculous cure of his severe rheumatism and, as a result, lost his wealth in investments, which were in the hands of his fellow Masons.[22] Julius contends that men are not always guided by self-interest and that there are disinterested actions, by which he means "gratuitous" (816). He goes on to maintain that evil may be just as gratuitous as good and that the evil action, the crime, if gratuitous, is nonattributable *(inimputable)* and its perpetrator uncatchable (818: "imprenable"). The irony is heightened when Julius later tells Lafcadio that he is planning to write a wholly new kind of novel: unlike his earlier ones, which were based on logic and consistency of character, this one would revolve around a young criminal who is led to commit a crime gratuitously. Lafcadio listens intently as Julius describes a person very much like himself and explains that he was simply waiting until an exemplary incident should occur to him as a plot device. Then, by a providential stroke, he has just found in the newspaper precisely the example he needed: the murder of his brother-in-law, if only the substantial sum he was carrying had not been taken. He is delighted when Lafcadio points out to him that the second page of the account makes it clear that the money was not missing and that the deed was therefore apparently gratuitous. But then, in a moment of sudden illumination, Julius realizes that a motive of a wholly different sort must have been involved, a motive that disabuses him of his theory of the *acte gratuit* and brings us to the second main theme of the work.

In 1893 a gang of confidence men in Lyon, in a scheme to swindle money from gullible believers, persuaded them that Pope Leo XIII had been imprisoned in the cellars of the Vatican by cardinals associated with the Freemasons, that a double was currently playing his role in the church, and that their contributions were needed to rescue the true pope.[23] The scheme was reported in several publications, one of which Gide footnoted in his work (749).[24] (The likelihood of such a scheme was not thought unreasonable because Pope Leo XIII was known for his opposition to Freemasonry, as expressed in his encyclical of 1884, *Humanum genus*. It was rumored, moreover, that his own secretary of state, Cardinal Mariano Rampolla, was an occult Mason.)

Gide used this widespread rumor as the basis for the second theme of his *sotie*, which opens with a reference to the Freemasons. Anthime's substantial investments in Egypt, the basis of his fortune, are managed by his fellow Freemasons. After his seemingly miraculous healing (which, in fact, is short-lived) he fears— correctly, as it turns out—that he will be financially ruined as a result of his conversion to Catholicism, despite promises of assistance from the church. Then we learn that Lafcadio's boyhood friend, known since schooldays as "Protos" because he won first place in Greek composition, has become the leader of a gang known as The Millipede ("le Mille-Pattes"), which is scheming to cheat credulous Catholics with the false story of the pope's imprisonment and their "Crusade for the Deliverance of the Pope" (785). Protos, a genius of disguise, approaches Julius's sister, the highly devout Comtesse Guy de Saint-Prix, dressed as a church canon with the (falsified) recommendation of her cardinal. With disarming eloquence and urgent warnings to secrecy he confides to her that the pope has been kidnapped by the Freemasons and is being held captive in the Castello St. Angelo while high offices in the Vatican have been seized by other Freemasons. A small group of loyal priests is working to liberate the pope, but it will cost a considerable sum. Protos skillfully plays on the comtesse's emotions in order to win her trust and the promise of a substantial donation. But, he warns, since neither the church nor the Freemasons want the rumor to be spread abroad and since few can be trusted, she must maintain absolute confidentiality. He instructs her to give him a check and to telegraph her banker to transfer the sum immediately to a Parisian bank.

After his departure and despite his warnings of secrecy the comtesse rushes to the house of her sister-in-law, Amédée's wife, eager to share the story. The latter in turn informs her naive husband, who—with absolutely no plan in mind—catches the next train to Rome in order to expose the plot and rescue the pope. When Protos finds out that the bumbling Amédée is in Rome, he fears that their elaborately conceived scheme will be exposed. Through a sequence of disguises and lies he manages to involve Amédée himself unwittingly in the machinations: warned that they are being watched by both Freemasons and Jesuits, Amédée is sent to cash a check and deliver the money to a (false) cardinal in Naples. At that point he encounters Julius, who is in Rome for a conference. After listening to Julius's theory of the *acte gratuit,* he reveals to him the alleged conspiracy surrounding the papacy and involving the Freemasons as well as the Jesuits. That evening, on the train from Rome to Naples, he enters the compartment where Lafcadio, embarked on his own journey to Java, is already seated and is pushed to his death in Lafcadio's *acte gratuit.*

When Julius learns from Lafcadio that the money was not taken by the murderer, he quickly concludes that Amédée must have been assassinated by those involved in the pope's kidnapping and now, fearing for his own safety, goes to the police. The following rapid dénouement involves further ironies. When Anthime learns from Julius that the current "pope" is allegedly a double, he renounces his earlier conversion and returns to the Freemasons and to his scientific research. Protos, who secretly followed Amédée on his errand, witnessed the murder and obtained a piece of evidence linking Lafcadio to his crime. With this information he tries to pressure his former schoolmate to blackmail Julius for his newly inherited fortune. Lafcadio, indignantly rejecting that demand, contemplates surrender to the police. But before Protos can take action, he is arrested for a different crime: he kills the young woman who has accused him of Amédée's murder. Lafcadio confesses his crime to Julius, who urges him not to surrender to the police but to make a full confession to the church. But Lafcadio's cynicism is confirmed when Julius rejects any further personal contact with him. Julius's daughter Genevieve, infatuated with Lafcadio, encourages him to flee and save his own life. Willing to accept the displeasure of her own family for his sake, she spends the night with him. The *sotie* leaves the ending open because Lafcadio, already disillusioned by the actions of Protos and the behavior of Julius, even loses his respect for Genevieve because she can love a man like him. As he wonders the following morning whether he really intends to surrender himself to justice, we instinctively know that he will not do so.

Again, then, we recognize a familiar pattern: a secret society, before its own collapse, controls the actions of several leading figures: Anthime, the comtesse, Amédée, Julius, and finally Lafcadio. In this case, however, the secret society is not a true order but a criminal gang. The irony of the *sotie* is intensified by the fact that the gang, to achieve its own criminal ends, exploits fears associated traditionally and popularly with both the Freemasons and the Jesuits.

The Sophistication of the Order

The "Cabala" designated in the title of Thornton Wilder's (1897–1975) early novel (*The Cabala* [1926]) is the precise opposite of Gide's sleazy gang: a coterie of members from Rome's high society, they carry out good works rather than crimes. The narrator, a young American student of antiquity (designated only by the nickname Samuele), hears of them for the first time as he approaches Rome by train from Naples. His friend James Blair, a slightly older American archaeologist, suggests that, before devoting himself to the ancients, he should experience some of the more interesting moderns in that city. He asks the narrator if he has ever heard of the Cabala, a group of rich and influential social and intellectual snobs living around Rome. "Everyone's afraid of them. Everybody suspects them of plots to overturn things" (11).[25] Their plots, however, are not so much political as cultural: "they hate what's recent." Dismayed at the thought, so prevalent after World War I, that the old Europe is dying, they long for the restoration of traditional norms: notably the divine right of kings, but also strict social protocol: "one duchess' right to enter a door before another" (12). Unlike eccentrics who can be ignored, they constitute a rich, powerful, and exclusive circle known by apprehensive Romans as The Cabala.

Samuele is introduced into the group by his friend Blair, who knows one of the members, the American heiress Miss Grier, because he cataloged her library for her. Fascinated, Samuele decides to become "the biographer of the individuals and not the historian of the group" (107). Accordingly, his narrative constitutes not so much a novel as, rather, a collection of short stories amounting in each case to a moral tragedy. In one episode the sex-crazed Marcantonio, the sixteen-year-old son of the Duchessa d'Aquilanera, commits suicide after succumbing to the taunting temptation to incest with his decadent sister. In another episode the lovely Princess Alix d'Espoli falls in love with James Blair and is humiliated and spiritually shattered when she is rebuffed. In response she flees with her dazzling conversation into a dizzying social round and becomes known to her friends as

"Alix aux Enfers" (148). The third episode links two stories, the first of which concerns the wealthy and naively devout Marie-Astrée-Luce de Morfontaine, "a Second Century Christian" (171), who, obsessed quixotically with the return of royalism in France and the revival of Catholicism, is so profoundly offended by the cynical rationalism of the famous Cardinal Vaini that she attempts to shoot him as the Devil incarnate. The second story focuses on Cardinal Vaini himself, once reputedly the greatest missionary known to the church since the Middle Ages, who has lost his faith and, seeking to recover it, returns to China in the hope of regaining touch with the people, dies en route, and is buried anonymously at sea.

Wilder's narrator, a sober-minded New England Protestant, survives the fantasies and tragedies of these European Catholic aristocrats, whose confidant he becomes. While he respects the cultural traditions they represent, he does not believe that their personal misfortunes mark the end of culture. As Samuele sails homeward at the end, the poet Virgil appears to him in a vision and reminds him that "Romes existed before Rome and when Rome will be a waste there will be Romes after her. Seek out some city that is young" (229).[26] In one sense, then, the novel constitutes yet another document of the sense, common in the 1920s among such pessimistic European thinkers as Oswald Spengler and optimistic American poets like Robert Frost and Allen Tate, that in the grand movement of history the course of cultural empire is moving westward: the *translatio imperii*. At the same time, it uses the form of the conventional lodge novel to achieve its ironic purpose.

Samuele is a typical quester, eager to enter the mysterious order of the novel and to learn its secrets. To be sure, the narrator introduces one episode that ridicules various familiar forms of secret society. He and Blair attend a séance arranged by a charlatan known as Sareptor Basilis, who as a young photographer's assistant in London had been vice president of the Rosicrucian Mysteries, Soho Chapter, a group of clerks, waiters, and idealistic barbers who found compensation for the humiliations they underwent by day in the glories they ascribed to themselves by night. They met in darkened rooms, took oaths with one hand resting on the works of Swedenborg, read papers on the fabrication of gold and its metaphysical implications, and elected one another with great earnestness to the offices of arch-adept and *magister hieraticorum* (156).

Now in Rome, he lives with two attendant sisters on the top floor of an old palace, where it is rumored that lightning plays around his left hand as he sits among the broken arcs of rainbows surrounded by hymns for unaccompanied voices and visited by women of every rank, who come away from their interviews reassured by words that make their faces shine. Samuele, annoyed by this nonsense, "invented opportunities for provoking his absurdity" but is unable to upset the serenity of the seer, who instructs him to "plan my life in harmony with the cosmic overtones" (155). In these few pages Wilder manages to deal ironically not only with Rosicrucianism but also with alchemy, theosophy, and the fascination with occultism in general.

While Samuele is almost obsequiously attentive to the interests and wishes of the members of the Cabala and eagerly accepts invitations to their palaces and villas, he remains objective enough to view their ideas with ironic detachment. When he asks Miss Grier to "throw some light on the Cabala" (219), she offers a theory of spiritual transmigration and reincarnation to explain their character and behavior. "The gods of antiquity did not die with the arrival of Christianity," she assures him. "When one of them died his godhead was passed on to someone else; no sooner is Saturn dead than some man somewhere feels a new personality descending upon him like a strait jacket" (219). Although Samuele is too tactful to ask her how these principles apply to the Cabala, it is clearly implied that the actions of the members of the Cabala can be interpreted as analogies to the gods they reincarnate: Miss Grier herself as Demeter, Cardinal Vaini as Jupiter, Marcantonio as Pan, and Alix and James Blair as Venus and Adonis.[27] She tells Samuele explicitly that "I sometimes think that you are the new god Mercury" (220), destined to serve as the messenger and secretary of the gods.

While the mythological analogy lends a certain unity to the episodic narrative and mystical coherence to the Cabala itself, Samuele soon realizes that he has "arrived on the scene in the middle of the decline of their power" (108)—at the moment, in other words, when the group's dissolution symbolizes the downfall of that same old Europe whose demise Hofmannsthal lamented. They still manage various trivial accomplishments. Miss Grier is able to use her influence with high church officials to obtain a sanctioned divorce for the devoutly Catholic Mrs. Roy, while Mrs. Roy, in turn, through her own connections, enables Miss Grier to ship a painting by Mantegna back to Vassar College in the United States without passing through customs (21–25). In other cases the Cabala blocks the canonization of various nonentities, arouses public indignation about the "faint smell of drains that is wafted through the Sistine Chapel," and summons a German expert to deal with tree disease in the Borghese Gardens. But their onetime political power is of no avail in the new postwar world. "At first they thought they could do something about the strikes, and about the Fascismo, and the blasphemies in the Senate." But they gradually realize that "the century had let loose influences they could not stem" (108). At the end, indeed, the group has dissolved to such an extent that even Miss Grier contemplates her departure from Rome and a return to Greenwich, Connecticut.

In sum, whereas the Rosicrucian manifestos portrayed the origins of a secret society and most of the later lodge novels the various political and cultural endeavors of their orders, the early twentieth century featured works by writers with no personal association with secret societies and in which such organizations are exploited for purely literary purposes: first etherealized (Hofmannsthal), then comically collectivized *(The Novel of the Twelve)* and criminalized (Gide), and finally made so effete and decadent that they virtually dissipate (Wilder).

German Ambivalence

Several writers whom we have already encountered noted similarities between the situation in Germany at the end of the eighteenth century and in the decades *entre deux guerres*. Hanns Heinz Ewers concluded the afterword to his continuation of *The Ghost-Seer* (1922) with an expression of astonishment at the utterly modern effect of Schiller's work:

> If one forgets the decorative daggers and powdered pigtails, one might think that
> it had been set in our own time. The same Knights of Abracadabra today as then,
> the same miracle-workers and bliss-makers of every variety, the same fantastic
> societies and orders that fight grimly with one another. Whether the leaders are
> serious or swindlers—or even, like most of them, both in one person—whether
> they are called Schröpfer and Stark, Cagliostro, Dr. Mesmer, Gassner; whether
> they call themselves Illuminati or Rosicrucians or, as today, Occultists, Spiritists,
> Christian Scientists, Theosophists, Anthroposophists and whatever: then as now
> all cities and lands are teeming with Ghost-Seers of every color.[28]

Arno Schmidt, we recall, labeled Meyern's *Dya-Na-Sore* a "prophetic description of a Super Third Reich" and "the ideal SS-Handbook."[29] Indeed, it seems hardly accidental—though the author makes no explicit reference to her own time—that in those same years Marianne Thalmann published the first and still standard account of the Romantic lodge novel in the context of the mystique of secret societies.[30]

Yet Germans of those years felt a profound sense of ambiguity regarding secret societies. As even such an outsider as André Gide observed in his preface
to the French translation of Hermann Hesse's *Journey to the East*, "something
primitive lingers in the Germanic soul when not ameliorated by culture, a sort of
functional availability" coupled with "a need to group themselves, to form *Bund,*
a more or less secret society, and to wend their way in company toward an end
often ill-defined, in appearance all the more noble because it is colored by mysticism and remains rather mysterious."[31] As evidence to the correctness of Gide's
observation, the period saw a growth-spurt of secret societies, especially on the
conservative right. The Thule-Gesellschaft (Thule Society), founded immediately after World War I in Munich purportedly as "a study group for Germanic
antiquity" but with its swastika-and-sword emblem actually an antirepublican
and anti-Semitic movement with occult tendencies, listed many members who
soon became leading figures in the National Socialist Party. The Nazis themselves recognized a number of smaller and often secret orders within the larger
party. This appetite for secret societies in the 1920s was, if anything, intensified
by the pronounced "hunger for myth" that stimulated so many German thinkers
from Nietzsche by way of Oswald Spengler, Ernst Cassirer, and Ludwig Klages
down to Alfred Rosenberg, the theoretician of National Socialism, in his *Myth of
the Twentieth Century (Der Mythus des 20. Jahrhunderts* [1930]).

At the same time, these right-wing societies mounted a vicious campaign
against the competition they sensed in such enlightened societies as the Freemasons. In his *Reflections of a Nonpolitical Man (Betrachtungen eines Unpolitischen*
[1918]) Thomas Mann, carried away by a wartime xenophobic patriotism, made a
sharp distinction between spirit and politics *(Geist* and *Politik),* culture and civilization, soul and society, cosmopolitanism and internationalism, and detected
the exemplar of the detested internationalized political democracy in Freemasonry. History will teach us, he argued, echoing earlier beliefs that the Masons
and Illuminati were responsible for the French Revolution, "what role international Illuminatism, the Freemasonic world lodge—excluding, of course, the
unsuspecting Germans—played in the intellectual preparation and actual un-
leashing of the world war, the war of 'civilization' against Germany."[32] He goes
on to claim that "the French lodge is political to the point of identity with the
radical party, that radical party which in France constitutes the nursery and
breeding ground for the spiritual hatred of Germany and German being." Germans in their naiveté had not suspected that "beneath the mantle of peaceful
international commerce in God's wide world, hatred, the inextinguishable

hatred of political democracy, of the Masonic-republican rhetorical bourgeois of 1789 was at its accursed work against us, against our form of government, the militarism of our souls, our spirit of order, authority and responsibility" (12:36).

These passages anticipate the more extended tirade against Freemasonry articulated six years later by the Jesuit Naphtha in *The Magic Mountain* (in the chapter "As a Soldier and Brave"), but in the novel Mann's wartime conservatism is tempered by the more liberal views of the enlightened Settembrini, himself a Mason. Other contemporaries were more virulent in their attacks.[33] Erich Ludendorff, an advocate of the "knife-in-the-back" theory to explain Germany's defeat, attributed responsibility to the Freemasons, whom he hoped to "destroy through the disclosure of their secrets" in his best-selling *Vernichtung der Freimaurerei durch Enthüllung ihrer Geheimnisse* (1927). His wife Mathilde Ludendorff in her account of "the unatoned sacrilege" against four famous Germans (*Der ungesühnte Frevel an Luther, Lessing, Mozart und Schiller* [1928]) revived such old rumors as the one that we have already encountered: that Goethe was party to the murder of his friend Schiller.

The Rehabilitation of the Lodge Novel

The writer who rehabilitated the traditional lodge novel, ridding it of the political baggage from left and right accrued in the course of two centuries and returning it to its religious-philosophical roots, was the least likely of candidates: the introspective outsider Hermann Hesse (1877–1962), who never belonged to an official organization of any sort and who spent his last forty years in the relative isolation of his villa in the mountains of southern Switzerland. Yet in the novels of his maturity, written in those years, the structure of the lodge novel is repeatedly evident in various ingenious modifications.

Hesse's acquaintance with mysteries, cults, orders, and secret societies was purely literary, and the fellows of the only order into which he was initiated consisted of the great writers, artists, and musicians of the past. He repeatedly stated that the period in which he felt spiritually most at home was the century from 1750 to 1850, precisely the years when the lodge novel flourished. His writings—notably his essay of 1929, "A Library of World Literature"—document his detailed knowledge of that period and, beyond that, his firsthand acquaintance with most of the writers we have considered: from Euripides and Apuleius by way of Wolfram von Eschenbach down to Goethe, Schiller, and the German Romantics. His reading specifically included "also much of lesser value, for to know a certain historical period richly and exhaustively has its advantages."[34] In this context he cites "certain writings that used to be called theosophical and in which an occult wisdom reputedly could be found" and comprising "in part thick tomes, in part tiny shabby tracts" (338). He was fascinated by these works because all their occult teachings *(Geheimlehren)*, he felt, pointed to a common source in India.[35] Finally, products of medieval monastic life particularly appealed to him "not for its ascetic aspect but because in monastic art and literature I found marvelous treasures and because the orders and monasteries appeared enviable as sanctuaries of a pious-contemplative life and highly exemplary as sites of culture and education" (342).

This fascination shows up initially in the novel *Demian* (1919), which was hailed as a literary sensation and cultural mirror by the younger generation emerging from the shattering experience of the First World War.[36] Written in 1917, the work was a direct response to Hesse's psychoanalysis, which had been necessitated by a breakdown caused by a combination of devastating personal and political factors and which forced Hesse to reexamine his previous values and beliefs. The novel is allegedly the first-person account of a young man named Emil Sinclair, who soon after war's end records certain crucial episodes from his life between the ages of ten and twenty. His boyhood revolved around his friendship with the mysterious Max Demian, an older boy who rescued him from a childhood bully and then challenged him to liberate himself from the sheltering confines of a narrow pietism by thinking boldly and independently. When Sinclair goes off to boarding school, he first drifts into profligacy. But the ethereal love he conceives for a girl glimpsed in the park sets him back on the path to self-discovery, a recovery abetted by the mystical teachings of the renegade theologian Pistorius. Later, at the university, Sinclair again encounters Demian and his friend's mother, who is known to her circle as Frau Eva. That year of happiness and spiritual maturity is ended by the war, which soon claims Demian as a victim. His friend's death forces Sinclair to the final stage of spiritual independence, where he discovers that he no longer has need of external mentors to guide him on his way.

The hero's development takes place in three stages. When we meet Sinclair he is still living in a state of childhood innocence, but he rapidly is plunged into a mood of doubt and despair, pendulating between two poles of light and dark, good and evil, until at the end he finds the ultimate synthesis of these conflicting ethical worlds within himself. In the Christian terminology that permeates the novel, these three stages would be the original state of paradise, the fall, and the ultimate redemption. As Hesse stated in his essay "A Bit of Theology" (1932), he regarded the individual's spiritual development or humanization *(Menschwer-dung)* as a three-stage process leading from innocence through guilt and an awareness of good and evil to a third kingdom of understanding beyond moral-ity and law: to faith. Only at the third stage do the questers begin to recognize one another no longer in their isolation but in their interdependency.[37]

In one sense the novel can be analyzed structurally, albeit not ideologically, as a form of gospel in which Sinclair's older friend Demian functions for him as a Jesus-figure and those surrounding him and his mother as disciples. Hesse, the son and grandson of missionaries to India, a boy who grew up in a home sur-rounded by the books and tokens of comparative religion, has affirmed more than once that he considered the religious impulse to be the decisive characteris-tic of his life and works.[38]

At the same time we recognize clearly the underlying structure of the lodge novel because the entire atmosphere surrounding the home of Demian and his mother is that of a secret society. "When I closed the gate behind myself," Sinclair recalls,

> indeed, as soon as I saw from afar the lofty trees of the garden rise up, I was rich and happy. Outside was "reality," outside were streets and houses, people and institutions, libraries and lecture halls—but here within were love and soul, here the fairy tale and the dream were alive. And yet we were not shut off from the world. In our thoughts and conversations we often lived in its midst but on a different plane. We were separated from the majority of people not by borders but only by a different manner of seeing. It was our task to represent in the world an island, perhaps a model, in any case the proclamation of a differ-ent possibility of living. Long alone, I became acquainted with the community that is possible among people who have tasted utter solitude. (236)[39]

In this context Frau Eva is the central symbol, the organizing principle of the order, and Demian the emissary who, from childhood on, watched over Sinclair and guided his steps after his liberation from the bully. After Demian's death Sinclair understands that he needs only to gaze into the dark mirror of his own soul to see "my own image, that now wholly resembles Him, my friend and my guide" (257).

The three stages of Sinclair's quest amount to three steps of initiation: first, Demian's exhortation to the young Sinclair to think independently and nota-bly to liberate himself from the narrow confines of his childhood pietism; then

Pistorius's indoctrination of the student Sinclair into the symbols, myths, and mysteries of the world religions. Finally, when he enters Frau Eva's garden and is introduced into her group, "I was slowly initiated into the secret of those who bore 'the sign'" (236). (This refers to the Mark of Cain, which, as Demian explained earlier to the young Sinclair, should be regarded as a mark of distinction rather than opprobrium.) He later recalls that period as "the first fulfillment of my life and my acceptance into the order *[Bund]*" (249). The circle of those who bore the mark or sign constituted "the awakened or awakening ones, and our striving was aimed at an ever more complete state of awareness. . . . For us humanity was a distant future toward which we were all under way, whose image no one knew, whose laws were nowhere written" (237). Among the members of the order were astrologers and cabalists, adherents of various sects, cultivators of Indian yoga, vegetarians, and others. "With all these we had nothing in common intellectually except for the respect that each acknowledged for the secret life-dream of the other." As in all the earlier cases, the order was founded in response to the perceived disorder of the world and in particular the desolation of the spirit. Europe, they felt, "had won the whole world only to lose its soul" (238). But here, in contrast to most of the earlier German and French works, the goal is not a political solution but a spiritual one.

A similar play with the form of the lodge novel may be seen in Hesse's *Steppenwolf* (1927). On one level the novel recounts a month in the life of the forty-eight-year-old intellectual Harry Haller, who is so totally alienated from the materialistic society surrounding him that he can endure life only by promising himself the luxury of suicide on his fiftieth birthday. During the month depicted in the novel Haller meets three individuals who introduce him to an utterly new world of experience: Hermine the nightclub hostess, Pablo the jazz musician, and their friend Maria. They initiate the all-too-earnest intellectual, who overreacts to the irritations of daily life with resentment and depression, into a carefree life of dancing, drugs, sex, and abandonment. He must learn to laugh, Hermine instructs him, and not to take life so seriously.

Haller, who in his ambivalent contempt for the bourgeois world regards himself as a "wolf from the steppes," enjoys—or is cursed with—the gift of double perspective. He has visions in which he projects into perfectly ordinary experiences a higher meaning and constantly imputes his own thoughts to others. Early in the novel, when a pamphlet of some sort—presumably a religious tract—is shoved into his hand by a placard-bearer on the street, it becomes in his imagination "The Tract of the Steppenwolf" and outlines a process of human development that precisely parallels the three stages of *Demian*. But rather than the stages of innocence, doubt, and independence and the extremes of good and evil that Sinclair experiences as he passes from childhood through adolescence into maturity, the tract suggests that for the adult Harry Haller the world is divided into three classes: at one extreme the staid majority with its bourgeois Judeo-Christian values, at the other the Immortals in a realm beyond good and evil, and torn between the two worlds the Steppenwolf: he has cast off the restraints of *Bürgertum* by means of humor and irony but not yet reached the heights of the Immortals. According to the tract, humor is the sole means that enables a Steppenwolf to live in the bourgeois world: "To live in the world as though it were not the world, to respect the law and at the same time stand above it, to possess 'as though one did not,' to renounce as though it were no renunciation—to realize all these popular and often formulated demands of a lofty worldly wisdom only humor is capable."[40] Perhaps he will find in one of their Magic Theaters, the tract continues, "whatever he needs for the liberation of his ravaged soul." Only a few are capable of making the leap into the cosmos, where they will join the Immortals.

It is precisely such a Magic Theater that Haller believes he is entering when, one evening, he wanders into the Black Eagle nightclub and encounters Hermine and Pablo. As he moves through his month of new experiences in the underworld of his new acquaintances, he sees himself on a quest to attain the realm of the Immortals—a realm that he experiences briefly in the Magic Theater of the third and final section of the novel. There, in an opium-induced vision, he enters a new world of experiences and encounters Mozart, Brahms, Wagner, and other Immortals he admires and cherishes. Since this encounter is induced by drugs, he soon returns to the everyday world in which Mozart is again transformed into Pablo. But now Haller is able to face reality with a new courage. "Someday I would learn how to laugh. Pablo was waiting for me. Mozart was waiting for me" (4:415).

In sum, the Immortals constitute the secret order to which Haller in his quest aspires. Like Parzival, Haller fails on his first encounter with the order and must return to everyday reality, but the novel suggests that, like his medieval counterpart, he will return with greater success—that, in other words, he will learn to transcend reality by regarding it with humor and by living in the eternal aesthetic realm of art, music, literature. In *Steppenwolf*, to be sure, the order of Immortals does not exist on the same level of reality as does the group of actual people surrounding Frau Eva in *Demian* or the societies of the earlier lodge novels. But structurally it fulfills the same role as do those earlier orders while Pablo and Hermine, as guide and figurehead of the order, represent precise counterparts to Demian and Frau Eva.

In Hesse's *The Journey to the East* (*Die Morgenlandfahrt* [1932]) we witness the ultimate rehabilitation of the lodge novel. In the two earlier works Hesse portrayed individuals striving out of their cultural and social malaise toward a vaguely sensed resolution. The individual—Emil Sinclair, Harry Haller—occupied the foreground; the resolution in the form of an order entered the novel only toward the end—notably the group surrounding Frau Eva and the Magic Theater—and was subsequently lost again. "In most of my work before *The Journey to the East*," Hesse acknowledged in 1935, "I gave evidence more of my weaknesses and difficulties than of the faith that, despite its weaknesses, made my existence possible and fortified it."[41] In *The Journey to the East* the emphasis shifts: the ideal itself moves to the center of the narrative—imperfectly observed yet still central—while the individual recedes toward the periphery. In its opening chapters the novel portrays a group assembled for the purpose of a pilgrimage to the East—the first trial of initiates into an as yet unspecified order—in a time specified as the period immediately following the Great War. The story is ostensibly limited both geographically and temporally. But the narrator, the musician H.H., soon realizes that it actually transcends those limitations, for in a higher sense this pilgrimage is only one wave in the eternal stream of souls striving homeward "to the home of light": "We were not wandering merely through space but likewise through time. We were journeying to the Orient, but we were also going into the Middle Ages or into the Golden Age; we passed through Italy or Switzerland, but we also sometimes spent the night in the tenth century and dwelled among the patriarchs or among fairies. . . . Our East was not only a land and something geographic; it was Everywhere and Nowhere, the unification of all times" (6:23). In this utopic and uchronic realm H.H. encounters childhood friends and figures of world literature (Parzival, Sancho Panza) all on the same level of reality. He sees writers who pale in existence beside their own lively creations.

The organization of the order emerges clearly in the course of the narrative. It has the traditional hierarchy with which we are familiar, ranging from a Superior and a High Tribunal down to the novices. Its four articles of faith, set forth in the Letter of the Order, are symbolized by the four stones in the ring presented to each novice. The novice is admitted to the order only after he has satisfied his superiors, through an interview, that his intentions are sincere; and he must still undergo a year of trial—in H.H.'s case the journey to the East—after absolving the oath of loyalty. The order itself, housed in a building more Kafkaesque than medieval, contains a vast archive housing a history of the order along with biographies of its members (a clear allusion to the archives of Goethe's Tower Society). The figures of the Superior as spiritual incarnation of the order and the emissary as its representative to the world outside are merged in the person of Leo. As emissary, he is the humble servant of the pilgrimage group who obliges everyone, yet he is characterized by the usual qualities of the genius of the order: he has the bright, penetrating eyes, the ageless appearance, the foreign origins, as well as the omnipotence and omnipresence of the traditional figure. The journey to the East undertaken by H.H. and other novices is the symbolic quest of the traditional hero, and its highpoints, festivals of the order, represent the counterpart of lodge celebrations with which we are familiar from earlier depictions in works from Apuleius's *The Golden Ass* to Sand's *The Countess of Rudolstadt*.

At the same time, the novel constitutes a symbolic autobiography because all the persons and places mentioned are based on Hesse's own life. The journey begins in the Swabia of Hesse's childhood and leads by way of the Tübingen of his early youth and Lake Constance (on which Hesse lived during the years of his first marriage) to "Noah's Ark" in Zurich and "Bremgarten" outside Bern (references to houses owned by Hesse's friends and benefactors) and the "Monday-Village" in the Ticino (Hesse's home in Montagnola) to Morbio Inferiore (an actual region on the Swiss-Italian border). Along the way he encounters, side by side with figures from his own novels and from world literature, such persons as Hans C. (Bodmer, owner of the house Zur Arch), Max and Tilli (Wassmer, owners of Schloss Bremgarten), Othmar (Schoeck, the composer), the astrologer Longus (Hesse's psychoanalyst Joseph B. Lang), Collofino (Hesse's friend Josef Feinhals), Ninon "the Foreigner" (Hesse's third wife, Ninon Ausländer [foreigner]), and others.

When the novices reach Morbio Inferiore, Leo disappears: the man whom all had regarded as a simple servant turns out to have been the spiritual center of the group. Without its motivating leader the entire undertaking disintegrates, and the novices depart one by one, convinced that the order has fallen apart and no longer exists. Ten years later, when H.H. tries to compose a history of the journey and of the order, he finds himself incapable of doing so: he cannot determine a common center linking his experiences, which seem to dissolve as soon as he tries to recollect and depict them. He begins to wonder if the story is even narratable. "I had either to write the book or to despair; it was the only possibility of my salvation from nothingness, from chaos, from suicide" (6:40). He seeks advice from his school friend Lukas, an experienced writer, who suggests that he should look up Leo, whose name keeps cropping up in H.H.'s account of the journey. They find a certain Andreas Leo in the address book, and H.H. visits him. Leo is unchanged in appearance, but he seems not to recognize or remember H.H., who has made himself unrecognizable as a lodge member through his own desertion of the order.

H.H. goes home despondently, but the next morning Leo appears in his rooms, sent by the order *(Bund)* to conduct H.H. to its High Seat. Along the way Leo relates to him episodes from the history of the order, founded in antiquity, and guides him into the vast lodge of the order, where he is welcomed by the assembled superiors as "a runaway lodge brother" who deserted the order at Morbio Inferiore and who feels hampered in his attempts to write its history by his oath of silence (6:57). Following consultation the superiors release him from his oath of silence and permit him to use the order's archives. There, as he revises his manuscript, he finds that he must delete as inaccurate sentence after sentence, whose letters vanish like incidental ornamentations. At this point, as he despairs at his own lack of understanding, the superiors enter again, and their verdict is spoken by the Most Superior, who turns out to be none other than Leo. His "novice's inanities," is the verdict, "are disposed of by laughing at them" (6:65). H.H. was led into despair by the failed trial of his initiation (at Morbio Inferiore): "Despair is the result of every serious attempt to fulfill life and its demands with virtue, with justice, with reason" (6:68). Children live on one side of despair, the Awakened Ones on the other. (Once again we recognize the three-stage process of humanization familiar from *Demian* and *Steppenwolf.*) H.H., no longer a child but not yet fully awakened, is still in the midst of despair. They offer him a second novitiate, welcome him back into the order, and return the ring that he lost years earlier.

Now a more difficult trial awaits him: the judgment of the archives about him. Reading other accounts of the same journey to the East, H.H. realizes that none of the other participants understood its meaning any more profoundly than he, but that all of them regarded him as a deserter from the order. When he finally works up the courage to look into his own rubric, he discovers no documentation but only a double figure, showing himself on one side, pale and morbid, back-to-back with a vigorous Leo into whose figure all his vitality was streaming. H.H. recalls a conversation with Leo from one of the order's festivals in which they remarked how much more vivid and real are the figures from literary works than the shapes of their creators. And with this ironic image—which recalls the ending of *The Novel of the Twelve,* when the twelve writers show up at the wedding reception of the figures they have created—the account ends.

The irony heightens Hesse's central theme: that the creators and creations of world culture constitute a higher order of being to which all may aspire and which encourages us to use humor and irony to deal with the irritations and frustrations of humdrum reality. To achieve this goal, Hesse uses the form of the lodge novel. H.H. is the quester who initially—like Parzival and Harry Haller—is admitted provisionally into the order (or Magic Theater) but fails the first trial. Ten years later H.H. is readmitted for a second trial, but like *Steppenwolf* the work ends ambivalently with regard to the future. Through his work of rehabilitation Hesse has restored to the secret society the larger cultural-intellectual-religious ideals that transcend the sociopolitical goals that for two centuries dominated the genre.

Hesse's last novel, *The Glass Bead Game* (*Das Glasperlenspiel* [1943]), may be viewed, paradoxically, as an expression of the author's ultimate disenchantment with even the loftiest utopian ideals toward which the secret societies of earlier periods aspired. The pedagogical province of Castalia as represented in his magnum opus is an extensive and rigidly hierarchical institution governed by a directorate of twenty members—an order dedicated to the abstract aestheticism of the Glass Bead Game. As a boy, Joseph Knecht is already initiated into the order and in the course of some thirty-five years achieves the supreme rank of Magister Ludi or Master of the Game. But Knecht, like Bulwer-Lytton's Zanoni, having recognized the limitations of an order dedicated narrowly and exclusively to intellect and the spirit, defects from the Castalian order to commit himself to life and service in the real world, where he soon dies.[42] The various stages of the quest that characterize the traditional lodge novel are lacking in Hesse's magisterial work, which portrays the goal—otherwise nowhere depicted in quest literature from Euripides to the present—but not the quest itself. Here we sense the sober conclusions of a writer whose ideals have been qualified by the events of the 1930s and of World War II and who now rejects the notion of a world governed by even the most spiritual elite.

The years preceding and following World War I betrayed as much activity by secret societies as did the revolutionary eras of the late eighteenth and mid-nineteenth centuries—activity that extended its scope from what Huysmans called the "madness of occultism" to the political ambitions of German nationalists. By this time the public curiosity about these activities and conspiracies had reached the point at which scholars began to take a lively interest in their existence and in their literary manifestations. Meanwhile, writers began to regard the lodge novel with both the fond familiarity of cultural commitment and the critical detachment of ironic modernity: an attitude that enabled them for the first time in the progression of the genre to engage in an uninhibited free play with its traditional and well-recognized forms. Accordingly the lodge novel underwent such radical transformations as its classicization in Hofmannsthal's hands, its collectivization by the authors of *The Novel of the Twelve,* its ironic criminalization by Gide, its dissipation in the effete society of Wilder's Cabala, and its rehabilitation and ultimate qualification in Hesse's fictions.

CHAPTER SEVEN

Interlude

The *Protocols of the Elders of Zion*

The Fabrication

It is ironic that the most widely ballyhooed conspiracy between the two world wars found virtually no contemporary literary resonance. The *Protocols of the Elders of Zion,* first published in 1903 in a St. Petersburg newspaper, had no impact outside Russia until the tract was brought to Western Europe after the Revolution by White Russian émigrés and then immediately (1920) translated—first into German, English, French, and Polish and soon thereafter into many other languages. The "document," allegedly the protocol of a meeting of the assembled Elders of Zion—that is, the leaders of international Jewry—notoriously lists in twenty-four articles the methods by which they propose to take over the world: by acquiring the financial establishments, controlling the press, infiltrating the political and cultural institutions, exploiting existing governments both capitalist and communist, and so forth.

The *Protocols* were almost immediately unmasked as a blatant fabrication.[1] As early as 1921 the American diplomat Herman Bernstein attacked the hoax in his book *The History of a Lie.*[2] In August of that same year the *Times* of London published a series of articles demonstrating that the publication was plagiarized extensively from Maurice Joly's *Dialogue in Hell between Machiavelli and Montesquieu, or the Politics of Machiavelli in the Nineteenth Century* (1864).[3] Joly's work, a satire by a liberal French lawyer composed in the traditional genre of "Dialogues of the Dead"[4] and directed against the despotic régime of Napoleon III, consists of twenty-five dialogues—mostly arguments by Machiavelli in which the political theorist expresses his skeptical view of constitutional government, denies the validity of morality and law in politics, adapts his Renaissance ideas to the new industrial society, advocates the role of terror, recommends the annihilation of the liberal press and secret societies, discusses the dangers of all collective agencies, and so forth. After ten years of this reign the nation has been transformed: Machiavelli has been crowned and is regarded by the people as greater than Louis XIV, Henry IV, and George Washington. In his closing line the horrified Montesquieu exclaims, "Eternal God, what have you permitted!"

In his articles Philip Graves, the correspondent for the *Times* in Constantinople, related the adventurous story of a mysterious "Mr X" who, wishing to remain anonymous, shared with him a copy of the still anonymous work, which the newspaper's researchers in London soon determined to be that of Joly. Detailed comparisons have revealed numerous and often verbatim parallels between the two works.[5] Often, indeed, the plagiarist simply replaced "France" with "the world" and "Napoleon III" with "the Jews." Fifteen years later, in a highly publicized trial in Bern, to settle a suit brought in 1934–35 by the united Jewish communities of Switzerland against the anti-Semitic National Front for distributing copies of the thirteenth (Nazi) edition of the *Protocols,* the judge again concluded that the work was clearly plagiarized from Joly's book. (His additional judgment that it was salacious and hence "indecent literature" was later quashed on technical grounds.)

In the course of time further details concerning the forgery emerged. Hermann Goedsche (1815–78), a onetime German postal official who lost his position because he fabricated documents incriminating a liberal politician, went on to become a journalist for conservative newspapers and achieved considerable popularity as the author of multivolume political-historical novels under the pseudonym of Sir John Retcliffe.[6] Only four years after Joly's satirical dialogues he published his episodic novel *Biarritz* (1868), which contains a chapter entitled "At the Jewish Cemetery in Prague" ("Auf dem Judenkirchhof in Prag").[7] According to the fiction of the episode, a young German scholar named "Dr. Faust," eager to add the secrets of the kabbalah to his learning, is taken by an Italian Jewish acquaintance, as a reward for saving his life three years earlier, to witness an unusual gathering in the Jewish cemetery on the festival of Succoth (October 8, 1860). Shortly before midnight the two men climb over the wall and watch from their hiding place as thirteen spectral figures, clad in white, gather at the tombstone of the Rabbi Simeon Ben Jehuda, which glows with a bluish light, and whisper a code word. "Out from this point goes the impulse which makes the exiles into the masters of the earth, the despised into the tyrants of the peoples" (144). It emerges that this meeting of the kabbalist Sanhedrin takes place every hundred years with representatives of the Jewish communities from twelve capitals of Europe and under the leadership of "the representative of the rejected and wanderers" (165)—none other than the Wandering Jew. Their goal is to recover the reign promised to their people by Abraham but stolen from them by followers of the Cross. When they have obtained all the gold in the world, they will have all the power: "Ours is the future" (167). One by one they report—in Chaldean, we are told—from their various cities on their vast and growing capital holdings and other progress: to corrupt the aristocracy by scandal and debt; to ruin the middle class by degrading them to artisans and factory workers; to undermine the church by encouraging free thought and doubt; to seize control of business and high positions in government, especially in law and culture; to promote the arts and sciences, in which the Jews excel; to corrupt Christian sacraments by seducing the women; and to exploit the press to justify their actions. In conclusion the leader exhorts them to renew their pledge as "Sons of the Golden Calf" and to go forth once more. Each one tosses a stone brought from various lands upon the tombstone, in whose bluish light the vague outline of an animal appears. A hundred years hence, their leader prophesies, they will have achieved their goal: "the new Canaan, mastery of the world" (143). The two onlookers, horrified by what they have seen, determine to oppose the Jewish conspiracy with all the means at their disposal. Subsequently, we learn (many chapters later) that Dr. Faust, on his way back to Berlin, suffers a (presumably induced) seizure in Dresden, whereupon the conspirators arrange for him to be permanently confined and helpless in the Saxon Insane Asylum.

Goedsche's work betrays two influences: it combines the secret meetings with which he was familiar from the tradition of the lodge novel from Schiller to George Sand with an agenda advanced by the despotic Machiavelli of Joly's satire. Joly, who never mentions the Jews, introduced the agenda satirically as a critique of the administration of Napoleon III and was duly arrested, tried, and sentenced to fifteen months imprisonment, his book banned and confiscated. Goedsche appropriated his words, often verbatim, but presented them seriously as the program of the conspiracy of the Elders of Zion.[8]

That chapter enjoyed a career of its own, quite independent of the lengthy fiction in which it first appeared.[9] In 1872 it was translated and published in St. Petersburg as a fictional work with a factual basis and again in 1876 under the title *The Jewish Cemetery in Czech Prague (The Jews, Sovereigns of the World)*. A year later it appeared in France in *Le Contemporain,* but at this point its original fictionality was ignored: it was introduced as an actual speech delivered by a chief rabbi to a secret meeting of his followers, and its source was cited as a forthcoming work by an English diplomat. In the confusion that followed, "John Readclif" [*sic*] was initially identified as the chief rabbi himself and only subsequently as the anti-Semitic Sir John Redclif [*sic*]—sometimes with the added tidbit that he was murdered for his heroic exposure of the conspiracy. Within ten years, in other words, a pure fiction came to be regarded as pure fact. Later this so-called *Rabbi's Speech* was frequently translated and republished—in France, Germany, Austria, Czechoslovakia, and Russia—and even cited as proof for the authenticity of the *Protocols.*

The *Protocols* themselves were presumably concocted between 1894 and 1899 in a France feverish with the anti-Semitism underlying the Dreyfus Affair.[10] On the basis of the available evidence it was long assumed that the forgery, written originally in French, was produced by a Russian journalist on the orders of the reactionary schemer Pyotr Ivanovich Rachkovsky, head of the Russian secret service *(Okhrana)* in Paris, in an effort to discredit liberal reformers in Moscow, and notably Sergey Witte, the minister of finance who was striving to modernize Russia. Recent findings in Soviet archives by the Russian historian Mikhail Lépikhine have provided evidence for the validity of a claim made years earlier by Catherine Radziwill during her US exile: that the chief fabricator was a skilled political propagandist named Mathieu Golovinsky, who worked for the Russian political police in France to influence the depiction of Russia in French newspapers.[11] However that may be, an abbreviated version of the original French text, inspired by the mysterious circumstances surrounding *The Rabbi's Speech* and based contextually on Joly's *Dialogues,* was published privately as early as 1897 and later appeared in August and September 1903 in the St. Petersburg newspaper *Znamya* (The Banner) of the militant anti-Semite Pavel Krushevan under the title "Programme for World Conquest by the Jews." Two years later the full version was published as a pamphlet entitled *The Root of Our Troubles* (1905) and was cited to justify and incite the efforts of the reactionary forces known as the Black Hundred to blame the Jews for the Russo-Japanese War, the revolution of 1905, and what they regarded as the abomination of the new liberal constitution. The work received further publicity when it was included as the final chapter in the second (or third) edition of the book *The Great in the Small: Antichrist Considered as an Imminent Political Possibility* (1905) by the renowned itinerant mystic Sergey Nilus. Initially, its effect was limited mainly to anti-Semitic fanatics.[12] Even though the Metropolitan of Moscow ordered that a sermon quoting the *Protocols* be read in all 368 churches of the capital, the work was generally rejected as a forgery by Tsar Nicholas II and most other influential Russians. (It was, however, found on the Tsaritsa's bed table following the murder of the royal family by the Bolsheviks in 1918.)

The Growing Influence

Despite imperial Russia's tradition and program of anti-Semitism—as witness the systematically planned and executed pogroms that took place between 1881 and 1920, when the Jews were blamed for the revolution of 1905 as well as the Great War—the *Protocols* had no wider impact until the 1917 Revolution, when once again the Jews were charged with their defeat by the White Russians, who took copies with them when they sought exile in the West. When the work finally reached Western Europe and the United States, the translations rapidly began.[13] Even before the war's end, in January 1918, the right-wing monthly *Deutschlands Erneuerung* (Germany's renewal) had included a version of *The Rabbi's Speech,* blaming Jewish bankers for plunging the world into war. Two years later the *Protocols* themselves were first published under the title *Die Geheimnisse der Weisen von Zion* (The secrets of the Sages of Zion), and the work was on its way to success despite all evidence of its forgery, such as the early articles in the *Times* of London and Herman Bernstein's *History of a Lie.* One editor, Gottfried zur Beek, claimed that the Sages or Elders were none other than the members who attended the First Zionist Conference at Basel in 1897. Another, Theodor Fritsch, maintained that the document was originally written in Hebrew, not French, and revealed to the public in Alsace by the wife of a prominent Freemason. Zur Beek's edition had such an immediate impact that it enjoyed six printings in 1920 and by 1938, after the Nazi Party had acquired the rights, could boast of some twenty-two editions. By 1933 Fritsch's version had separately achieved thirteen editions.

It is unnecessary to rehearse in detail the unsavory history of the document's success as a factor in Nazi policy. Hitler cited it frequently, as in *Mein Kampf* (1925):

> How very much the entire existence of this people is based on a continuing lie is shown in an incomparable manner by the "Protocols of the Wise Men of Zion," which is so endlessly hated by the Jews. It is supposed to be based on a forgery, as the *Frankfurter Zeitung* never tires of moaning into the world—the best proof that it is genuine. What many Jews may do unconsciously is here exposed consciously. That's what matters. It is all the same from what Jew-head these revelations come; definitive is the fact that they expose with a virtually horror-stirring certainty the nature and the activity of the Jewish people and depict them in their innermost connections as well as in their ultimate goals. The best criticism, however, is reality itself. Whoever examines the historical development of the past hundred years from the standpoint of this book will immediately understand the outcry of the Jewish press. For if this book becomes the common property of a people, the Jewish menace will be seen as broken.[14]

Heinrich Himmler later claimed that "the Führer [had] learned it by heart,"[15] and the work was exceeded in sales only by *Mein Kampf.* Hannah Arendt has argued that the Nazis took the *Protocols* as "a model for the future organization of the German masses for 'world empire'" because they "presented world conquest as a practical possibility [and] implied that the whole affair was only a question of inspired or shrewd know-how. . . . The Nazis started with the fiction of a conspiracy and modeled themselves, more or less consciously, after the example of the secret society of the Elders of Zion."[16] Long before he wrote his more famous *Myth of the Twentieth Century* (*Mythus des zwanzigsten Jahrhunderts* [1930]), Nazism's chief ideologue, Alfred Rosenberg, published what became the principal party doctrine on the *Protocols: Die Protokolle der Weisen von Zion und die jüdische Weltpolitik* (1923), a work that became required reading for students after 1933. Even before the Holocaust the *Protocols* were at least partly responsible for such criminal acts as the political murder of Walther Rathenau, the highly accomplished (Jewish) minister for foreign affairs of the fledgling Weimar Republic, whose young assassins admitted that they regarded him as one of the Elders of Zion.[17]

We should not console ourselves with the thought that the influence of the *Protocols* was limited to Nazi Germany. In the United States, where the translation enjoyed a remarkable success, Henry Ford's newspaper the *Dearborn Independent* published a series of articles coauthored by Dr. August Müller and a Russian refugee named Boris Brasol, a German-Russian collaboration promoting the view of the *Protocols* as a genuine document of Jewish conspiracy. Republished as a book under the title *The International Jew: The World's Foremost Problem* (1920) under the name and auspices of Henry Ford, the work was widely circulated and translated and spread the ideas of the *Protocols* to hitherto unknowing audiences.[18] Even a stance of alleged impartiality could have its drawbacks. In her book *Secret Societies and Subversive Movements,* which surveys "associations working through nineteen centuries to undermine social and moral order and above all Christian civilization,"[19] Nesta H. Webster appends an allegedly unbiased discussion (408–14) in which she professes inconclusiveness about the authenticity of the *Protocols* but adds her conviction that the ideas expressed in the document, legitimate or not, reflect widespread Jewish doctrines—a conclusion that neatly fits her thesis that "an Occult Power" is at work in the world in the eternal conflict between the powers of darkness and the powers of light (405).

In France the *Protocols* benefited from the literary genius of the aggressively anti-Semitic Louis-Ferdinand Céline,[20] who blamed Jewish powermongers, with their "globulous eyes," along with the Freemasons they controlled, for everything he detested: from the reigning governments of the world and the obscenities of the "Jewish-Masonic Exposition of 1937" in Paris to modern French literature, written by his account almost wholly by Jews; Jewish literary critics who condemned his works; and contemporary art, which was sponsored and purchased by Jews. In his venomous, obscene, and rabidly anti-Semitic rant of more than three hundred pages, *Trifles for a Massacre (Bagatelles pour un massacre* [1937]), an invective dominated wholly by his idée fixe, Céline devotes a lengthy section to the *Protocols,* calling it "a Jewish divinatory hysteria" that initially appears to be sheer fantasy but that, when one looks around at the contemporary world, is precisely confirmed by the evolution of events.[21] Echoing Hitler, he writes that "The *Protocols* of 1902 [*sic*] predict almost exactly all that the Jews have accomplished in the world since then." Following a tradition naming the speaker of *The Rabbi's Speech* Rabbi Eichhorn or Rabbi Reichhorn, Céline attributes the *Protocols* to "one Rabbi Rzeichhorn" and states that they were subsequently reproduced by Sir John Radcliff [*sic*], who was killed for having communicated the secret doctrine. He then recapitulates the primary passages of the *Protocols* and, in conclusion, confirms the accuracy of the prophecy by naming the Jewish chiefs of both capitalism and its communist opposition, Rothschild and Karl Marx, and listing other "Jews of the Great Golden Calf" who command the world in war and peace, including specifically the principal leaders of the Bolshevik Revolution.

The Literary Response

In contrast to the voluminous vitriol of the Nazis and such anti-Semites as Céline the absence of literary responses is striking. This is due in part no doubt to the fact that fiction could hardly match the weirdness of the innumerable "serious" responses to the *Protocols* and in part to the perhaps misguided assumption that it would simply dignify the ridiculous subject to mention it. In Germany another factor played a significant role: the very real fear of inner-emigration writers of irritating the Nazi authorities and the parallel caution of exile authors not to offend the censors so that their works might continue to be published in Germany. When Ludwig Lewisohn asked Thomas Mann in 1933 for an unequivocal statement about the Nazi takeover, Mann replied from his recent exile in Switzerland: "If I told you what you wish to hear, my capital and property in Germany would be taken from me tomorrow, my son would be arrested as a hostage, I do not know what would happen to my old parents-in-law, who are Jewish, no more of my books could be sold in Germany, and I do not know what the other consequences would be."[22] However, at least two literary responses were published by German exile writers living abroad.

Stefan Heym (1913–2001), known today as one of the most prominent writers in the German Democratic Republic, was born to a Jewish family in Chemnitz as Helmut Flieg. An early anti-Nazi, he was expelled from his gymnasium in Chemnitz for publishing an antimilitaristic poem in a socialist newspaper and then studied journalism in Berlin. Immediately after Hitler's accession to power in 1933 he fled to Czechoslovakia, where, under the pseudonym Stefan Heym, he became a frequent contributor to the short-lived Prague satirical weekly *Der Simpl* (1934–35; initially *Simplicius*). Emigrating to the United States in 1935, Heym continued his studies at the University of Chicago, became a U.S. citizen, served in the army, and published his first novels. Following his return to Europe in 1952 (simultaneously with Thomas Mann, Bertolt Brecht, and other German writers suspected of being communists) and despite repeated conflicts with the East German government, he established himself as one of postwar Germany's leading literary voices.

It was in *Der Simpl* that, at the age of twenty-two, he published his grotesque "Interview with the Sages of Zion,"[23] which plays on all the common prejudices about Jews as expounded in the *Protocols*. (As a result of Nazi propaganda and the publicity attached to the trials in Bern the *Protocols* were once again conspicuously in the news.) When the interviewer meets six of the sages in Prague—the seventh is due to arrive shortly by chartered flight from Berlin—they have just finished a fine breakfast of tender cutlets prepared from the flesh of Christian maidens slaughtered according to kosher rules. They readily explain their activities. The first, a bearded rabbi who writes under the pseudonym "Vandevelde" (Theodoor van de Velde achieved an international reputation in the 1920s with his semipornographic sex manuals), seeks to ensure with his writings that the pure races are thoroughly watered down with Jewish blood. "Why else are all the Jewish shop assistants running around in the world?" A second, named Löwenfisch, is preparing a world financial crisis by destroying useful capital and seizing control of the economy. Tartokower, the representative from Moscow who under a pseudonym occupies a high office, concerns himself with the collectivization of the farm economy and the socialization of women in the pursuit of communism. Isaac Sternschuss, who holds a position in the League of Nations, uses his Talmudic skills to teach the other delegates how to utter a thousand words without saying a word. The American "Selfmademan" Rechabeach (pronounced "rich bitch") is responsible for stealing the Lindbergh baby and controlling the Jewish press as he prepares the public for the coming world war. When the interviewer asks about the traffic in white slaves, Vandevelde reports that such trivialities are handled locally—even though virgins are no longer what they used to be! For his final question the interviewer wonders what they intend to do about Germany, where the government is beginning to shake off the Jewish domination. At this they all smile knowingly and introduce the representative from Berlin, who has just arrived: a small, club-footed man who apologizes for being late, saying that his wife Magda did not want to let him go. (Contemporary readers would instantly have recognized the allusion to the chief Nazi propagandist Joseph Goebbels.) It is easy to understand why Heym, who contributed other equally satirical poems and stories to *Der Simpl*, felt it necessary to escape from the Nazis—first at home in Germany and later in Czechoslovakia.

Wolfgang Cordan (1909–66) was a novelist and translator who spent his later years in Latin America, becoming an acknowledged specialist in Mayan archaeology and mythology.[24] Born in Berlin as Heinrich Wolfgang Horn—his father was a director in the Prussian Ministry of Education, and his mother was related to Nietzsche—he received a solid grounding in classics at the famous Schulpforta and then, after his expulsion (for reading Nietzsche during chapel), at the public gymnasium in Dessau, where he also attended drawing classes at the Bauhaus. In 1927 he began his studies in classics, philosophy, and music at the University of Berlin, followed in 1931 by a year in the Balkans and Turkey, where he studied Middle Eastern languages and culture. Back in Berlin, he was intimately involved in the lively cultural life of the city, especially the theater, knew most of the prominent and largely Jewish figures, and contributed to liberal journals. Shortly after Hitler came to power, he left Germany, going first to Paris, where he translated for the communist newspaper *L'Humanité* and published a pamphlet, *L'Allemagne sans masque* (1933), with a preface by André Gide, against the Nazi terror. Later that year he moved to the Netherlands, where he published his novella *The Sages of Zion* (*De Wijzen van Zion* [1934]), which was based in part on the autobiographical account of a Hungarian Jewish friend and for which he used for the first time the pseudonym Wolfgang Cordan.[25] From 1935 to 1938 he resided alternately in Berlin and Amsterdam. In 1938 he moved permanently to Amsterdam and following the German occupation of Holland was active with the resistance, in which capacity he rescued a number of Jewish children.

The Sages of Zion is related by a nameless young man—his former girlfriend, Helen, calls him "Teddy"—who, from his exile, recalls a shattering episode that took place on an autumn day in his German past (in an unspecified city that is clearly Berlin). He claims not to know whether it was "one year or ten years ago," but the time is irrelevant, he says, because evil occurred on the earth three thousand years ago and "after three thousand more years people will still kill, burn, torture" (1). On that day he strolled with Helen to the university, where they took their places in the classroom for a lecture on Goethe's theory of colors. Before the professor enters, a fellow student approaches and asks him if he's a Jew. When Teddy says "Yes," the colleague, backed up by other students, orders him to go and sit in the front of the room so that the others can keep their eyes on the Jews. The situation rapidly worsens. Teddy moves to the front with another Jewish student but then decides to leave the room during the lecture. When his tormentor follows, Teddy knocks him down and tries to flee from the university building, but the various exits are guarded. He finally gets out to the garden by helping to carry another Jewish student, who has apparently been killed, and later makes his escape. Outside he discovers that the world is going on its normal way. "The chauffeur steers his automobile, the Führer is perhaps signing death sentences,

His Magnificus issues a proclamation, and the students break ribs and make work for the eye-glass factories" (18).

Teddy eventually makes his way home, reluctant to tell his parents what has happened, but his mother quickly discerns the truth and urges him not to inform his father. "He always believed that his son would be spared the torments of his own youth. But the time of the persecutions has come again, more terrible than ever before. He won't survive this . . ." (27). Teddy retreats to his room, where he first relives the day in a dream and then realizes that "it was not even a year ago that I saw everything that happened in the past twelve hours taking place on the stage" (31). At this point Teddy interpolates a chapter entitled "Dialectical Intermezzo," in which he recapitulates in detail the scenario of a wildly expressionistic play, allegedly written by a Jewish author and produced by a renowned socialist director, that he had attended some months earlier: "Revolution, inflation, putsches . . . everything that our great country endured after the war was supposed to be unrolled in a single evening like a kaleidoscope. One heard that film, loudspeakers, moving sets and all imaginable technical innovations were going to be used, and even before the performance the critics vehemently discussed the pros and cons in the newspapers" (31). The first half does just that in a "fantastic orgy," showing "decorated generals, grenade explosions, hand-to-hand combat, dead soldiers, beaten Jews, murdered workers, mass meetings, ecstatic demagogues—everything that a desperate, collapsing, chaotic age produces" (35). Thinking back, Teddy realizes that "this century has no place for humanists" (34)—such as, for instance, the Goethe who was the subject of that morning's lecture.

Following an intermission, the highpoint of the second part, allegedly to explain the preceding, is "A Sermon about the Seven Sages of Zion (based on the communications of Julius Streicher and General Ludendorff)" (36). According to that notorious Nazi propagandist and the puppet president of Hitler's régime, several German professors obtained the protocol of a meeting of the Seven Sages of Zion that took place in Krakow in 1865 and outlined their program for world domination: "Without delay we must poison the mutual relations of peoples, states, and classes; through hatred and envy, through strikes and war, yes even through privation, hunger, and the spread of contagious diseases we must weaken all the peoples so greatly that they find no other remedy than to submit wholly to our domination" (87–88). Their schemes not only caused the war between Prussia and Austria in 1866 and the Franco-Prussian war of 1870–71 but also systematically brought all heavy industry and banking into Jewish hands while continuing to penetrate the intellectual professions with the goal of destroying the culture of humanity. Since the meetings of the Seven Sages take place every seven-times-seven years, the most recent one occurred in 1914. Although the protocol of that meeting was so closely guarded that it could not be discovered, it is reasonable to attribute to their plots the Great War as well as the revolutions, financial turmoil, and social upheavals that followed—in sum, everything depicted in the first part of the play. This threat brought forth the Brown Shirts, who are then depicted in a drunken scene, planning to expose and resist the Jews, France, and other archenemies of the Holy Mother of God.

Shocked by what he has seen and heard, Teddy no longer recalls how the play ended. Afterward, he reluctantly accompanied several friends to a wine restaurant to discuss the success of the socialist play. Teddy is dismayed to learn that his liberal friends have been persuaded by what they saw. The Social Democrat Groning confesses that he was "overwhelmed, and converted"—that it was "soothing, even fascinating to understand the historical process of development as determined by eternal and unwavering fundamental laws" (41).

Disillusioned more by the acquiescent response of his friends than by the play itself, Teddy goes home, where his father is conferring with a group of friends about their own futures. When Teddy realizes that the group consists of seven elderly men, he asks them if they constitute a gathering of the Seven Sages of Zion—and then collapses in a feverish state in which he lies for some ten days. When he learns that one of his friends has already departed to study in Switzerland, he decides to leave, too, and his memoir concludes with the notation that the mountains are now nearby.

The closing "Lamentation à la Jeremias (along with a contemplation of the 3 elements)" (53–67) begins with a survey of the manners in which humankind through its technological advances has abused the earth (with economic exploitation of its resources), the water (with destructive submarines, like the one that sank the *Lusitania*), and the air (with bombers that destroy cities). It ends with a spectral vision anticipating the Holocaust. "The corpses lay bundled in sheafs. Or hung like puppets from their frame. The sound of the zoo animals was ear-deafening. And slowly the blast furnaces were extinguished" (67).

Cordan's dazzling novella is remarkable and moving not so much for its depiction of the by now familiar propagandistic use of the *Protocols* but particularly for its analysis of the manner in which even non-Nazis such as Teddy's socialist and communist friends were persuaded by the conspiracy theory that promised to explain the chaotic world *entre deux guerres*. It is compelling not least, finally, for the concluding vision of the horrors that in 1934 lay ahead for a humankind that not only abused nature but had even lost its own humanity.

The Continuing Fascination

It will have occurred by now to every reader who has followed my argument to this point that the phenomenon of the *Protocols* displays remarkable parallels to that of the Rosicrucian manifestos. Both works, almost exactly three hundred years apart, were perpetrated as literary hoaxes—albeit one as a student prank and the other for more sinister political purposes. Both, despite their immediate identification by rational readers as fabrications, had an enormous impact on their contemporaries, catching as they did the mood of their respective times, and generated countless pamphlets exploring their implications. To both were attributed deplorable historical consequences: the manifestos were blamed, as we saw, for the Thirty Years' War and, two centuries later, the French Revolution, and they exacerbated antipapal sentiments in Protestant lands. The *Protocols* were held accountable by many Germans for the "stab in the back" in World War I, for the financial disasters of the 1920s, as well as for the immoral deviations of modernist music, art, and literature; and they contributed directly to genocidal acts against the Jews, both the pogroms in Russia and the Holocaust in Nazi Germany. Although neither work generated notable or extensive contemporary literary responses, both fascinated later generations. The Rosicrucians inspired writers from Goethe to Umberto Eco. And at least two prominent postwar European authors have devoted their attention to the history of the *Protocols*.

In one of his best-known works, a collection of largely fantastic novellas based on history entitled *Encyclopedia of the Dead* (1983), the Yugoslav writer Danilo Kiš (1935–89) included a tale entitled "The Book of Kings and Fools,"[26] which amounts to a fictionalized retelling of the history of the forgery, beginning with the circumstances and personalities surrounding its composition and following it to its inevitable and disastrous consequences in the Nazi concentration camps. As Kiš explains in his postscript, he originally conceived of the story as an essay, a form whose traces it still distinctly betrays. "It was my intention to trace briefly the true and fantastic—'unbelievably fantastic'—history of the birth of the *Protocols of the Elders of Zion* and of their insane influence on generations of readers and the tragic consequences that they had" (187). But the essay disintegrated as he sought to imagine the parts missing from the troubled history. So he decided to focus on the personages in the history whose lives were lost in the shadows and to give them a new life. To make clear the new fictional intention he changed the name of the central work from *Protocols* to the more general label "Conspiracy." "Undertaken at the margin of the facts—without betraying them altogether—the tale began to develop precisely in those places where the historical data were spotty and the facts unknown" (188). Among the sources he consulted, Kiš cites Norman Cohn's *Warrant for Genocide* (1967), as well as Henri Rollin's *Apocalypse de notre temps* (1940).

The account begins with a statement anticipating its conclusion: the crime that was going to be perpetrated forty years later was already announced in a St. Petersburg newspaper of 1906 (actually 1903) in a series of articles signed by the editor in chief, P. A. Krushevan. Kiš relates with obvious delight the strange saga of Sergey Nilus in his pilgrimage from one monastery to another and his inclusion of "The Conspiracy" in his book *Antichrist* (drawing for further details on an account by Maria Dmnitrievna Kashkina, dictated years later for the Bern trial, and on the biography by N. D. Zhevakhov). He then briefly discusses the role of "The Conspiracy" in stirring up the pogroms in Russia before describing how Nilus's book made its way west in the baggage of White Russian officers alongside copies of the New Testament and monogrammed napkins. At this point the action of his "novel with multiple ramifications" leads the author to Constantinople and the mysterious "Mr X," who reputedly first alerted the *Times'* correspondent, Philip Graves, to Joly's book as a source for the *Protocols*.[27] Since nothing was known about Mr X, Kiš was free to use his imagination to fill in the blanks. Those pages lead back in turn to an account of Joly and his *Dialogues*. The narrative finally returns to the "atelier of Rachkovsky," where the "Conspiracy" was cobbled together. "The noise made by this 'masterpiece of calumny' spread throughout the world at a speed with which only rumor circulates and the Fever of Malta" (158).

The tale continues with an account of the document's influence. "In Germany, belief in the authenticity of the *Conspiracy* is 'unshakeable and solid as a rock'" while the American translation reaches a circulation of half a million copies thanks to the name of Henry Ford, a man of "two passions: automobiles and secret societies" (160). After citing the work's influence on Hitler and Stalin, "the former amateur painter" and "the anonymous Georgian seminarist," Kiš's tale ends with a sobering account of the Nazi concentration camps by Kurt Gerstein, who was already known to many theatergoers as the hero of Rolf

Hochhuth's controversial and highly acclaimed drama *The Deputy* (*Der Stellver-treter* [1963]).

While Kiš is clearly concerned with the disastrous historical consequences of the *Protocols*—first the pogroms in Russia and then the Holocaust in Germany—Umberto Eco in *Foucault's Pendulum* (1988), which will be discussed more appropriately and thoroughly in the next chapter, focuses on the phenomenon of conspiracy in general and on the *Protocols* as a literary construct. Here it suffices to point out that, among the examples featured in the conversations of the three central figures—editors at a fashionable publishing house who become obsessed with various world conspiracies from antiquity to the present—the *Protocols of the Elders of Zion* occupy six entire, albeit short chapters (chaps. 91–96). The work is introduced in connection with the anti-Semitic campaigns initiated at the end of the nineteenth century (chap. 91). In this context the friends consider the introduction of the *Protocols* in Russia by the itinerant monk Nilus (chap. 92). The next episode (chap. 93) constitutes a brief recapitulation of the ideas of the *Protocols.* In chapter 94 Eco introduces his own (unfounded) theory that the *Protocols* were anticipated by a document that plays a role in the last chapter of Eugène Sue's novel *Les mystères du peuple* (1849–57; not to be confused with the more famous *Les mystères de Paris*). He goes on to cite Joly's pamphlet and Goedsche's (Retcliffe's) novel *Biarritz,* for whose source he proposes a scene from the beginning of Alexander Dumas' *(père)* novel *Joseph Balsamo,* in which Balsamo/Cagliostro attends a secret meeting in the forests of three hundred initiates of an unnamed conspiratorial group (chap. 95).[28] The last of the six chapters brings them to Rachkovsky's role in creating the forgery. According to Eco the Russian secret agent, in a house search, finds a pamphlet written by the Jew Elie de Cyon, which uses Joly's book as the basis for an attack against the progressive minister Witte. Rachkovsky, substituting the Jews for Witte, turns his own text against Cyon, whose very name suggests Zion. Eco has taken a number of fictional liberties with his sources in the effort to make a more exciting narrative of the various episodes that constitute the history of the *Protocols* as a literary fiction, and his account, while making use of primary texts and secondary sources, should not be taken as a reliable history of the *Protocols.*

A few years later Eco recapitulated his account, often verbatim, in the chapter "Fictional Protocols" of his Charles Eliot Norton lectures at Harvard.[29] There he analyzes the human temptation to read the actual world as fiction, since fictional worlds are more comfortable and comprehensible than reality, and demonstrates the historical consequences that can occur when fiction intrudes into life. The *Protocols,* of course, provide the most vivid and tragic modern example.

Obsessed as are few other writers with conspiracies generally and the *Protocols* in particular, Eco returned to the subject yet again in 2010 in his novel *The Prague Cemetery,* a fanciful mélange of fact and fiction.[30] The title is misleading to the extent that the *Protocols* play a central role only in the final twenty pages of the 440-page novel, where it represents the culmination of the protagonist's encounters with various texts and personalities. Up to that point Eco provides, through the eyes of his protagonist(s)—the schizophrenic Italo-French lawyer and forger Simone Simonini and his alter ego, Abbé Dalla Piccola—a capsule tour through revolutionary and conspiratorial Europe during the second half of the nineteenth century: from the Italian *risorgimento* with Garibaldi's Thousand and the Carbonari by way of the Paris Commune down to the Dreyfus Affair in France along with lengthy discussions of the Freemasons, Jesuits, Illuminati, and various Satanic cults (e.g., Palladism and a meticulously depicted Black Mass). The novel features walk-on appearances by such personalities as Sigmund Freud (who inspires Simonini/Dalla Piccola's diary confessions), the French neurologist Jean Martin Charcot, Garibaldi, Alexandre Dumas, the Italian patriot and novelist Ippolito Nievo, the French anti-Semitic propagandist Edouard Drumont, the French anti-Catholic forger Léo Taxil and his supposed creation Diana Vaughn, and Alfred Dreyfus, as well as figures we have already encountered in connection with the *Protocols:* Hermann Goedsche, Maurice Joly, P. I. Rachkovsky, and Mathieu Golovinsky. The narrative is enlivened by the polyhistoric author's detailed descriptions of street scenes in Paris, clothing and sartorial fashions, and elaborate menus and recipes.

This often exhaustively encyclopedic whole is held together by the protagonist—surely with his vicious anti-Semitism and general misanthropy and racism one of the most warped and contemptible monsters in modern literature. Simonini, allegedly the grandson of a "Captain Simonini" known historically only as the author of a letter attributing the French Revolution to the machinations of the Jews—creates masterful forgeries and acts, often as a traitor and double agent, for Cavour's diplomatic manipulations, for schemes of the Jesuits, for successive French regimes as well as the Prussian and Russian secret services—in sum, for anyone or any group that offers a sufficient reward. In this capacity he is said not only to have murdered Nievo, Joly, Diana Vaughn, and others; he is also reported to have written the initial account of the secret meeting in the Prague cemetery—allegedly of Jesuits, not Jews—that was then appropriated by Goedsche for his novel *Biarritz;* to have forged the document responsible for Dreyfus's indictment; and ultimately—in a chapter entitled with ominous foreshadowing "The Final Solution"—to have drafted the French document on which Golovinsky based his *Protocols.* Because the novel ends at this point—Simonini is killed when he attempts as an act of terrorism to blow up an early excavation for the Paris *métro*—he does not live to witness the eventual worldwide success of his greatest forgery. Eco's historical fantasy adds nothing to the account of the *Protocols* that he presented in earlier works; it simply illustrates with a predictable repetitiveness the author's thesis that "people believe only what they already know, and this is the beauty of the Universal Form of Conspiracy" (79). In this case, however, truth is truly stranger than fiction.

The use of their history in such prominent works of postmodern fiction exemplifies the continuing fascination of the *Protocols.*[31] The lasting obsession with the destructive fabrication into the twenty-first century, finally, is illustrated by Will Eisner's *The Plot: The Secret Story of the Protocols of the Elders of Zion* (2005), which features an introduction by Umberto Eco and an afterword by the political scientist Stephen Eric Bronner. Eisner (1917–2005), creator of the graphic novel and an acclaimed master in the use of comics for educational purposes, exploits all the potentialities of sequential art in what Eco calls his "courageous, not *comic* but *tragic* book" (vii).[32] Eisner's own acknowledgments and the bibliography document the extent to which his lively graphic portrayal is based on a detailed acquaintance with the history of the forgery and, in particular, the lives of the various perpetrators. (For the sake of narrative simplicity Eisner skips certain episodes, such as the role of Goedsche's German story, and focuses on the more entertaining biographical elements.)

Eisner's depiction begins with Maurice Joly's anti-Napoleonic *Dialogue* of Machiavelli and Montesquieu, and notably the author's subsequent life—his trial, imprisonment, and exile—as told by the police officer who discovers his body following his suicide in 1878. The scene then shifts to Moscow of 1894, where Rachkovsky is plotting to undermine Witte and his modernizing ideas by exposing them as a Jewish plot. To this end he employs Mathieu Golovinski [*sic*], whose earlier career as a cunning fabricator of political forgeries is depicted in considerable detail and who encounters Rachkovsky in Paris in 1898. Golovinski's work pleases Rachkovsky, who arranges to have it published in 1905 in the book of the mystic Sergius Nilus, whose anti-Semitic ravings are portrayed vividly.

The scene then jumps forward to Constantinople in 1921, where Philip Graves is approached by a Russian émigré who introduces himself as Mikhail Raslovlev and offers to sell the correspondent a copy of Joly's *Dialogues,* from which the *Protocols* were obviously plagiarized. The following fifteen pages (73–89) reproduce parallel passages from the two works, which clearly expose the plagiarism. Graves's editor at the *Times,* delighted with the exposé, is convinced that the world will now hear no more of this particular fraud. But the skeptical Graves points out that the anti-Bolsheviks have published thousands of copies, that translations have appeared worldwide, and that Henry Ford has serialized the work in his *Dearborn Independent.* At a Nazi rally in 1921 a reporter who challenges the validity of the *Protocols* is beaten by Hitler's hoodlums, who revile him as a communist Jew. Two years later Hitler's associates send him a copy of the *Protocols* to read in prison, and he cites the work in *Mein Kampf.* Following the 1934–35 trial in Bern and the rejection of the appeal in 1937, the newspapers again are convinced that the *Protocols* will be unable to survive their judicial exposure as nonsense and defamatory trash—even though a translation has just been published in Brazil while leaflets in Poland quote from the *Protocols.* Even after World War II, in 1964, the U.S. Senate felt compelled to issue a report for the Committee on the Judiciary, based on analyses by authorities in several countries and signed by Senators Thomas J. Dodd and Kenneth B. Keating, "in order to lay to rest any honest question concerning the nature, origin, and significance of this ancient canard" (111).[33]

When Eisner, who at this point introduces himself into his work, begins to undertake his own research in 1993, a librarian shows him many examples confirming that "the worldwide use of publication of the 'Protocols' has continued" (114). Even in 1999, when a Russian historian proved that Golovinsky was the forger of the document—"an unquestionable disclosure that erases any claim to legitimacy" (121)—the use of the *Protocols* continued, not only in the Middle East but also in Louisiana, where the Christian Defense League distributed copies of Henry Ford's *The International Jew* (122). Even in 2002, when Eisner hands in his manuscript, his publisher reminds him that an Egyptian weekly recently praised a state-sponsored Arab television series proving that the *Protocols* provide "the central line dominating Israel's policy" (125). But the U.S. State Department called on Egypt to stop the broadcasts, and the penultimate panel shows the publisher and editor shaking hands in their hopeful belief that this finally marks the end of the *Protocols.* The novel concludes with a dismaying page of headlines from 2003 reporting anti-Semitic acts in France and the United States and the continuing sale of the *Protocols* in bookstores around the world.

Eisner created his morally compelling work in conscious contrast to the scholarly books and articles "written mostly by academics and . . . designed to be read by scholars or by persons already convinced of their fraudulence" (3).[34] It was his hope to employ the medium of the graphic novel to "drive yet another nail into the coffin of this terrifying vampire-like fraud" (3). Unfortunately, the *Protocols* continue to be widely disseminated in the Middle East, where the fabrication is accepted by many as truth, serving the same destructive propagandistic purposes as it did, a century earlier, in Imperial Russia and Nazi Germany.[35] The legend persists tenaciously among anti-Semites in other parts of the contemporary world, as demonstrated by the publications of Oleg Platonov, the blatantly anti-Semitic director of Moscow's Institute for the History of Russian Culture, who blames Jewish-Masonic conspirators for the Russian Revolution, praises Stalin for saving Russia from Jewish Bolshevism, and denies the Holocaust. Even in the twenty-first century, fiction continues to trump historical reality.

CHAPTER EIGHT

The Playfulness of Postmodernism

The fear of conspiracy, whether justified or not, has been a factor in politics at least since Pentheus worried that Dionysus and his maenads were undermining his authority in ancient Thebes. In the Middle Ages kings and popes were anxious lest the Knights Templar with their vast resources usurp their power. Papists of the early seventeenth century were convinced that the Rosicrucians had instigated the Thirty Years' War for their own insidious purposes. In the late eighteenth century it was widely believed that the Illuminati lay behind the unrest that precipitated the French Revolution. Mid-nineteenth-century monarchies attributed the social-democratic movement to the Carbonari and other secret societies of the working classes. This apprehension regarding secret societies—for instance, the thesis of a Jewish world conspiracy generated by the spurious *Protocols of the Elders of Zion,* the hoax concerning the alleged Priory of Sion, the real threat of Al Qaeda and its worldwide cells—has continued unabated down to the present. Karl Popper suggests that the "conspiracy theory of society" is akin to Homer's ancient theory of society, according to which the action in the Trojan War was simply an earthly reflection of conspiracies among the deities on Olympus. By analogy, the conspiracy theory of society is simply a version of that theism. "It comes from abandoning God and then asking: 'Who is in his place?' His place is then filled by various powerful men and groups—sinister pressure groups, who are to be blamed for having planned the great depression and all the evils from which we suffer."[1]

In the 1960s scientific research into this long-standing and international phenomenon began to be systematically undertaken and conspiracy scrutinized with the eyes of critics and scholars rather than always from the suspicious standpoint of those affected.[2] This critical detachment corresponded, in turn, to the tenor of the times, which tended to cast a postmodernist, deconstructive, often satirical gaze on all aspects of the past. This tendency led in Western literature to a pronounced inclination to re-view the myths of the past with an analytical and often humorous eye. Günter Grass in his novella *Cat and Mouse* (1961) and John Barth in *Giles Goat-Boy or, The Revised New Syllabus* (1966) are among several writers who used the New Testament Gospels as the structural basis for modern parodies.[3] In Tom Robbins's novel *Skinny Legs and All* (1990) the biblical tale of Salome is secularized, and in Ulrich Holbein's novel *Isis Unveiled* (2000) the myth of Ishtar is deconstructed out of any religious meaning through satire.[4] So it is hardly surprising that conspiracy theory should also, at this stage in its evolution, be deconstructed and satirized. These parallel developments produced predictable results: first, that every secret society began to be regarded as a conspiracy; and, second, that conspiracy fiction evolved into satire, parody, and sheer playfulness.

The Model

The imagination of Jorge Luis Borges anticipated the general development of playfulness by several decades. Despite its brevity his tale "Tlön, Uqbar, Orbis Tertius" (1940) contains several of the features that mark the lengthier and sometimes ponderous treatments of the 1960s. Borges's tale is openly based on the Rosicrucian *Fama*. According to the author's "Postscript" the idea of inventing an imaginary country, Uqbar, was conceived in the seventeenth century by a (wholly fictitious) "secret and benevolent society" including such (historical) members as the linguist George Dalgarno and the philosopher George Berkeley.[5] From that same period dates the (again fictitious) work *Lesbare und lesenswerthe Bemerkungen über das Land Ukkbar in Klein-Asien* (1641) by none other than Johannes Valentinus Andreä (5). "After a few years of secret conclaves and premature syntheses it was understood that one generation was not sufficient to give articulate form to a country." They resolved that each of the masters should elect a disciple who would continue his work—an arrangement that lasted until, in 1824, a Tennessee millionaire proposed that they should invent an entire planet, Tlön, and agreed to fund the enterprise, stipulating that the idea should be kept secret, and commissioned the members to undertake a "methodical encyclopedia of the imaginary planet." In 1914 the last of forty volumes was delivered to three hundred collaborators in the enterprise. At this point of the narrative (postdated to 1947) the entire world, we are informed, "enchanted by its rigor," has yielded to "the minute and vast evidence of an orderly planet" and its harmonious history, which has replaced the traditional history of the world. With its two references to Andreae, the tongue-in-cheek scholarly rigor of its narrative, and the fiction of a secret society that gradually embraces the world Borges's tale constitutes a consciously playful modern counterpart to the original (and, as we saw, equally playful) Rosicrucian *Fama*. But the interest in the Latin American master and his influence on European and North American writers did not begin until 1961, when Borges shared with Samuel Beckett the first International Publishers Prize (Prix Formentor) and began to be widely translated.

Meanwhile, literary adaptations of secret societies continued to look back to the established tradition of the lodge novel. In Germany, for instance, Martin Walser's acerbic satire of the *Wirtschaftswunder, Marriages in Philippsburg* (*Ehen in Philippsburg* [1957]), for instance, includes the parody of a secret society in the form of a realistically plausible social organization: an elegant nightclub (formerly an antique shop specializing in sacral art objects), called "Sebastian" because it features a statue of the saint, and to which membership is restricted to keyholders. It shares various features of the traditional secret order, to be sure. Its members are formally initiated, in an elaborate ceremony involving maids of honor (barmaids and dancers) holding candles and an oath, to become Knights of Sebastian, otherwise known as Chevaliers de l'Établissement Sebastian or Comes Sebastiensis. But the society, introduced only in the last pages of the novel, plays no role in the plot and betrays no hint of Borgesian playfulness. Most of the central figures in the four parts turn out to have been members of the club, to which the young opportunist Hans Beumann is finally inducted. But there is no suggestion that he was on a quest to be initiated or that the members guided his path. The motif of the secret society provides little more than a familiar narrative device for a novel written by an author educated in the literary tradition including Schiller and Karl Gutzkow.[6]

Three American Re-visions

The introduction of Borges in the United States in the 1960s is due in large measure to the publicity following the award of the International Publishers Prize and John Barth's appreciation of the Latin American master in his frequently cited and anthologized essay "The Literature of Exhaustion" (1967), which singles out "Tlön, Uqbar, Orbis Tertius" for special comment.[7] It is not surprising that conspiracy fiction emerged at the same time in the United States, where conspiracy theory was driven by widespread speculation into the assassinations of American leaders during that decade. The years from 1966 to 1975 saw the publication of three major literary works revolving around conspiracies—works that are widely regarded as landmarks in the genre of conspiracy fiction and that display, regarded in retrospect, a pronounced similarity of theme and style, as well as the influence of Borges.

The earliest of the three, Thomas Pynchon's *The Crying of Lot 49* (1966)—the title, as we learn on the last page, refers to the auctioneer's crying, or announcement, of a lot at an auction—resembles Walser's novel to the extent that it is biting social satire, but it moves a step beyond Walser as a study not of a social institution but of the paranoia revolving around a conspiracy that may or may not exist. The heroine, a young California housewife named Oedipa Maas, learns to her surprise that she has been named executor of the will of a former lover, a wealthy real estate tycoon. Her efforts to fulfill that obligation lead her through a number of highly improbable encounters that enable the author to satirize in brief snapshots multiple aspects of California life in the 1960s: the hippie youth culture, a rock band named the Paranoids, the nascent aerospace industry, the gay bars, university careerism, theater life, and others. The loose connection among these various groups is provided by Oedipa's (imagined?) discovery of a conspiracy linking them all: W.A.S.T.E. ("We Await Silent Tristero's Empire"), a secret postal system for citizens who choose deliberately not to communicate by U.S. mail. "It was not an act of treason, nor possibly even of defiance. But it was a calculated withdrawal, from the life of the Republic, from its machinery. Whatever else was being denied them out of hate, indifference to the power of their vote, loopholes, simply ignorance, this withdrawal was their own, unpublicized, private" (124).[8]

When she goes to San Narciso—the name, of course, suggests the self-centeredness of all the figures—near Los Angeles, where her former lover had his offices, she begins to note mysterious references to what she labels The Tristero System: a message on the latrine wall of a bar with an allusion to WASTE and an image of its sign, "a loop, triangle and trapezoid" (52), which turns out to be the symbol of the order: a post horn with a mute; she spots the symbol on trash bins and in telephone booths; she meets a man who is writing a history of private mail delivery in the United States since 1845; she attends a Jacobean revenge play, *The Courier's Tragedy* by a (fictitious) writer named Wharfinger, that features a conflict between the Thurn und Taxis family and the hero Trystero; at a stockholders meeting she meets a young engineer who is doodling the order's symbol on his notepad; at a used-book store she obtains and studies a copy of *The Courier's Tragedy* in an edition of Jacobean revenge plays; she is shown what appears to be the WASTE symbol in the watermark of a 1940 U.S. stamp; she hears the name Tristero in the rhymes of little girls jumping rope. Finally, after various other encounters she finds a college professor who is an expert on Wharfinger and his plays, from whom she learns the alleged history of the Tristero System.

Founded in the late sixteenth century by a Spanish nobleman/madman/rebel/con artist, it competed for two centuries with the official postal service of Europe maintained since the late Middle Ages by the family of Thurn und Taxis. It was even rumored that Tristero staged the French Revolution in his attempt to end the postal monopoly of Thurn und Taxis in France and the Lowlands (165). When the Holy Roman Empire came to an end, "possibilities for paranoia became abundant" (165) because, given the partial secrecy of Tristero, Thurn und Taxis no longer had a clear idea about its adversary, which meanwhile had supposedly moved to the United States, where it was competing with the Pony Express. As she strives to learn more about her new obsession, Oedipa discovers that most of her earlier informants, who now seem to have had some connection with her former lover, have disappeared—died, or run off with other women, or gone mad—or to have been in collusion with him. She begins to wonder: "Either Trystero did exist, in its own right, or it was being presumed, perhaps fantasied by Oedipa, so hung up on and interpenetrated with the dead man's estate" (109). Finally it is suggested to her that the whole affair is nothing but an elaborate hoax that her former lover set up before his death: "some grandiose practical joke he'd cooked up, all for her embarrassment, or terrorizing, or moral improvement" (170) or even as his attempt "to survive death, as a paranoia, as a pure conspiracy against someone he loved" (179). When she learns that his collection of stamps—unusual because it consists entirely of forgeries with the WASTE watermark—is going to be auctioned off and that a secret bidder has mysteriously appeared, she goes to the auction in the hope of learning more. As the novel ends, the auction room is locked shut, the auctioneer "spread his arms in a gesture that seemed to belong to the priesthood of some remote culture," and Oedipa "settled back to await the crying of lot 49" (183). The novel ends on this totally ambivalent note, leaving us uncertain whether the secret society of Tristero exists or whether it is simply a delusion of Oedipa's paranoid imagination: a "forgery," like the stamp collection.

We recognize here the parody of a form traditional at least since Lucius's quest for the cult of Isis in Apuleius's *The Golden Ass*—a form with which Pynchon, among the most well-read of American postmodernist writers, was no doubt familiar in one or another of its manifestations. In particular, in Pynchon's invention of the secret society Tristero we sense the influence of Borges's "Tlön, Uqbar, Orbis Tertius."[9] The shift of scene to California in the 1960s provides the author with a large and tempting target for his satire. The paranoia of the heroine constitutes a postmodern intensification of the uncertainty and anxiety of heroes and heroines since Schiller's prince and George Sand's Consuelo. And the suggestion that the secret society may be simply a paranoid delusion is a heightening of Borges's invention. The originality of the novel is evident in various twists. Rather than a radical novelty, as it was regarded by its early readers, *The Crying of Lot 49* may be seen, then, as another stage in the progression of a genre—quest and secret society—conventional in literature for some two thousand years and here updated with all the trappings of the postmodernist 1960s.[10] In the works of his successors Pynchon's realistic setting, within which his heroine's paranoia emerges, evolves into an atmosphere approaching magical realism.

Ishmael Reed's *Mumbo Jumbo* (1972) is not so much a novel as a fulminating and sometimes sparkling diatribe against Western civilization, here designated as "Atonic"—that is, sterile, monotheistic, lacking sensuality and vitality, encumbered by logic, order, and restraint. The background draws heavily on Afrocentric theories according to which much of Egyptian, Greek, and biblical myth is derived from black African sources. The work fits into the present context because its sketchy plot, which takes place in the 1920s—when Haiti was under a sometimes violent U.S. occupation and rumors circulated that President Warren Harding had black ancestry—is based on the notion that a secret society of enforcers calling itself "The Wallflower Order" is striving to combat a "psychic epidemic"[11] known as "Jes Grew," which is infecting the black community as it moves from New Orleans toward New York—an illness that "knows no class no race no consciousness" and, in contrast to Western Atonism, is marked by "ebullience and ecstasy" (6).

To achieve its goal the Wallflower Order joins forces with Hinckle Von Vampton, the last surviving Knight Templar, to suppress the spreading plague. He attempts to do so by founding a journal to ridicule black culture through exaggeration and by training a "Talking Android" to convert other African

Americans to become New Negroes and resist the insidious virus of jazz, dance, polytheism, personal freedom, and the other manifestations of Jes Grew. The author offers a history of the Knights Templar according to which the order was simply a European imitation of the Assassins of the black Arab Hasan-ibn-al-Sabbah with its Grand Masters, Priors, Knights, Esquires, Lay Brothers, symbols, and rituals. Following their dismantling in the early fourteenth century, the Templars went underground and "a corrupt form of their rites continued as Masonry" (189).

Egyptian mythology and the Bible come into this zany history because Hinckle Von Vampton, as librarian of the original Templars, discovered in an ancient room beneath the Temple of Solomon the Book of Thoth, "the sacred Work Isis had given to Moses" (188), which itself was the work of the Black Birdman, an assistant to the black Osiris, and which provided the Templars with their secret rites and ceremonies. The Wallflower Order is eager to recover and destroy the Work because it proves the black African origin of much of Western civilization, including its Judeo-Christian religion and secret societies. The order and the Templars are opposed by an elderly voodoo priest known as PaPa LaBas (a tribute to Huysmans?) and a group of Harlem radicals bearing the unsubtle faux-Arabic name *Mu'tafikah* who rob museums in their scheme to return to Africa various treasures looted by Western archaeologists and art dealers. Accordingly, the novel involves a struggle between competing secret societies representing an effete Western civilization and a vibrant African culture to recover a mythic object: the Work.

In its form the book, which refers to many actual places and introduces various figures from African American history, mimics Western scholarship with its frequent allusions to Freud, Jung, and other representatives of Western civilization; with its interpolations of quotations from scholarly works; with its (often irrelevant) illustrations; and with its bibliography of works on Western and African American history and culture. Although the history is far-fetched and the plot disjointed, the narrative is carried along irrepressibly by the inventiveness of its language, which combines street slang with higher diction. With its realism heightened into fantasy, in which all such secret orders are playfully satirized, it constitutes a step beyond Pynchon in the progression from cult to conspiracy.

It is revealing that *The Illuminatus! Trilogy,* coauthored by Robert Shea and Robert Anton Wilson and initially published in 1975 as three separate volumes— *The Eye in the Pyramid, The Golden Apple,* and *Leviathan*—begins with a (loosely paraphrased) motto taken from Reed's *Mumbo Jumbo:* "The history of the world is the history of the warfare between secret societies."[12] For the trilogy, despite its enormous and increasingly tedious length, displays a number of conspicuous parallels to Reed's fantasy, as well as reminiscences of Pynchon's novel.

A minor figure in the work, a book critic reviewing a book that sounds suspiciously like the novel under consideration here, calls it "a fairy tale for paranoids. That refers to the ridiculous conspiracy theory that the plot, if there is one, seems to revolve around" (381)[13]—appropriate reading for Pynchon's Oedipa. Earlier, that same critic, who only has time to skim the "dreadfully long monster of a book," describes the novel as precisely as any plot précis: "It starts out as a detective story, switches to science-fiction, then goes off into the supernatural, and is full of the most detailed information of dozens of *ghastly* boring subjects. And the time sequence is all out of order in a very pretentious imitation of Faulkner and Joyce. Worst yet, it has the most raunchy sex scenes, thrown in just to make it sell, I'm sure, and the authors—whom I've *never* heard of—have the supreme bad taste to introduce real political figures into this mishmash and pretend to be exposing a real conspiracy" (239).

The work does begin as a detective story, when two New York City detectives are assigned to investigate the bombing of a leftist magazine's office and the disappearance of its editor. In the magazine's files they discover letters from various readers obsessed by imagined conspiracies and a series of numbered internal memoranda headed "Illuminati Project," which alert them to the fact that the editors were investigating secret societies and various conspiracies: notably the Illuminati, whose symbol is the great Eye of Providence familiar from the $1 bill and whose motto is *Ewige Blumenkraft* ("eternal flower power").[14] This still reasonably realistic plotline, while loosely continued and leading to Las Vegas and Chicago, is gradually overshadowed by a second and more fantastic one when one of the reporters falls into the hands of a group known as the Discordians, whose base is a golden submarine in the Atlantic Ocean and whose allies are such groups as the Erisian Liberation Front (ELF), headed by the mystic Dealy Lama; the Justified Ancients of Mummu (JAMs), an order founded in ancient Babylon and led by John Dillinger, who was not killed by the FBI; and the Legion of Dynamic Discord, with its symbol: the Golden Apple of Discord.

The Discordians, we learn, have been engaged for centuries in a continuing battle against the Illuminati. While we are initially reminded of Pynchon's contest between the two postal services, this one is remarkable as "the longest war in history, the battle for the freedom of the human mind waged by the Illuminati against the forces of slavery, superstition and sorcery" (530). From the perspective of the Discordians, of course, the situation looks quite different: for them "the pentagon of the Illuminati, the Satanists, and the U.S. Army . . . represents the anal, authoritarian, structural, law 'n' order values which the Illuminati have imposed, through their puppet governments, on most of the peoples of the world" (280).

This struggle, which is also defined as one between the "neophobes" (the Illuminati) and "neophiles" (the Discordians) of world history and in which without difficulty we recognize a recasting of the battle in *Mumbo Jumbo* between "Jes Grew" and the Wallflower Order, comes to a head in Ingolstadt (the Bavarian town where in 1776 Weishaupt founded the Illuminati): the third of three "crises" that take place during the roughly one week of actually narrated time. The Discordians' submarine surfaces in a lake outside the town and, at the first European Woodstock festival, where the Illuminati plan to raise thousands of Nazis from their deathlike state by the "life-energy" of their rock 'n' roll, succeed in killing the four leaders of the Illuminati, who are there in the guise of the rock group American Medical Association. (In one passage the authors list scores of absurd names for the participating bands.) This is followed by an encounter with Leviathan, a gigantic pyramid-shaped (like the symbol of the Illuminati) sea monster threatening to destroy the submarine until one of the passengers reveals herself to be the Great Mother—"the first transcendentally illuminated being, the mother worshipped in the matrist religions which ancient foes of the Illuminati first followed" (728). At her request Leviathan returns to the bottom of the sea with her promise to lay an underwater cable that will enable him to communicate with their master computer. Then the leader of the Discordians reveals himself to be the fifth Illuminatus Primus, who was always working against the others: "'While they were a worldwide conspiracy infiltrating every other organization, you were infiltrating them'" (730) in the attempt to demonstrate "'that it's possible to get involved in this world without being corrupted by the crimes of this world. And I failed.'" At this point, sixty years after *The Novel of the Twelve,* the figures realize that they are actually characters in a book. The leader has programmed the computer to "'correlate all the data on this caper and its historical roots . . . and to put it in the form of a novel for easy reading'" (722).

The novel, long recognized as an underground classic, was hailed on the dust jacket by an enthusiastic Timothy Leary as "more important than *Ulysses* or *Finnegans Wake.*" Readers less entranced by nostalgia for the psychedelic 1960s and perusing the eight-hundred-page tome with greater objectivity, will soon note the all-too-visible seams of this obviously contrived literary construct and recognize that the devices that impressed many contemporary readers and critics are actually the tried and tested tricks of the genre.

In the first place it betrays the weaknesses of most collective fiction, as I noted in the preceding chapter.[15] Into this floppy bag of a book the two authors stuffed pell-mell the notes and clippings collected during three years of composition (1969–71), including memos from their research assistants at *Playboy* magazine, where they were both associate editors, as well as letters from conspiracy-obsessed readers, extensive excursuses on numerology, and large chunks of unassimilated and often hallucinatory material: for instance, the history of the world from the prehistoric invasions from outer space and the rise and fall of Atlantis to the founding of the Illuminati in 1776 by Adam Weishaupt; the sensationalized killing of John Dillinger in 1934 outside a Chicago movie theater; the hippie riots in Chicago during the 1968 Democratic Party convention; and much more. This method of composition accounts for the sudden shifts of narrative focus and the frequent lack of transition from paragraph to paragraph or even within sentences. Often transition is effected simply by means of puns, wordplay, and chronological simultaneousness, as parallels are drawn, for instance, between the founding of the Illuminati in 1776 and the American Revolution or when it is suggested that George Washington died early and was replaced by Weishaupt.

In the second place the frequent references to an international cold war conflict on an island off the coast of Equatorial Africa play the same role here as do the allusions in *Mumbo Jumbo* to the turmoil in Haiti, suggesting broader international implications. In one case precisely the same paragraph is used to characterize the president of the United States, the premier of the Soviet Union, and the chairman of the Chinese Communist Party. Similarly, the references to Hassan i Sabbah (to whom an appendix is devoted) remind us of the central role of that same figure in Reed's account of the Knights Templar. The work includes many references to other secret societies, including the Knights Templar, the Thule Society, and the Order of the Golden Dawn. Along with allusions to such authors of Gothic fiction as "Monk" Lewis, Horace Walpole, and Mary Shelley (426), the frequent literary references include works I discussed earlier: *Parzival*, Huysmans's *Là-bas*, Hesse's *Journey to the East*, and Pynchon's *The Crying of Lot 49*.

A semblance of order is imposed on this baggy monstrosity by various external devices. It is divided into three books. These are divided, in turn, into five parts with portentous German titles: "Verwirrung" (confusion), "Zweitracht" [*sic!*] (Zwietracht, or discord), "Unordnung" (disorder), "Beamtenherrschaft" (bureaucratic rule), and "Grummet" (aftermath; literally "second crop")—terms that are elucidated in the appendix (742–56) as the five stages of "the Illuminati theory of history," which in turn is said to be an improved expansion of the three stages in the philosophies of history from Joachim of Floris to Hegel and Marx. A further division is provided by the ten chapters or "trips," each of which bears a title from the kabbalist Sephirot. The work concludes with a fourteen-part appendix, each part of which is numbered according to the letters of the Hebrew alphabet.

What remains is, finally, a construct displaying familiar features, including the collective authorship; the occult data that can be traced back by way of *Mumbo Jumbo* to Huysmans's *Là-bas;* the self-consciousness of characters who realize that they are actually fictional figures—a literary device marking a stage well beyond Oedipa's paranoia; and, above all, the clash of sinister secret societies. While the work demonstrates the combinatory ingenuity of the authors, it is less persuasive on the matter of their literary imagination. Less compelling than the equally long novels of Eugène Sue, George Sand, and Karl Gutzkow, it nevertheless marks a stage in our development of conspiracy fiction despite its sometimes heavy-handed playfulness.

A Magisterial Summation

At first glance Umberto Eco's *Foucault's Pendulum* (*Il pendolo di Foucault* [1988]) appears to be a more ordered version of *The Illuminatus! Trilogy,* using as it does the ten Sephirot, the emanations of God according to the kabbalah (and depicted in an illustration facing the title page), as headings for its ten parts and containing 120 chapters—a numerologically charged number that we recall from the Rosicrucian *Fama* as the years that must elapse before the secret may be revealed: *post CXX annos patebo.* The novel is similarly replete with esoteric information: the history and practices of various secret societies, contemporary occult rituals in Brazil, numerology, kabbalistic and alchemistic lore, and so forth. Yet despite its length, which matches that of the earlier novel, Eco's work is more coherently narrated, its knowledge is truly synthesized, and it never moves into the realm of the fantastic or science fiction. These differences enable his "polyphony of ideas" (50) to become a critically acknowledged masterpiece and an international popular success rather than simply a cult classic.

The basically simple plot involves three friends—Belbo, whose life since childhood has been motivated by a depressing sense of failure; Diotallevi, a devout Jewish mystic and kabbalist; and Casaubon, a young scholar of medieval history driven by a serious desire for knowledge (with a name borrowed from the pedantic scholar in George Eliot's *Middlemarch*)—who work for a publisher in Milan,

Garamond, whose firm combines a serious scholarly line (Garamond) with a vanity press (Manuzio, or Manutius) for SFAs (self-financing authors). One day a prospective author, a former Nazi officer, offers them the manuscript of a book about the Knights Templar based on what he claims to be a coded fourteenth-century manuscript in Old French outlining the Templars' conspiracy, following their dispersal in 1314, to meet in various cities at intervals of 120 years to combine the segments of knowledge with which they intend to take over the world. Casaubon, who is writing his doctoral thesis on the Templars, recommends that they reject the book as nonsense. When the author mysteriously disappears, a police inspector interviews the editors in his investigation of the case. Soon thereafter Casaubon follows his Brazilian Marxist girlfriend, Amparo, to Brazil, where he learns about Caribbean religious cults and attends an occult candomblé ritual. Returning to Italy two years later, he is hired by Garamond to search libraries and archives for images to illustrate a coffee-table history of metals. The growing public interest (in the 1970s and 1980s) in the occult and conspiracies, meanwhile, encourages the publisher to inaugurate two new lines: a series of studies of the occult for serious readers at Garamond and a second one at Manutius, called "Isis Unveiled" (in a clear reference to Mme Blavatsky's theosophical work) to attract vanity authors (who pay handsome subsidies to see their works printed). Garamond engages as consultant the mysterious Agliè, who claims among other things to be the notorious Comte de Saint-Germain.

Overwhelmed by the submissions they receive, the editors begin to refer to the authors of occult works as the "Diabolicals" and, for their amusement, develop a conspiracy theory of their own: "The Plan": "to transform into fantasized reality that fantasy that others wanted to be real" (337). Using their new computer and their own ingenuity—notably numerological play with such symbolic Rosicrucian numbers as 36 and 120 and orthographic identifications based on the initials R. C. (e.g., René des Cartes [*sic*], René Clair, Raymond Chandler, and others [464])—they begin to establish the most far-fetched connections linking the Knights Templar to other conspiracies of the world, from the Rosicrucians, Freemasons, and Jesuits down to the Elders of Zion and the Nazis. They conclude that their plan, which originated with the Templars, was taken over first by the Jesuits and then successively by other orders: "a blueprint that migrated from one conspiracy to another" (490). In their decoding of the old fragment, they believe that they have discovered the Templars' ancient secret: "telluric currents" of subterranean energy whose power will enable them to take over the world. Gradually, as they become more obsessively involved with their game, the three editors begin to believe in its reality and to think that there is really a conspiracy that they call "TRES" (*Templi Resurgentes Equites Synarchi,* or "Resurgent Knights of the Synarchic Temple"). Casaubon's new girlfriend, Lia, a rational historical researcher, reads their alleged Templar document and explains in sober detail that it is really nothing but the order-and-price list of a late medieval merchant. But the three editors, each for his own credulous reasons, are obsessed and refuse to capitulate: Belbo because he hopes finally for a success in his life, Diotallevi for religious-mystical reasons, and Casaubon in the hope for new knowledge.

When Diotallevi is diagnosed with the cancer that rapidly kills him, he becomes convinced that the disease is his punishment for dealing sacrilegiously with mysteries that should have remained unveiled. Belbo goes to Agliè and claims to have in his possession the Templar's map showing the location of the "telluric currents" and explaining that it must be used in conjunction with Foucault's Pendulum—the device invented in the mid-nineteenth century by Léon Foucault to demonstrate the rotation of the earth—which is suspended in the Paris Conservatoire des Arts et Métiers. When Belbo refuses to share the (nonexistent) map with him, Agliè, who turns out to be a member of an actual conspiracy mirroring the editors' project, frames Belbo as a terrorist and threatens him with exposure. In that manner he forces him to attend a meeting of the brotherhood in the Paris museum, a meeting that turns out to include, along with Garamond, many Diabolicals from the Manutius publications. There in the museum, following an elaborate Rosicrucian initiation ceremony, he is expected to hand over the map and reveal its secret. When he refuses—since no such information exists—the conspirators hang him from the pendulum. Casaubon, who has secretly and helplessly observed these proceedings from a hiding place in the museum, flees back to Milan—actually to Belbo's house in the hills of Piedmont—where he relates the story as we have read it and awaits what he is convinced will be his inevitable murder by the conspirators.

The relatively straightforward plot is interrupted by numerous episodes: a lengthy account of Casaubon's two-year stay in Brazil (chaps. 23–33); the love affairs of Casaubon and Belbo; a dozen files (interpolated at intervals) containing Belbo's autobiographical memories and fragments of an autobiographical novel that Casaubon discovers on Belbo's computer in his Milan apartment; elaborate (and factually reliable) histories of the Knights Templar (chaps. 13–14), the Rosicrucian manifestos (chap. 70), the establishment of the Freemasons (chap. 76), the hoax of the Protocols of the Elders of Zion (chaps. 91–96), and various other orders; and more.

The novel also contains references to many of the authors and works that have figured in earlier chapters here, beginning with Apuleius and the mysteries of Isis (184).[16] Wolfram's *Parzival* is cited twice in chapter mottoes (chaps. 21 and 22) and mentioned twice more (184, 313), taking for granted Wolfram's identification of the *templeise* with Templars, mentioning Wolfram's *lapis exillis* (444), and identifying the Grail as a source of enormous tellurian energy. We hear that *The Magic Flute* was a product of "mystical neo-Templarism" (476). Eugène Sue, about whom Eco has written at length and appreciatively,[17] is mentioned several times—for instance, "History is closer to what Sue narrates than to what Hegel projects" (495–96)—as well as his figure "Rodin, the secret general of the Jesuits," in *The Wandering Jew* (502). Indeed, Casaubon states that their Plan, "novelized by Sue, is rehashed by others, who are not Jesuits" (488). Huysmans is cited twice: first in a chapter motto (chap. 43) and later when one figure accuses another, who has been describing a Black Mass, of reading too much Huysmans (279; a clear allusion to *Là-bas*). In sum, Eco, as a skilled literary scholar, is keenly aware of the tradition within which he is working.

In several other instances the literary references are structurally more significant. Eco has repeatedly indicated his admiration for Borges, notably in his essay "Borges and My Anxiety of Influence."[18] The figure of the librarian in *The Name of the Rose,* the blind Benedictine monk Jorge of Burgos, is patently modeled after Borges. And Borges's story "The Golem" provides the motto for chapter 6 of *Foucault's Pendulum.* But a larger influence is also evident. Eco has stated that the idea for his novel was triggered when he read "a totally stupid book on the Rosicrucians" and "got the idea of doing a Bouvard and Pécuchet for occult idiocy"[19]—an allusion to Flaubert's unfinished novel *Bouvard et Pécuchet,* in which two autodidactic copy clerks devote their years of retirement to the quixotic challenge of compiling an encyclopedic survey of human knowledge. Taking up such disparate fields as agriculture, archaeology, aesthetics, science, and metaphysics, they determine in each case that their understanding collapses in the face of everyday reality and move on to a new topic. In that sense Eco intended to satirize works by "second-rate occultists," but he was distracted in the process by his recollections of Borges's "Tlön, Uqbar, Orbis Tertius," which provided the pattern for the conspiracy invented by the three collaborators—an imaginary society that in each case becomes real.

A second striking instance of intertextuality is evident in Eco's repeated use of Andreae's *Chymical Wedding.* He refers frequently to Rosicrucians generally, to such early defenders of the movement as Michael Maier (epigraph to chap. 4), and to the *Fama* (epigraphs to chaps. 12, 70, 71; pages 31, 170, 189–90, 394–97, 470). The editors' enterprise is compared explicitly to Andreae's invention of the Rosicrucian order: Belbo's files include a note concerning his ambition: "Like Andreae: to create, in jest, the greatest revelation of history and, while others are destroyed by it, swear for the rest of your life that you had nothing to do with it" (529). But the *Chymical Wedding* holds a special position. First, quotations from it are taken as the epigraphs for several chapters (chaps. 9, 56, 57, 104, 119). The most conspicuous manifestation occurs when the three editors visit the castle owned by a rich Rosicrucian in the hills near Turin, where they have been invited to attend an alchemistic celebration and later to witness in the hills a druidic rite. The ceremony, which is described in detail (chap. 58), turns out to be a precise reenactment of the wedding in *Chymical Wedding,* where the three royal couples are beheaded, and then of the succeeding alchemistic procedure, in which an egg is generated in a golden sphere, then a bird decapitated and reduced to ashes, which in turn are placed and baked in a mold from which the figures of a youth and maiden appear. Later that evening, when they journey higher into the hills to observe the druidic rite, the scene is based (again without acknowledgment) on the scene in *The Bacchae* in which Pentheus spies on the dance of the maenads. Here, too (chap. 62), the three editors, guided by Agliè, hide in bushes and watch the Druidesses, who have come from many European countries and are dressed in white tunics, as they move ecstatically in a mist that obscures the scene. Suddenly one of the Druidesses breaks away and rushes toward their concealment. But she does not discover them, as the maenads noticed Pentheus, and the men are able to leave safely as the women begin their ritual—a slaughter of pigs—that is reminiscent of the bacchantes who invade the countryside below Mount Cithaeron, killing the flocks and kidnapping the children.

The novel displays various features that remind us of other contemporary playful fictions. The collaboration of the three editors in their enterprise is reminiscent not only of *The Novel of Twelve* and other collective works, but also of the actual collaboration of Shea and Wilson in their *Illuminatus! Trilogy,* whose figures are similarly obsessed with numerology, as are Eco's. Belbo's novel features a hero, like the figure in Breier's *Rosicrucians in Vienna,* who pretends to be the incarcerated Cagliostro (496). Eco's depiction of the growing obsession of the three editors is analogous to Pynchon's description of Oedipa's intensifying paranoia. As Casaubon writes at one point, "I was prepared to see symbols in every object I came upon" (381). At the end, wholly subject to his semiotic delusions, he decides that "every earthly object, even the most squalid, must be read as the hieroglyph of something else, and that there is nothing, no object, as real as the Plan" (576). Like *The Crying of Lot 49,* the ending is left ambivalently open: has the entire plot been a paranoid delusion, or is Casaubon seriously in danger of death at the hands of the conspirators? But these features are presumably unwitting and simply reflect tendencies implicit in the genre itself.

With his brilliance as a semiotician and his authentic learning as a scholar of medieval literature and culture, Umberto Eco has written in *Foucault's Pendulum* a novel that both recapitulates the history of conspiracy literature from Euripides to the present and transcends it.[20] His three editors are questers in search of a secret that they identify with the Holy Grail. His magisterial summation, which may well be designated along with *The Name of the Rose* as the "carnivalization of genres and conventions,"[21] is at the same time a summa. At this point the genre is ripe for its appropriation by the conspiracy thrillers of the twenty-first century.

The Rounding of the Circle

The year 2009 produced what in retrospect seems virtually inevitable: a historical novel set in the Roman Empire—four centuries after Euripides and a century before Apuleius—with a plot inspired by modern conspiracy theory. Yorick Blumenfeld's *The Waters of Forgetfulness,* which takes place in Cumae and Baeae in the decade preceding Virgil's death in 19 BCE, is allegedly the memoir of Rufus Longius, elder of the Orphic sect and member of a *familia* that for generations has operated "the most long-running and audacious fraud thus far perpetrated by any culture" (8).[22] The clan manages "the Oracle of the Dead," a make-believe but utterly convincing underworld—an ancient Disneyland—beginning with an interview with an ecstatic Sibyl and continuing by way of subterranean passages down to Charon (a part played by Rufus), who ferries the visitors across the River Styx, one of whose tributaries is Lethe, the fabled River of Forgetfulness. "My own perspective on these dread waters is that if they exist in our imaginations, they possess a reality of their own" (10). There the trembling visitor, encountering figures of the dead projected as shadows on the walls of Hades, seeks wisdom from their souls. Skeptical patrons are carefully screened out in advance, and participants are drugged with hallucinogens to make them more receptive to the performance. The occasional doubter is drowned or poisoned so that the lucrative scam will not be exposed.

One of the most prominent visitors, and the catalyst for the fraud's exposure, turns out to be Virgil. Seeking inspiration for book 6 of his *Aeneid*—Aeneas's renowned journey to the underworld—the aging poet desires to undertake the experience. Old and weak, he is partially persuaded by what he sees and in his epic, according to Rufus, "accurately describe[d] the parts of Hades that we showed him" (217) and "immortalised" their Sibyl. But for verification he later sends a friend with further questions for the dead souls in Hades. When the skeptical friend is poisoned by the schemers, the consul Marcus Vipsanius Agrippa sends investigating magistrates who carefully interrogate the *familia*. Though they find no firm proof of criminal acts, they conclude that the entire group has "set a poor example for both the worship of the gods and the practice of citizenship" (213). These doubts prompt the authorities to suspend the undertaking, seal off the underground passages with gravel, and exile most members of the *familia*. The elderly Rufus, who at his advanced age is merely fined and placed under observation, admits that he does not miss "the play of bogus wraiths in our make-believe underworld" (218) but wonders how Charon will be portrayed a few millennia in the future. Realizing that the Roman institution of slavery must be abolished and that the anomalous attitude toward women needs to be changed, he continues to "envision Orphism as the great hope for Rome if we are to rise to those heights that are in us to attain" (221).

The ingenious but skimpy plot is filled out with the customary trappings of historical fiction: descriptions of sexual orgies and discussions of such utopian topics as Lucretius's philosophy or the Augustan and Orphic conceptions of community. Rufus explains, for instance, that "as an Orphic, I could see a grave danger in formal religions, like that of the Jews. The Orphic offer the myths of Apollo and Bacchus; the Jews offer a vengeful god, a chosen people, and a history of their suffering" (88). Blumenfeld takes the novelist's usual liberties with history: he makes Catullus, who died in 54 BCE, a contemporary and critic of Virgil (143); and readers admire Ovid's "arousing sensuality" (168) at least two decades before his poems began to appear. Basically, nevertheless, we recognize once again the traditional pattern of a quest for the secrets of an arcane society. But here the quester is none other than Virgil, while the secret order, like Gide's, is a conspiratorial fraud. The narrative circle enclosing some two and a half millennia of the genre has been neatly rounded.

Conclusion

Our literary quest has led us from Greek antiquity to the postmodern present and, with the heroines and heroes of the various works, through the most culturally varied mysteries. Has the journey brought us to a goal? Initiated us into the secret? "A secret that, if we only knew it, would dispel our frustration, lead us to salvation; or else the knowing of it in itself would be salvation. Does such a luminous secret exist?"[1] As Eco's Casaubon realizes at the end of his quest, "the most powerful secret is a secret without content" (621). Like the figures in the many works we have considered, we have learned that the mystery, or at least its content, its message, is never disclosed. But the fact that we have gained no insight into an arcane content does not mean that we have learned nothing. Like Eco's three editors, we have been able to establish multiple connections—not contextual but semiotic and structural—linking our cults and conspiracies.

Students of the Gothic novel and Rosicrucian fiction have stressed the alienation of their heroes, arguing that such literature is "not ahistorical but a product of its own socio-economic context"—specifically, the period of social upheaval produced by the early Industrial Revolution.[2] They cite Karl Marx's theory adumbrating the various types of human alienation: the alienation of man from his labor, from his species, and from himself. They point to heroes who exemplify the various types: Mary Shelley's monster (in *Frankenstein*) as alienation of man from the product of his labor or Bulwer-Lytton's Mejnour (in *Zanoni*) as alienation of man from humankind. As pure description this argument is quite persuasive for the fiction with which it is concerned. Yet is it not too restrictive in its historical limitations? Long before Marx and the Industrial Revolution Lucius's transformation into an ass offered a vivid example of alienation from one's species, not to mention the scores of metamorphoses that have made Ovid such a popular source for postmodern adaptations.[3]

At the same time, we have seen repeatedly that it is precisely the sense of alienation that motivates individuals to seek solidarity in association. Christian Rosencreutz, in the Rosicrucian *Fama,* established his order—initially of three, then of eight, fellow members—to provide companions with whom to share the secret knowledge that led originally to that sense of alienation from the European intellectual community. Even Zanoni and Mejnour, the only two remaining members of their order, constantly seek new initiates to assure continuity of their occult lore. The socially alienated heroes and heroines of romantic socialism sought through their secret societies to bring about democratic utopias. And their individual senses of alienation provide the common factor that unites Eco's three editors in their quest for the Templars' "Plan." Even the most radical alienation finds its solace. The Eternal Wanderer, cited as exemplary for the alienated outsider,[4] gains companionship with Herodias in Sue's *The Wandering Jew,* just as Zanoni, forsaking the alienation of immortality, achieves union in spiritual eternity.

Alienation stems, *pace* Marx, not just from the conditions of the Industrial Revolution. It can emerge, as we have observed, during any age of social upheaval. Our earliest examples stemmed from periods when religion and politics were brought into conflict, causing individuals to reexamine their values and loyalties. Pentheus, recognizing his alienation from the majority of his people who are embracing the new Dionysian ecstasy, is forced to worry about the impact of the imported beliefs upon his city. Lucius, in his condition of asinine alienation, is attracted for redemption to the cult of Isis, which along with other alien sects was threatening the Roman Empire at the beginning of its decline. Parzival, as the "pure fool" alienated from society by his upbringing and garb, encounters the opposing forces of state (King Arthur's Court) and church (the Temple of the Holy Grail) that were rending the fabric of late twelfth-century European culture. The Rosicrucian manifestos were produced, albeit in a spirit of play, by young intellectuals alienated by the crisis generated by the Reformation and the ensuing struggle between Protestants and Catholics.

It was only in the eighteenth century that the factors that caught Marx's attention began to play a prominent role. The Freemasons, Illuminati, and new forms of Rosicrucianism depicted in the lodge novels arose as bases for the intellectual turmoil in the new bourgeoisie—turmoil that eventually resulted in the French Revolution. It was their disappointment in the results of the Revolution that led the newly formed socialists of the mid-nineteenth century, as portrayed in the fiction of romantic socialism, to undertake the broader European revolutions of 1848. In the years preceding and following the First World War, religion again entered the equation as the consequences of Darwinism and the Higher Criticism of the Bible prompted many thoughtful Europeans to forsake their religious beliefs and search for a new faith, as depicted by writers from Huysmans and Hofmannsthal to Hesse. And the figures of *Mumbo Jumbo, The Illuminatus! Trilogy,* and *Foucault's Pendulum* are all engaged in a search for a quasi-religious meaning to compensate for their social alienation. A vivid corollary to the loss of religious faith was often evident in fictions from antiquity to the present in the phenomenon of sinister priestly maneuvering, which debased the image of the religion: in the manipulation of Lucius by the priests of Isis; in the rejection of Rosencreutz's learning by the savants of Christian Europe; in the malevolent schemes of Jesuits in works from Schiller's *Ghost-Seer* to Sue's *The Wandering Jew;* and parodistically in the plot of the criminal gang pretending to be church officials in Gide's satire.

The historical sequence of texts revealed a progression as the pagan religious cults of antiquity (Dionysus and Isis) developed, first, into the religious orders of the Middle Ages and Renaissance (Knights Templar and Jesuits), then into the societies of the Enlightenment (Rosicrucians, Freemasons, Illuminati) and the Industrial Revolution (the Carbonari, the Compagnons du Tour de France, and other French and German unions), and finally into the nonaffiliated conspiracies of the twentieth and twenty-first centuries.

Despite these transformations a conspicuous continuity of effects is evident. *The Magic Flute* refers explicitly to rituals based on the ancient cult of Isis— parallels that were exploited in the stage décor of the classic set designed by Karl Friedrich Schinkel for the Berlin State Opera in the early nineteenth century. The German lodge novels make prominent use of Masonic practices, both real and imagined. The novels of Sand and Bulwer-Lytton are clearly based on the earlier lodge novels, and the name of Sand's "Invisibles" alludes to a characteristic under which the Rosicrucians initially introduced themselves into Paris. Hofmannsthal's *Andreas* was constructed as a witting parallel to Schiller's *The Ghost-Seer.* Borges alludes to Andreae's *Fama* in "Tlön, Uqbar, Orbis Tertius." The very title of *The Illuminatus! Trilogy* suggests the most obvious source for patterns in that work. Eco based two central scenes of *Foucault's Pendulum* on the *Chymical Wedding* and *The Bacchae* respectively. All these writers were keenly aware of the tradition within which they located their works.

Many other continuities are apparent. The journey motif constitutes a significant component of the quest from Lucius, Parzival, and Christian Rosencreutz down through the heroes of the German lodge novels to Hofmannsthal's Andreas, H.H. in Hesse's *Journey to the East,* Pynchon's Oedipa, and Eco's Casaubon. While most of the works are concerned with existing cults and orders, several depict the creation of fictitious secret societies: the Rosicrucian *Fama* and Gutzkow's *Knights of the Spirit* for idealistic goals; Tieck's *William Lovell* and Gide's *Lafcadio's Adventures* for criminal purposes. The numerological playfulness that characterizes the works by Shea/Wilson and Eco has its source in the Rosicrucian manifestos. One can observe striking similarities among the rituals and ceremonies that are described in *The Bacchae, The Golden Ass, Parzival,* the *Chymical Wedding,* the various lodge novels, Sand's *The Countess of Rudolstadt,* Huysmans's *Là-bas,* the *Novel of the Twelve,* Hesse's fictions, and *Foucault's Pendulum.* It has even been proposed that Euripides' *Bacchae* provides a model that can illuminate the sinister appeal of the Jones cult or People's Temple at "Jonestown" in Guyana and the subsequent mass suicide or "white night" of its more than nine hundred members in 1978.[5]

By their very nature, finally, all these works depend for their effect on the lure of the arcane: we thrill to share in the ecstatic dances of the maenads in *The Bacchae* and the rituals of Isis in Apuleius's *The Golden Ass* down to the esoteric lore that constitutes large segments of *The Illuminatus! Trilogy* and *Foucault's Pendulum.*

The form that has emerged overlaps with such genres as the Gothic novel, the lodge novel, detective fiction, and conspiracy thrillers. But it transcends those genres to the extent that its underlying pattern links them all among themselves and, in turn, exposes their ties to such older forms as the Baroque *ludibrium* of the Rosicrucian manifestos, the medieval verse epic of *Parzival,* the Latin romance of *The Golden Ass,* and the Greek tragedy of *The Bacchae.* In all these works, from Euripides to Umberto Eco and Dan Brown, we detect the pattern of a quest attracted by some arcane lore possessed by a secret group, whether that group be labeled cult, order, lodge, society, or criminal conspiracy. Inevitably, as I noted at the outset, this lore, this secret, remains ineffable—even nonexistent. And the group may guide seekers or, as in the case of the higher levels of many societies and most conspiracies, lead them astray or oppose them. Yet the pattern remains constant almost to the point of being what has been called an archetype or myth.

In the thought of C. G. Jung the archetype is a primordial type, a product of the collective unconscious, that has "not yet been submitted to conscious elaboration."[6] The archetype remains unconscious, he explains, until it is given conscious expression in such genres as myth and fairy tale. According to Joseph Campbell's well-known pattern for the monomyth of the hero, "the standard path of the mythological adventure of the hero is a magnification of the formula represented in the rites of passage: *separation—initiation—return*."[7] Campbell's separation is essentially identical with what I have called alienation. But the heroes and heroines of the works I have examined, although they may or may not undergo an initiation, do not usually return: the point of their adventure is the quest itself—not an Odyssean return with new knowledge to the former life. Similarly, Northrop Frye's discussion of the quest that underlies his understanding of the romance is not applicable—or applicable only to the more narrowly conspiratorial thrillers cited in my introduction—because it involves successful violence: the hero and an enemy, typified by dragon-killing, rather than a search for secret knowledge.[8]

The pattern that we have been observing might be characterized more precisely as a paradigm: that is, inflectional variations of the basic form as it develops from cult through order to secret society and from drama through epic and opera to novel. The paradigm of our quester searching for arcane knowledge, a search ending in an encounter without revelation, is perhaps more appropriate for ages of disillusionment than Campbell's monomyth of the hero or Frye's archetype of romance. For that reason it tends to emerge in periods of religious-intellectual-social-political disenchantment. Readers seek the traditional assurances of cults, orders, secret societies—the promise of knowledge that will make sense of the chaos confronting them—only to find, like Lucius, that they must undergo yet another trial; like the first Rosicrucians, that the mystery must remain veiled for another 120 years; like the heroes and heroines of the German Romantic lodge novels and romantic socialism, that the world goes on as before without the promised fulfillments; or, like the heroes and heroines of the postmodern *ludibria* and thrillers, that at the end of the quest the secret remains unknown. Is it, in the last analysis, a melancholy commentary on our own society and its belief, or lack thereof, that so many millions of us lie in bed each evening perusing conspiracy thrillers that revolve around what Eco called "a secret without content"?

Notes

INTRODUCTION

1. On Brown's "esoterico-religious" thrillers and other manifestations of popular culture since 1970 and their relationship to right-wing theories concerning plots by occult powers, see Pierre-André Taguieff, *La foire aux "Illuminés": Ésotérisme, théorie du complot, extrémisme* (Paris: Mille et une nuits, 2005). Taguieff is concerned with ideology rather than literary form and thus deals with very few novels.

2. For further discussion of Brown's fictional formula see Jan Auracher, "Erleuchtung und Bevormundung—Die Rolle der Geheimgesellschaften in den Bundesromanen von Friedrich Schiller und Dan Brown," *Doshisha Studies in Language and Culture* 12 (2010): 665–90, esp. 665–71.

3. In "Erleuchtung und Bevormundung" Auracher exposes similarities between Brown's novel and the lodge novels of German Romanticism. But there is no indication that Brown was aware of that genre; it is my thesis, in contrast, that both contemporary conspiracy novels and the lodge novels (which I discuss in chapter 5) belong to an older and longer tradition of works involving both illumination *(Erleuchtung)* and mentoring *(Bevormundung)*.

4. See John Ayto, *Twentieth Century Words* (New York: Oxford University Press, 1999), 16; Ayto provides the date without citing the source.

5. See Ted Goertzel, "Belief in Conspiracy Theories," *Political Psychology* 15 (1994): 731–42.

6. Richard Hofstadter, *The Paranoid Style in American Politics, and Other Essays* (New York: Knopf, 1965), 3–40, here 14 and 4.

7. Michael Barkun, *A Culture of Conspiracy: Apocalyptic Visions in Contemporary America* (Berkeley: University of California Press, 2003), 3–4.

8. On the tension between "good" and "evil" secret societies see Marco Frenschkowski, "Politik, Paranoia, Projektion: Geheimgesellschaften und Weltverschwörungen in der literarischen Imagination des 18. und 19. Jahrhunderts," in *Macht und Mythos: Tagungsband 2004*, ed. Thomas Le Blanc and Bettina Twrsnich (Wetzlar: Phantastische Bibliothek, 2005), 56–76.

9. Daniel Lyons, *Newsweek*, Feb. 8, 2010, 16. In this connection see also Theodore Ziolkowski, *Modes of Faith: Secular Surrogates for Lost Religious Belief* (Chicago: University of Chicago Press, 2006).

10. Thomas De Quincey, "Secret Societies" (1847), in his *Historical and Critical Essays*, 2 vols. (Boston: Ticknor and Fields, 1959), 2:276.

11. C. G. Jung, *Memories, Dreams, Reflections*, ed. Aniela Jaffé, trans. Richard and Clara Winston (New York: Vintage/Random House, 1963), 342.

12. See in this connection David V. Barrett, *A Brief History of Secret Societies* (Philadelphia: Running Press, 2007), xi–xv.

13. Georg Simmel, "Das Geheimnis und die geheime Gesellschaft," in his *Soziologie: Untersuchungen über die Formen der Vergesellschaftung* (Leipzig: Duncker und Humblot, 1908), 337–402, here 391–402.

14. Goertzel, "Belief in Conspiracy Theories," 739.

15. Timothy Melley, *Empire of Conspiracy: The Culture of Paranoia in Postwar America* (Ithaca, NY: Cornell University Press, 2000), vii, see esp. 7–16. In this connection see also Taguieff, *La foire aux "Illuminés,"* 17–23, 126–32.

16. Edmund Burke, *A Vindication of Natural Society or, a View of the Miseries and Evils Arising from Every Species of Artificial Society*, ed. Frank N. Pagano (Indianapolis: Liberty Classics, 1982), 83.

17. See Pagano's introduction to his edition of Burke's *Vindication*, xvii–xxiii.

18. Melley's *Empire of Conspiracy* is based on the thesis that, while conspiracy theory has a long history in the United States, "its influence has never been greater than now" (vii). Barkun, *Culture of Conspiracy*, also limits his discussion to such "apocalyptic visions in contemporary America" as millennialism, fear of New World Order conspiracies, and anxiety about UFOs and invaders from outer space. Hofstadter, *Paranoid Style*, takes a broader view: "the phenomenon is no more limited to American experience than it is to our contemporaries" (6), citing (without discussion) earlier fears of Jesuits and Freemasons.

19. See Hofstadter, *Paranoid Style*, 32–33.

20. Theodore Ziolkowski, *Fictional Transfigurations of Jesus* (Princeton, NJ: Princeton University Press, 1972), 182–224.

21. Melley, *Empire of Conspiracy*, cites in passing various literary examples (e.g., Margaret Atwood and Don DeLillo) without discussing the phenomenon of conspiracy-based thrillers.

22. Ralf Klausnitzer, *Poesie und Konspiration: Beziehungssinn und Zeichenökonomie von Verschwörungsszenarien in Publizistik, Literatur und Wissenschaft, 1750–1850* (Berlin: De Gruyter, 2007), 600.

CHAPTER ONE: The Mystery Cults of Antiquity

1. See Ursula Kästner, "Attische Vasen mit Dionysosdarstellungen: Gefäßform und Dekoration," in *Dionysos: Verwandlung und Ekstase*, ed. Renate Schlesier and Agnes Schwarzmaier (Berlin: Staatliche Museen zu Berlin—Stiftung Preußischer Kulturbesitz, 2008), 54–69; and Britta Özen-Kleine, "Dionysos, Hermes, Herakles—Die Verjüngung," in *Die Rückkehr der Götter: Berlins verborgener Olymp*, ed. Dagmar Grassinger, Tiago de Oliveira Pinto, and Andreas Scholl (Berlin: Staatliche Museen zu Berlin—Stiftung Preußischer Kulturbesitz, 2008), 138–61, esp. 151–52.

2. See Walter F. Otto, *Dionysus: Myth and Cult*, trans. Robert B. Palmer (Bloomington: Indiana University Press, 1965), 52–64.

3. Lewis R. Farnell, *The Cults of the Greek States*, 5 vols. (Oxford: Clarendon, 1896–1909), 5:151; Otto, *Dionysus*, 125; R. P. Winnington-Ingram, *Euripides and Dionysus: An Interpretation of the Bacchae* (1948; repr. Amsterdam: Hakkert, 1969), 1–2, 150–51; and Hans Oranje, *Euripides' Bacchae: The Play and Its Audience* (Leiden: Brill, 1984), 110. Jane

Harrison, *Prolegomena to the Study of Greek Religion* (1903; repr. New York: Meridian, 1957), 397–400, suspects that men in Macedonia were afraid to stop the orgies and that even the Athenians had difficulties restraining their women. But she relies principally on such earlier sources as Solon and Epimenides. A. Henrichs, "Between Country and City: Cultic Dimensions of Dionysos in Athens and Attica," in *Cabinet of the Muses: Studies in Honor of T. G. Rosenmeyer*, ed. Mark Griffin and D. J. Mastronarde (Atlanta: Scholars Press, 1990), 257–77, stresses the diversity of Dionysian cults in different regions and periods.

4. E. R. Dodds, introduction to *Euripides' Bacchae*, ed. by E. R. Dodds, 2nd ed. (Oxford: Clarendon, 1960), xx–xxv, here xxii. See also Farnell, *The Cults of the Greek States*, 150–239 ("Dionysiac Ritual"), esp. 208–9.

5. See Otto Kern, *Die Religion der Griechen*, 2 vols. (Berlin: Weidmann, 1935), 2:287–302 ("Der Ausgang des fünften Jahrhunderts").

6. I cite the translation of Thucydides' *History of the Peloponnesian War* by Rex Warner (1954; repr. London: Penguin, 1972).

7. P. Foucart, *Des associations religieuses chez les Grecs* (Paris: Klincksieck, 1873), 55–66; Walter Burkert, *Greek Religion: Archaic and Classical*, trans. John Raffan (Oxford: Blackwell, 1985), 176–79; and Kern, *Religion der Griechen*, 2:225–42 ("Fremde Gottesdienste").

8. Strabo, *Geography: Books 1–12*, trans. Horace Leonard Jones (Cambridge, MA: Harvard University Press, 2000), 109 (bk. 10.3.18).

9. See Martin P. Nilsson, *Greek Popular Religion* (New York: Columbia University Press, 1940), 121–22.

10. William Arrowsmith, "Euripides' Theater of Ideas," in *Euripides: A Collection of Essays*, ed. Erich Segal (Englewood Cliffs, NJ: Prentice-Hall, 1968), 13–33, here 15–16.

11. Dodds, introduction, xxv; Winnington-Ingram, *Euripides and Dionysus*, 171; and Charles Segal, *Dionysiac Poetics and Euripides' Bacchae* (Princeton, NJ: Princeton University Press, 1982), 55–56.

12. Dodds, introduction, xl–xli. For a historical review of interpretations see especially Oranje, *Euripides' Bacchae*, 7–19.

13. Nietzsche, in *The Birth of Tragedy* (chap. 12), was one of the most prominent advocates; see Friedrich Nietzsche, *Werke in drei Bänden*, ed. Karl Schlechta (München: Hanser, 1954), 1:70–71.

14. Winnington-Ingram, *Euripides and Dionysus*, 114–15.

15. Winnington-Ingram, *Euripides and Dionysus*, offers the most extensive and systematic exploration of this transformation.

16. See Burkert, *Greek Religion*, 276.

17. *Euripidis Fabulae*, ed. Gilbert Murray, 2nd ed., vol. 3 (Oxford: Clarendon, 1949). Unless otherwise noted, all citations of *The Bacchae* refer to this edition and are my own translations.

18. J. A. Hartung, as quoted by Dodds, introduction, xliii.

19. Sarolta A. Takács, *Isis and Sarapis in the Roman World* (Leiden: Brill, 1995), 8.

20. See Hans Kloft, *Mysterienkulte der Antike: Götter, Menschen, Rituale* (Munich: Beck, 1999), 17–25.

21. Hugh Bowden, *Mystery Cults in the Ancient World* (London: Thames and Hudson, 2010), even suggests that the cults had no "secret" to transmit and that their mysteries were imagistic rather than doctrinal.

22. Kloft, *Mysterienkulte der Antike,* 25–32.

23. Ibid., 31.

24. Takács, *Isis and Sarapis in the Roman World,* 8–11. For a detailed historical account of the specific occasion for Livy's version see Sarolta A. Takács, "Politics and Religion in the Bacchanalian Affair of 186 BCE," *Harvard Studies in Classical Philology* 100 (2000): 301–10.

25. Cited here in my own translation according to the text in Livy, *History of Rome,* books 38–39, trans. Evan T. Sage (1936; repr. Cambridge, MA: Harvard University Press, 2000), 240–74. Although Livy's account of the Senate action is historically accurate, his depiction of the events that triggered it is reshaped for dramatic effect and makes use of literary elements from other works. See Adele Scafuro, "Livy's Comic Narrative of the Bacchanalia," *Helios* 16 (1989): 119–42; and P. G. Walsh, "Making a Drama out of a Crisis: Livy on the Bacchanalia," *Greece and Rome* 43 (1996): 188–203.

26. Plutarch, "Über Isis und Oriris," in *Drei religions-philosophische Schriften,* ed. and trans. Herwig Görgemann (Düsseldorf: Artemis, 2003), 154–71. The remaining chapters contain a discussion of various possibilities of interpretation (chaps. 22–44), Plutarch's exposition of his own interpretation (chaps. 45–64), and his examination of theological misunderstandings (chaps. 65–78). E. A. Wallis Budge, *Book of the Dead* (1901; repr. London: Arkana, 1985), 119–94, contains a full account, based on all the various sources, including many images from the legend, the hymns to Osiris from *The Book of the Dead* and other sources, the names of Osiris with the corresponding hieroglyphic symbols, and a translation of Plutarch's relevant chapters.

27. See Kloft, *Mysterienkulte der Antike,* 44–45, who cites the Russian historian Michael Rostovtzeff; and Reinhold Merkelbach, *Isis regina—Zeus Sarapis: Die griechisch-ägyptische Religion nach den Quellen dargestellt* (Stuttgart: Teubnier, 1995), 121–30.

28. Takács, *Isis and Sarapis in the Roman World,* 56–70, emphasizes the fear of political destabilization.

29. Josephus, *The Complete Works,* trans. William Whiston (1737; repr. Nashville: Thomas Nelson, 1998), 576–77.

30. See Merkelbach, *Isis regina—Zeus Sarapis,* 134–38.

31. Kloft, *Mysterienkulte der Antike,* 46–47; and Takács, *Isis and Sarapis in the Roman World,* 5–7, and esp. 130–203.

32. See his *Apologia* 55.8: *sacrorum pleraque initia in Graecia participavi.*

33. Reinhold Merkelbach, *Roman und Mysterium in der Antike* (Munich: Beck, 1962), and in his later *Isis regina—Zeus Sarapis,* 355–484, argues persuasively that the stories of Lucius and Psyche are basically quite similar and that Lucius's fate precisely mirrors Psyche's because both are ultimately redeemed by deities (1–2).

34. Ulrike Egelhaaf-Gaiser, *Kulträume im römischen Alltag: Das Isisbuch des Apuleius und der Ort von Religion im kaiserlichen Rom* (Stuttgart: Steiner, 2000), 57–60, provides a chart that conveniently outlines the sequence of cult events in book 11.

35. I refer here to the text and (freely modified) translation in the Loeb edition of Apuleius, *The Golden Ass,* trans. W. Adlington (1566), rev. S. Gaselee (Cambridge, MA: Harvard University Press, 1971), here 545.

36. For the debate on this topic see S. J. Harrison, *A Latin Sophist* (Oxford: Oxford University Press, 2000), 240–43. For a detailed explanation of the entire proceedings see Merkelbach, *Isis regina—Zeus Sarapis,* 266–304.

37. On the "public solemnities and mystery rites" of the cult of Isis see Robert Turcan, *The Cults of the Roman Empire*, trans. Antonia Nevill (Oxford: Blackwell, 1996), 114–21.

38. For a detailed analysis of the three stages as "Psychogramm eines Mysten" see Egelhaaf-Gaiser, *Kulträume im römischen Alltag*, 84–91. Altogether the author provides the most elaborate discussion of the cult of Isis, its spaces, and its practices, in their Roman context.

39. The extreme positions are well represented by Merkelbach, who argues both in *Isis regina—Zeus Sarapis* and in his earlier *Roman und Mysterium in der Antike* ("Vorwort") that "the novels [of Greek and Roman antiquity] are actually mystery texts"; and by Harrison, *A Latin Sophist*, who sees in the novel only "intellectual display and satirical entertainment" (238).

40. J. J. Winkler, *Auctor & Actor: A Narratological Reading of Apuleius's "Golden Ass"* (Berkeley: University of California Press, 1985).

41. Harrison, *A Latin Sophist*, 245.

42. On the continuing popularity of *The Golden Ass* see Robert H. F. Carver, *The Protean Ass: The Metamorphoses of Apuleius from Antiquity to the Renaissance* (Oxford: Oxford University Press, 2007). With the notable exception of Spenser's *Fairie Queene* (393–98), however, the Isis episode appears to have had little afterlife: sometimes the goddess was simply omitted (254–55) and elsewhere replaced by Ceres (318).

CHAPTER TWO: The Order of Knights Templar in the Middle Ages

1. Theodore Ziolkowski, "The Mystic Carbuncle: Transmutations of an Image," in *Varieties of Literary Thematics* (Princeton, NJ: Princeton University Press, 1983), 34–85, here 65–70.

2. There are many histories of the Templars. For my brief overview I take my information primarily from Edward Burman, *The Templars: Knights of God* (Wellingborough, Northamptonshire: Crucible, 1986); and Malcolm Barber, *The New Knighthood: A History of the Order of the Temple* (Cambridge: Cambridge University Press, 1994).

3. Quoted in Burman, *The Templars*, 32.

4. Ibid., 37.

5. Ibid., 25.

6. Ibid., 138.

7. Henry Osborn Taylor, *The Medieval Mind: A History of the Development of Thought and Emotion in the Middle Ages*, 2 vols., 3rd ed. (New York: Macmillan, 1919), 1:538.

8. Ibid., 1:551.

9. See Walter Johannes Schröder, *Der Ritter zwischen Welt und Gott: Idee und Problem des Parzivalromans Wolframs von Eschenbach* (Weimar: Böhlau, 1952), 118–26.

10. Quoted in Albert Blaise, *Lexicon Latinitatis Medii Aevi: Presertim ad res ecclesiasticas investigandas pertinens* = Dictionnaire latin-français des auteurs du Moyen-Âge (Turnholti [Turnhaut, Belgium]: Typographi Brepols, 1975), 423. On other etymologies see Konrad Burdach, *Der Gral: Forschungen über seinen Ursprung und seinen Zusammenhang mit der Longinuslegende*, ed. Johannes Rathofer (1938; repr. Stuttgart: Kohlhammer, 1974), 471–76.

11. Chrétien de Troyes, *Le Roman de Perceval or Le Conte du Graal: Edition critique d'après tous les manuscrits*, ed. Keith Busby (Tübingen: Niemeyer, 1993), 136 (vv. 3233–34) and 272 (v. 6422).

12. See Richard Barber, *The Holy Grail: Imagination and Belief* (Cambridge, MA: Harvard University Press, 2004), 246–48.

13. Blaise, *Lexicon Latinitatis Medii Aevi*, 423.

14. Nigel Bryant, in the introduction to his translation, *Merlin and the Grail: The Trilogy of Prose Romances Attributed to Robert de Boron* (Cambridge: Brewer, 2001), 7. On Robert de Boron see esp. Burdach, *Der Gral*, 450–502.

15. Bryant, *Merlin and the Grail*, 17–19.

16. Jessie L. Weston, *From Ritual to Romance* (1920; repr. Garden City, NY: Doubleday Anchor, 1957), 203.

17. Roger Sherman Loomis, *The Grail: From Celtic Myth to Christian Symbol* (1963; repr. Princeton, NJ: Princeton University Press, 1991), 271–73.

18. The principal account of the Grail occurs in book 9 of Wolfram's *Parzival*, which I cite according to the first three volumes in *Wolfram von Eschenbach*, ed. Albert Leitzmann, 5 vols., 5th ed. (Halle: Niemeyer, 1948). There is a readable and reliable translation of *Parzival* by A. T. Hatto (New York: Penguin, 1980).

19. On the "neutral angels," who refused to take sides in God's battle with Lucifer, and Wolfram's ambivalence regarding whether or not they were permitted to return to heaven, see Hermann J. Weigand, "Wolfram's Grail and the Neutral Angels: A Discussion and a Dialogue," *Germanic Review* 29 (1954): 83–95; repr. in Weigand, *Wolfram's Parzival: Five Essays with an Introduction*, ed. Ursula Hoffmann (Ithaca, NY: Cornell University Press, 1969), 120–41.

20. Schröder, *Der Ritter zwischen Welt und Gott*, 34, is one of the few scholars who describe the Grail society and its ceremony as a "cult."

21. On "templeise" and Templars see Schröder, *Der Ritter zwischen Welt und Gott*, 118–26. Barber, *The Holy Grail*, 179, 306–9, denies any connection in the Middle Ages between Templars and the Grail and, on the basis of incomplete familiarity with the Middle High German vocabulary, argues that *templeise* does not mean "Templar."

22. On the complementary relationship between the two powers in Wolfram's work see esp. Julius Schwietering, *Die deutsche Dichtung des Mittelalters* (Darmstadt: Gentner, 1957), 160–72.

23. Joachim Bumke, *Wolfram von Eschenbach*, 6th ed. (Stuttgart: Metzler, 1991), 135–36, observes that the negative portrayal of courtly life on Parzival's first visit to Arthur's court is based directly on Chrétien's text. The more appreciative depiction in later books (esp. 14 and 15) appears to reflect Wolfram's own view. This would correspond to the shift in his view of the knights of Munsalvaesche, who only in the later books are called "templeise."

24. The following paragraphs are based in part, with significant cuts and additions, on the *Parzival* chapter in Theodore Ziolkowski, *Hesitant Heroes: Private Inhibition, Cultural Crisis* (Ithaca, NY: Cornell University Press, 2004), 54–73.

25. On Parzival's character and development see David Blamires, *Characterization and Individuality in Wolfram's "Parzival"* (Cambridge: Cambridge University Press, 1966); and Benedikt Mockenhaupt, *Die Frömmigkeit im "Parzival" Wolframs von Eschenbach: Ein Beitrag zur Geschichte des religiösen Geistes in der Lebenswelt des deutschen Mittelalters* (1942; repr. Darmstadt: Wissenschaftliche Buchgesellschaft, 1968).

26. Schröder, *Ritter zwischen Welt und Gott*, 49, separating Herzeloyde's instruction on religion and on knightly behavior, sees four degrees of initiation; but in principle he views Parzival's development as a gradual initiation into the cult.

27. It is worth noting that another contemporary work, the anonymous Old French prose romance *Perlesvaus,* also known as *The High Book of the Grail,* possibly identifies its hero and the Grail with the Templars. At the beginning of the story a maiden presents King Arthur with a shield displaying a red cross and a boss of gold, which belonged to Joseph of Arimathea, saying that a knight will come for it and use it to conquer the Grail—the very shield that Perlesvaus bears at the end to reconquer the Grail Castle that has been won by an evil king. The Grail, which had disappeared upon the death of the Fisherman, reappears in the chapel and Perlesvaus, the Good Knight, sets out to restore the New Law, which had been overturned in parts of the world. The plot has little to do with Wolfram's slightly earlier *Parzival:* in the French romance it is Gawain who fails to ask the question; and Lancelot, because of his secular character, is unable to see the Grail (like Feirefiz). See *The High Book of the Grail. A Translation of the Thirteenth-Century Romance of Perlesvaus,* trans. Nigel Bryant (1978; repr. Cambridge: Brewer, 1996).

CHAPTER THREE: The Rosicrucians of the Post-Reformation

1. Hajo Holborn, *A History of Modern Germany: The Reformation* (Princeton, NJ: Princeton University Press, 1959), 249–304.

2. See Richard van Dülmen, *Die Utopie einer christlichen Gesellschaft: Johann Valentin Andreae (1586–1654),* Part 1 (Stuttgart-Bad Canstatt: Frommann-Holzboog, 1978), 15–22; and Will-Erich Peuckert, *Das Rosenkreutz,* 2nd ed. (Berlin: Erich Schmidt, 1973), 7–18.

3. Peuckert, *Das Rosenkreutz,* 11–12.

4. Ibid.

5. Hans Schick, *Das ältere Rosenkreuzertum: Ein Beitrag zur Entstehungsgeschichte der Freimaurerei* (Berlin: Nordland, 1942), 17–42. A useful overview is provided by Christopher McIntosh, *The Rosicrucians: The History, Mythology, and Rituals of an Esoteric Order,* 3rd ed. (York Beach, ME: Samuel Weiser, 1997), 9–18. Illustrations of several of the important precursors, along with an informed commentary, are available in the handsome exhibition catalog *Cimelia Rhodostaurotica: Die Rosenkreuzer im Spiegel der zwischen 1610 und 1660 entstandenen Handschriften und Drucke,* ed. Carlos Gilly (Amsterdam: Pelikaan, 1995), 2–24.

6. See C. G. Jung, *Psychology and Alchemy,* trans. R. F. C. Hull, 2nd ed. (Princeton, NJ: Princeton University Press, 1968).

7. See John Warwick Montgomery, *Cross and Crucible: Johann Valentin Andreae (1586–1654), Phoenix of the Theologians,* vol. 1 (The Hague: Martinus Nijhoff, 1973), 16–19; and the separate entries in *Alchemie: Lexikon einer hermetischen Wissenschaft,* ed. Claus Priesner and Karin Figala (Munich: Beck, 1998). All three alchemists, along with Paracelsus, are frequently cited by Jung in *Psychology and Alchemy.*

8. Peuckert, *Das Rosenkreutz,* 12–16.

9. McIntosh, *The Rosicrucians,* 39–40.

10. Many studies deal with the history of Rosicrucianism; see, e.g., McIntosh, *The Rosicrucians.*

11. I base my biographical information primarily on the two most reliable accounts: the earliest and still valuable biography by Wilhelm Hossbach, *Johann Valentin Andreä und sein Zeitalter* (Berlin: Reimer, 1819); and Martin Brecht, *Johann Valentin Andreae,*

1586–1654: Eine Biographie (Göttingen: Vandenhoeck und Ruprecht, 2008). Briefer treatments in English, useful but to be used with caution because of their pronounced thematic slants, include Montgomery, *Cross and Crucible;* and Frances A. Yates, *The Rosicrucian Enlightenment* (London: Routledge and Kegan Paul, 1972). See in this connection Brian Vickers, "Frances Yates and the Writing of History," *Journal of Modern History* 51 (1979): 287–316.

12. *Mariae Andreanae Merita Materna* (1632), in Johann Valentin Andreae, *Gesammelte Schriften,* ed. Wilhelm Schmidt-Biggemann, vol. 2 (Stuttgart-Bad Canstatt: Frommann-Holzboog, 1995), 111–97.

13. For accounts of his teachers and friends see, in addition to Hossbach and Brecht, Montgomery, *Cross and Crucible;* McIntosh, *The Rosicrucians,* 19–30; and Schick, *Das ältere Rosenkreuzertum,* 96–113.

14. Andreae, *Gesammelte Schriften,* 2:147–215.

15. Unpublished letter quoted in Montgomery, *Cross and Crucible,* 52.

16. See the bibliography in Montgomery, *Cross and Crucible,* 489–505.

17. Andreae, *Gesammelte Schriften,* 2:54 and 62.

18. I have not had access to the Latin original, which is quoted extensively in the various biographical works cited here. Montgomery, *Cross and Crucible,* 37, renders *ludibrium* as "fantasy." See also Vickers, "Frances Yates and the Writing of History," 292–96, for an insightful discussion of *ludibrium* and of Andreae's critique of the Rosicrucians.

19. I cite the text in my own translation from Joh. Valentin Andreae, *Fama Fraternitatis (1614) Confessio Fraternitatis (1615) Chymische Hochzeit: Christiani Rosencreutz. Anno 1459. (1616),* ed. Richard van Dülmen (Stuttgart: Calwer Verlag, 1973). English translations of all three works are available in *A Christian Rosenkreutz Anthology,* ed. Paul M. Allen (Blauvelt, NY: Rudolf Steiner, 1968), which reproduces the classic 1690 version of *The Chymical Wedding,* by Ezechiel Foxcroft, and the 1652 versions of *The Fame and Confession of the Fraternity of the Rosie Cross,* by Thomas Vaughan. A more readable version of *The Chemical Wedding of Christian Rosenkreutz* has been published by Joscelyn Godwin, *Magnum Opus Hermetic Sourceworks,* no. 18 (Grand Rapids, MI: Phanes, 1991).

20. Dülmen, *Die Utopie einer christlichen Gesellschaft,* 64–73.

21. Brecht, *Johann Valentin Andreae, 1586–1654,* 71.

22. Stanley W. Beeler, *The Invisible College: A Study of the Three Original Rosicrucian Texts* (New York: AMS Press, 1991), 73–88.

23. The most detailed interpretation is still that of R. Kienast, *Johann Valentin Andreae und die vier echten Rosenkreutzer-Schriften* (Leipzig: Mayer und Müller, 1926), 37–98. On the "sevenfold architecture" of the work see especially McLean's commentary in Godwin's translation of *Chemical Wedding,* 107–57.

24. Yates, *The Rosicrucian Enlightenment,* 30–40 and passim.

25. See, most recently, Gilly, *Cimelia Rhodostaurotica,* 22.

26. Kienast, *Johann Valentin Andreae und die vier echten Rosenkreutzer-Schriften,* 64–65.

27. For a detailed day-by-day commentary on the alchemistic details of the narrative see the edition by Bastiaan Baan: Johann Valentin Andreä, *Die Chymische Hochzeit des Christian Rosencreutz,* trans. by Agnes Dom-Lauwers (Stuttgart: Urachhaus, 2001); and McLean's commentary to Godwin's translation.

28. For an appreciation of Andreae as an important writer of the early Baroque, a role generally ignored in literary histories, see Christoph Brecht, "Johann Valentin Andreae: Zum literarischen Profil eines deutschen Schfritstellers im frühen 17. Jahrhundert," in Martin Brecht, *Johann Valentin Andreae, 1586–1654,* 313–48.

29. It should be mentioned that Rudolf Steiner and his anthroposophic followers take the work quite seriously as "gates into the spiritual world" and "genuine spiritual experience." See Steiner's essay "The Chymical Wedding of Christian Rosenkreutz" (1917–18), in Allen, *A Christian Rosenkreutz Anthology,* 19–59.

30. Montgomery, *Cross and Crucible,* 228. For a sense of the disagreements among those who take the work seriously see Adam McLean's contemptuous rejection in his introduction and commentary to Godwin's translation of *The Chemical Wedding,* esp. 107–10: Montgomery's "appalling attempt" to explain its Lutheran orthodoxy; Steiner's "vague waffling" in his "disappointing attempts" to align its ideas with his anthroposophy; the equally "uncompromising" and "slavish" adherence of other anthroposophists to Steiner's "idiosyncratic views"; and the "convolutions" of Frances Yates's allegorically historical interpretation. The path to the Palace is indeed treacherous terrain.

31. On the still unresolved problem of authorship see Dülmen, *Die Utopie einer christlichen Gesellschaft,* 73–79.

32. See the detailed commentary in Kienast, *Johann Valentin Andreae und die vier echten Rosenkreutzer-Schriften,* 112–27.

33. The *Confessio* also contains an allusion to the supernova, when it states that the Lord God has already sent various premonitions of his will, namely "several new stars that arose in the sky in the constellation of Serpens and Cygnus" (38: "etliche newe Sterne, so am Himmel in Serpentario und Cygno entstanden").

34. Kienast, *Johann Valentin Andreae und die vier echten Rosenkreutzer-Schriften,* 113, believes that the initials cannot be identified with any certainty with Andreae's circle of acquaintances but that their characterization may be based on them.

35. McIntosh, *The Rosicrucians,* 32–33, points to other (less convincing) analogies to *Parzival:* the secret castle, the stone, the astrological reference, the well-preserved old man.

36. C. G. Jung, *Memories, Dreams, Reflections,* ed. by Aniela Jaffé, trans. by Richard and Clara Winston (New York: Vintage/Random House, 1963), 342.

37. Brecht, *Johann Valentin Andreae, 1586–1654,* 80: "Medienereignis." On the response see especially Schick, *Das ältere Rosenkreuzertum,* 159–277; Yates, *Rosicrucian Enlightenment,* 91–102; and McIntosh, *The Rosicrucians,* 53–59.

38. See his extensive review-essay on Templars, Freemasons, and Rosicrucians published in 1782 in *Teutscher Merkur,* in: J. G. Herder, *Sämtliche Werke,* ed. Bernhard Suphan, 33 vols. (repr. Berlin: Weidmann, 1967), 15:57–81, 82–120, esp. 59–64.

39. Gilly, *Cimelia Rhodostaurotica,* reproduces the title pages of more than 250 responses from the earliest years: here 87–88 (ills. 84 and 89).

40. Ibid., 75 (ill. 76).

41. Ibid., 135 (ill. 211).

42. Ibid., 147 (ill. 249).

43. Ibid., 149 (ill. 255), 153 (ill. 265), 155 (ill. 271).

44. Hossbach, *Johann Valentin Andreä und sein Zeitalter,* 95.

45. Ibid., 96. See also Peuckert, *Das Rosenkreutz,* 126–35 ("Das Rosenkreuz auf der Straße").

46. Quoted in Peuckert, *Das Rosenkreutz*, 132.
47. Yates, *The Rosicrucian Enlightenment*, 15–29.
48. Gilly, *Cimelia Rhodostaurotica*, 159 (ill. 285); see also Brecht, *Johann Valentin Andreae, 1586–1654*, 87–88.
49. Quoted in Hossbach, *Johann Valentin Andreä und sein Zeitalter*, 97.
50. McIntosh, *The Rosicrucians*, 109–17.

CHAPTER FOUR: The Lodges of the Enlightenment

1. Jürgen Habermas, *Strukturwandel der Öffentlichkeit: Untersuchungen zu einer Kategorie der bürgerlichen Gesellschaft* (1962; repr. Frankfurt am Main: Suhrkamp, 1990), 90–107, here 95–96.
2. Reinhard Koselleck, *Kritik und Krise: Eine Studie zur Pathogenese der bürgerlichen Welt* (Freiburg: Karl Alber, 1959), 49–61. On the intellectual sources of secret societies see also Dirk von Petersdorff, *Mysterienrede: Zum Selbstverständnis romantischer Intellektueller* (Tübingen: Niemeyer, 1996), 49–54.
3. See Manfred Agethen, *Geheimbund und Utopie: Illuminaten, Freimaurer und deutsche Spätaufklärung* (Munich: Oldenbourg, 1984), 303; and, most recently, Ritchie Robertson, "Freemasons vs. Jesuits—Conspiracy Theories in Enlightenment Germany," *Times Literary Supplement*, Oct. 12, 2012, 13–15.
4. The secondary studies of Freemasonry are innumerable. On the literary influence see especially Marianne Thalmann, *Der Trivialroman des 18. Jahrhunderts und der romantische Roman: Ein Beitrag zur Entwicklungsgeschichte der Geheimbundmystik* (Berlin: Ebering, 1923); Michael Voges, *Aufklärung und Geheimnis: Untersuchungen zur Vermittlung von Literatur- und Sozialgeschichte am Beispiel der Aneignung des Geheimbundmaterials im Roman des späten 18. Jahrhunderts* (Tübingen: Niemeyer, 1987); and Scott Abbott, *Fictions of Freemasonry: Freemasonry and the German Novel* (Detroit: Wayne State University Press, 1991).
5. Michael Titzmann, "Strukturen und Rituale von Geheimbünden in der Literatur um 1800 und ihre Transformation in Goethes Wilhelm Meisters Lehrjahre," in *Jeux et fêtes dans l'œuvre de J. W. Goethe*, ed. Denise Blondeau, Gilles Buscotane, and Christine Maillard (Strasbourg: Presses universitaires de Strasbourg, 2000), 197–224, here 199.
6. For detailed information see Richard von Dülmen, *Der Geheimbund der Illuminaten: Darstellung, Analyse, Dokumentation* (Stuttgart-Bad Canstatt: Frommann, 1975).
7. Voges, *Aufklärung und Geheimnis*, 112–46.
8. On Weishaupt and Knigge see Martin Mulsow, "Adam Weishaupt als Philosoph," in *Die Weimarer Klassik und ihre Geheimbünde*, ed. Walter Müller-Seidel and Wolfgang Riedel (Würzburg: Königshausen und Neumann, 2002), 27–66; and Theo Stammen, "Adolf Freiherr von Knigge und die Illuminatenbeweung," in ibid., 67–89.
9. Hans-Jürgen Schings, *Die Brüder des Marquis Posa: Schiller und der Geheimbund der Illuminaten* (Tübingen: Niemeyer, 1996), 11–12, quotes the pledge as signed by Goethe on Feb. 11, 1783.
10. Johann Wolfgang Goethe, *Sämtliche Werke*, ed. Karl Richter (Munich: Hanser, 1998), vol. 11, pt. 1, sec. 1, 157.
11. Adolf Freiherr von Knigge, *Ueber den Umgang mit Menschen*, in vol. 3 of his *Schriften*, 10th ed. (Hannover, 1822), 167–75, here 167; and the more recent edition by

Michael Rüppel in vol. 2 of Knigge's *Werke,* ed. Pierre-André Bois et al. (Gőttingen: Wallstein, 2010), 408–13.

12. A. F. G. Rebmann, "Wanderungen und Kreuzzüge durch einen Teil Deutschlands" (1795), in Rebmann, *Jena fängt an, mir zu gefallen: Stadt und Universität in Schriften und Briefen,* ed. Werner Greiling (Jena: Leipziger Universitäts-Verlag, 1994), 119. In this connection generally see Voges, *Aufklärung und Geheimnis,* 112–23.

13. Richard Hofstadter, *The Paranoid Style in American Politics, and Other Essays* (New York: Knopf, 1965), 10–12.

14. James H. Billington, *Fire in the Minds of Men: Origins of the Revolutionary Faith* (New York: Basic Books, 1980), 4. Later he writes that "the real innovators were not so much political activists as literary intellectuals, on whom German romantic thought in general—and Bavarian Illuminism in particular—exerted great influence" (87).

15. J. M. Roberts, *The Mythology of the Secret Societies* (London: Secker and Warburg, 1972). On the continuing obsession with the Illuminati as a sinister conspiracy see Pierre-André Taguieff, *La foire aux "Illuminés": Ésotérisme, théorie du complot, extrémisme* (Paris: Mille et une nuits, 2005), which focuses on popular culture since the "retour de l'ésotérisme" (27) of the 1970s.

16. The term *Bund* designates leagues, orders, societies, and associations generally; more narrowly, as *Geheimbund,* it refers to secret societies. But since the Bundesroman so often concerns such groups organized into Masonic-like lodges and meeting in elaborately described lodges with their various ceremonies and symbols, and also for the sake of brevity, I choose to call them simply "lodge novels" (rather than, more cumbersomely and unclearly, "order novels," "secret society novels," or—as I did in *The Novels of Hermann Hesse*—"league novels").

17. Thalmann, *Der Trivialroman des 18. Jahrhunderts* (see note 4 above). Jan Auracher, "Erleuchtung und Bevormundung—Die Rolle der Geheimgesellschaften in den Bundesromanen von Friedrich Schiller und Dan Brown," *Doshisha Studies in Language and Culture* 121 (2010): 665–90, is vitiated by its neglect of Thalmann's standard work on *Der Trivialroman,* of Voges's *Aufklärung und Geheimnis,* and of Abbott's *Fictions of Freemasonry,* which enables his belief that the Bundesroman has remained "bisher für die Literaturwissenschaft kaum erschlossen" (688).

18. Reinhold Taute, *Ordens- und Bundesromane: Ein Beitrag zur Bibliographie der Freimauerei* (Frankfurt am Main: Mahlau, 1907), lists almost 450 works from Thomas More's *Utopia* to Tolstoy's *War and Peace,* but most of them are not lodge novels in the more precise sense of the word.

19. See Albert Schweitzer, *The Quest of the Historical Jesus* (1906), trans. W. Montgomery (New York: Macmillan, 1968), 38–44.

20. *Dya-Na-Sore, oder die Wanderer: Eine Geschichte aus dem Sam-skritt übersetzt,* 2nd ed., 3 vols. (Vienna, 1791), 1:68.

21. Arno Schmidt, *Dya Na Sore: Gespräche in einer Bibliothek* (Karlsruhe: Stahlberg, 1958), 14–53, here 19 and 53.

22. On Schiller and secret societies, though not in *Der Geisterseher,* see Schings, *Die Brüder des Marquis Posa.* On *The Ghost-Seer,* specifically, see Auracher, "Erleuchtung und Bevormundung," 677–80. On the novel, generally, see Jeffrey L. Sammons's knowledgeable introduction to Friedrich Schiller, *The Ghost-Seer,* trans. Henry G. Bohn (Columbia, SC: Camden House, 1992), v–xv.

23. Dennis F. Mahoney, "*Der Geisterseher:* A Princely Experiment or, the Creation of a 'Spiritualist,'" in *Schiller's Literary Prose Works: New Translations and Critical Essays,* ed. Jeffrey L. High (Rochester, NY: Camden House, 2008), 234–49.

24. On Friedrich Wilhelm II and the occult see Christopher McIntosh, *The Rosicrucians: The History, Mythology, and Rituals of an Occult Order* (Wellingborough, Northamptonshire: Crucible, 1987), 95–100.

25. *Berlinische Monatsschrift* (May 1786): 391–94, here 391–92.

26. Ibid., 395–96.

27. *Berlinische Monatsschrift* (July 1786): 1–9. On Elisa von der Recke and the prince see Adalbert von Hanstein, *Wie entstand Schillers Geisterseher?* (Berlin: Duncker, 1903), esp. 33–80.

28. Letters cited from vol. 2 of *Schillers Briefe,* ed. Fritz Jonas, 7 vols. (Stuttgart: Deutsche Verlags-Anstalt, 1892–96).

29. I cite the text in my own translation, from Friedrich Schiller, *Sämtliche Werke,* ed. Gerhard Fricke and Herbert G. Göpfert, 5 vols. (Munich: Hanser, 1967), 5:48–182. The novel has been widely discussed in the secondary literature; see, e.g., Abbott, *Fictions of Freemasonry,* 41–58; Voges, *Aufklärung und Geheimnis,* 343–98; Rüdiger Safranski, *Friedrich Schiller oder Die Erfindung des Deutschen Idealismus* (Munich: Hanser, 2004), 238–51; and Auracher, "Erleuchtung und Bevormundung," 677–80.

30. [Ernst Friedrich Follenius,] *Friedrich Schillers Geisterseher: Aus den Memoiren des Grafen O**. Zweiter und Dritter Theil, von X**Y**Z**,* 2 vols. (Strassburg, 1796). I have not seen the original; I have used the English translation by the Reverend W. Render, *The Armenian, or the Ghost Seer: A History Founded on Fact,* 4 vols. (London, 1800).

31. *Der Geisterseher: Aus den Papieren des Grafen O***. I. Teil herausgeben von Friedrich von Schiller; II. Teil herausgegeben von Hanns Heinz Ewers* (Munich: Müller, 1922), 518.

32. In fact, it was rumored at the time that Schiller was murdered by Freemasons to punish him for revealing secrets of the order. See Eugen Lennhoff and Oskar Posner, *Internationales Freimaurerlexikon* (1932; repr. Munich: Amalthea, 1966), col. 1392.

33. Kai Meyer, *Die Geisterseher: Ein unheimlicher Roman im klassischen Weimar* (1995; repr. Berlin: Aufbau, 1999), 334.

34. I take the biographical information from Günter Dammann's "Nachwort" (afterword) to his edition of Carl Grosse, *Der Genius* (Frankfurt am Main: Zweitausendeins, 1982), 725–835.

35. Titzmann, "Strukturen und Rituale," 202, provides a chart demonstrating graphically the enormous surge of such novels in the decade from 1790 to 1799.

36. For a discussion of the novel in its various aspects see Dammann, "Nachwort," 762–808; and Marianne Thalmann, *Die Romantik des Trivialen: Von Grosses "Genius" bis Tiecks "William Lovell"* (Munich: List, 1970), 58–92.

37. I cite in my own translation the text of the first edition—Carl Grosse, *Der Genius: Aus den Papieren des Marquis C* von G*** (1791–94)—as reprinted by Zweitausendeins.

38. Letter of July 12, 1792, to Christian Otto, in *Jean Pauls Sämtliche Werke: Historisch-kritische Ausgabe, Dritte Abteilung: Briefe,* ed. Eduard Berend, vol. 1 (Berlin: Akademie Verlag, 1956), 360.

39. In the *Neue allgemeine deutsche Bibliothek* (1794), 316–18; repr. *Jean Paul im Urteil seiner Kritiker: Dokumente zur Wirkung Jean Pauls in Deutschland,* ed. Peter Sprengel (Munich: Beck, 1980), 3–4.

40. Jean Paul, *Werke*, ed. Norbert Miller, 6 vols. (Munich: Hanser, 1960), 1:20.

41. Voges, *Aufklärung und Geheimnis*, 538–51, analyzes what he regards as hints in the text regarding the possible function of the order in the still unwritten volume of the novel.

42. I quote in my own translation from the abbreviated version of the 1828 edition of *William Lovell*, ed. Manfred Schlösser (Darmstadt: Agora, 1961).

43. Hölderlin, *Sämtliche Werke*, ed. Friedrich Beissner, vol. 3 (Stuttgart: Kohlhammer, 1958), 36.

44. There have been countless books and articles on the subject. See, e.g., Paul Nettl, *Musik und Freimaurerei: Mozart und die Königliche Kunst* (Esslingen: Bechtle, 1956); Jacques Chailley, *"The Magic Flute," Masonic Opera: An Interpretation of the Libretto and the Music*, trans. Herbert Weinstock (New York: Knopf, 1971); and Jan Assmann, *"Die Zauberflöte": Oper und Mysterium* (Munich: Hanser, 2005).

45. Matt Rees's historical thriller, *Mozart's Last Aria* (London: Corvus, 2011), is based on the notion that Mozart was poisoned as the result of a complicated political conspiracy involving his membership in the Freemasons.

46. On these terms see Hans Joachim Kreutzer, "Die Krönung von Schönheit und Weisheit—Die Zauberflöte," in *Die Zauberflöte. Facsimile of the Autograph Score*, ed. Hans Joachim Kreutzer and Christoph Wolff (Los Altos, CA: Packard Humanities Institute, 2009), 35–37.

47. See the survey by Chailley, *"The Magic Flute," Masonic Opera*, 21–29.

48. Assmann, *"Die Zauberflöte,"* 261, 289. Chailley, *"The Magic Flute," Masonic Opera*, makes a similar case for the essential unity of the opera, albeit without the same theoretical justification. It should be noted that Maynard Solomon, in *Mozart: A Life* (London: Hutchinson, 1995), 505–19, takes a much more negative view of Sarastro and his "authoritarian utopia" (590n12).

49. Accordingly, Solomon, *Mozart: A Life*, 514–15, goes much too far when he characterizes Sarastro as a "lustful" kidnapper asserting his "droit du seigneur"—traits for which there is absolutely no textual justification.

50. See Chailley, *"The Magic Flute," Masonic Opera*, 74–79.

51. I cite the libretto in my own translation according to the original version of 1791 as reprinted in Wolfgang Amadeus Mozart, *Die Zauberflöte: Oper in zwei Aufzügen*, ed. Wilhelm Zentner (Stuttgart: Reclam, 1976).

52. See esp. Chailley, *"The Magic Flute," Masonic Opera*, 83–157; and Assmann, *"Die Zauberflöte,"* 167–258.

53. In his idiosyncratic critique of Romanticism—*Zur Romantik* (Hamburg: Konkret, 2001)—the prominent East German dramatist and essayist Peter Hacks suggests provocatively that Sarastro is "an Illuminist prince" engaged in a dispute with "a Rosicrucian princess," the Queen of Night (82).

54. Johann Wolfgang Goethe, *Dramen, 1791–1832*, ed. Dieter Borchmeyer and Peter Huber (Frankfurt am Main: Deutscher Klassikerverlag, 1993), 221–49.

55. Ibid., 1043–77, for Goethe's notes on the continuation.

56. Rosemarie Haas, *Die Turmgesellschaft in "Wilhelm Meisters Lehrjahren": Zur Geschichte des Geheimbundromans und der deutschen Romantheorie im 18. Jahrhundert* (Frankfurt am Main: Peter Lang, 1975), 21–28.

57. *Goethes Werke*, ed. Erich Trunz, 14 vols. (Hamburg: Wegner, 1956), 2:271–84. That Goethe was familiar with the *Chymische Hochzeit*, of which the new edition of 1781 was

circulated among his Weimar friends, is evident from a letter of June 28, 1786, to Frau von Stein.

58. Goethe, *Dramen, 1791–1832,* 21–109.

59. On the influence of "conspirationist projections" on the bildungsroman generally see Ralf Klausnitzer, *Poesie und Konspiration: Beziehungssinn und Zeichenökonomie von Verschwörungsszenarien in Publizistik, Literatur und Wissenschaft, 1750–1850* (Berlin: De Gruyter, 2007), 401–3.

60. See esp. Haas, *Turm-Gesellschaft,* 54–56, 83–86; and Abbott, *Fictions of Freemasonry,* 71–74, who analyzes the architectural imagery of the passage.

61. Eric A. Blackall, *Goethe and the Novel* (Ithaca, NY: Cornell University Press, 1976), 115.

62. Nicholas Boyle, *Goethe: The Poet and the Age,* vol. 2 (Oxford: Clarendon, 2000), 372–77, here 374.

63. Voges, *Aufklärung und Geheimnis,* 563–70, here 563 and 564. For the most exhaustive study see Wilfried Barner, "Geheime Lenkung: Zur Turmgesellschaft in Goethes *Wilhelm Meister,*" in *Goethe's Narrative Fiction,* ed. William J. Lillyman (Berlin: De Gruyter, 1983), 85–109. Rejecting the view of the Tower Society as prosaic and routine, Barner sees it as a guiding force operating beyond the antinomies of rationality and irrationality and employing elements of Freemasonry as "zitierte Signale im Sinne eines Modells" (108).

64. *Der Briefwechsel zwischen Schiller und Goethe,* ed. Hans Gerhard Gräf and Albert Leitzmann, 3 vols. (Leipzig: Insel, 1955), 2:191–96, here 191–92.

65. I quote in my own translation from the text in vol. 7 of *Goethes Werke,* ed. Erich Trunz, 3rd ed. (Hamburg: Wegner, 1957).

66. On *Bildung* see Hans-Jürgen Schings, "'Wilhelm Meister' und das Erbe der Illuminaten," in Müller-Seidel and Riedel, *Die Weimarer Klassik und ihre Geheimbünde,* 179–203.

67. Novalis, *Schriften,* ed. Paul Kluckhohn and Richard Samuel, 2nd ed. (Stuttgart: Kohlhammer, 1960), 3:646.

68. On the structure of the lodge novel and Goethe's adaptation see Titzmann, "Strukturen und Rituale" (see note 5 above).

69. Trunz, *Goethes Werke,* 1:340.

CHAPTER FIVE: Secret Societies of Romantic Socialism

1. Archives Parlementaires, Chambre des Députés, Jan. 15, 1848; quoted by H. A. C. Collingham, *The July Monarchy: A Political History of France, 1839–1848* (London: Longman, 1988), 402.

2. See Jonathan Beecher, *Victor Considerant and the Rise and Fall of French Romantic Socialism* (Berkeley: University of California Press, 2001), esp. 1–8; and Sigmund Rubinstein, *Romantischer Sozialismus: Ein Versuch über die Idee der deutschen Revolution* (Munich: Drei Masken Verlag, 1921), esp. 118–28. Petra Röder, "Romantischer Sozialismus— eine aktuelle Alternative zum real existierenden Kapitalismus und dessen postmodernen Apologeten?" in *Sozialismus in Geschichte und Gegenwart,* ed. Richard Faber (Würzburg: Königshausen and Neumann, 1994), 133–46, analyzes Marx's indebtedness to the Romantic philosophy of nature and Ludwig Feuerbach's theory of religion.

3. Novalis, *Schriften,* ed. Paul Kluckhohn and Richard Samuel, 4 vols., 2nd ed. (Darmstadt: Wissenschaftliche Buchgesellschaft, 1960–75), 3:507. On this essay generally see

Theodore Ziolkowski, *Vorboten der Moderne: Eine Kulturgeschichte der Frühromantik* (Stuttgart: Klett-Cotta, 2006), 144–52.

4. Beecher, *Victor Considerant*, 1–2, points out that others had used the word earlier but that Leroux gave the term currency.

5. David Friedrich Strauss, *Das Leben Jesu für das deutsche Volk bearbeitet*, 3rd ed. (Leipzig: Brockhaus, 1874), 207 (chap. 34).

6. Beecher, *Victor Considerant*, 2. See also Collingham, *The July Monarchy*, 258–68.

7. See Jost Hermand's afterword to *Der deutsche Vormärz: Texte und Dokumente*, ed. Jost Hermand (Stuttgart: Reclam, 1967), 357–94, here 370. See also Hermand's edition *Das Junge Deutschland: Texte und Dokumente* (Stuttgart: Reclam, 1966).

8. Georg Kloss, *Bibliographie der Freimaurerei und der mit ihr in Verbindung gesetzten geheimen Gesellschaften* (Frankfurt am Main, 1844); repr. Graz: Akademische Druck- und Verlagsanstalt, 1970), 266–71.

9. Thomas De Quincey, *Historical and Critical Essays*, 2 vols. (Boston: Ticknor and Fields, 1859), 2:276–341.

10. Quoted here and elsewhere by volume and page in my own translation from the usefully annotated three-volume edition: George Sand, *Consuelo: La Comtesse de Rudolstadt*, ed. Léon Cellier and Léon Guichard (Paris: Garnier, 1959).

11. Alain (Emile Auguste Chartier), *Propos de littérature* (Paris: Hartmann, 1934), 223: "C'est notre *Meister*, plus courant, plus attachant par l'aventure, et qui va au plus profond par la musique, comme fait l'autre par la poésie."

12. René Jacques Baerlocher, "'Le nom insifflable du Grand Goethe'. Anmerkungen zum Goethe-Bild von George Sand," *Goethe-Jahrbuch* 112 (1995): 309–20, discusses her preface to the 1845 translation of *Werther* and her "Essai sur le drame fantastique: Goethe—Byron—Mickiewicz" (1839) but does not take up the *Wilhelm Meister* analogy.

13. For a list of the principal sources see Sand, *Consuelo*, 1:lxxxiii–lxxxvii.

14. For further detail on music and theater see Léon Guichard's introduction, "Pauline Garcia et la musique dans *Consuelo* et *La Comtesse de Rudolstadt*," in Sand, *Consuelo*, xxxi–xlvi; and the six essays in the section "Opéra, fêtes, musique," in *Lectures de Consuelo: La Comtesse de Rudolstadt de George Sand*, ed. Michèle Hecquet and Christine Planté (Lyon: Presses universitaires de Lyon, 2004), 165–248.

15. The standard study is Cellier, "Le roman initiatique en France au temps du romantisme," in his *Parcours Initiatiques* (Neuchatel: Presses universitaires de Grenoble, 1977), 118–37. Cellier states (129) that the "chef-d'oeuvre du genre," which he distinguishes from the *Bildungsroman*, is *The Magic Flute*; but since he and his followers—for instance, Isabelle Hoog Naginski, *George Sand: Writing for Her Life* (New Brunswick, NJ: Rutgers University Press, 1991), 202–4—do not realize that Mozart's work is not the starting point but the sublimation of an existing genre in Germany, French critics fail to establish the obvious links between the "roman initiatique" and the *Bundesroman* and, hence, the continuity of the genre—a topic worthy of more extensive study.

16. On Sand's use of the Gothic novel and the parallels with Radcliffe's *Udolpho* see Naginski, *George Sand*, 190–220, here 191–202.

17. On Sand's sources see Claude Rétat, "Parler aux yeux: Entre épreuves physiques et épreuves morales (La Comtesse de Rudolstadt)," in Hecquet and Planté, *Lectures de Consuelo*, 367–86, here 372–74; on Consuelo's symbolic descent see ibid., 381; and, also in the same volume, Martine Watrelot, "Femmes et sociétés secrètes: de la maçonnerie des

héroïnes dans *La Comtesse de Rudolstadt*," 387–400, here 393; on the descent as a journey into the subconscious see Naginski, *George Sand,* 192.

18. Léon Cellier, "L'Occultisme dans *Consuelo* et *La Comtesse de Rudolstadt*," in his edition of *Consuelo,* 1:lxxviii; repr. in his *Parcours initiatiques,* 138–63, here 139.

19. George Sand, *Le Compagnon du Tour de France,* ed. René Bourgeois (Grenoble: Presses universitaires de Grenoble, 1979), 35.

20. Letter of June 1843 to Pierre Leroux, in George Sand, *Correspondance,* ed. Georges Lubin (Paris: Garnier, 1969), 6:179.

21. Letter of June 1843 to Ferdinand François; *Correspondance,* 6:175.

22. Ibid., 6:174.

23. Letter of July 1843 to Ferdinand François; *Correspondance,* 6:208. Cellier, "L'Occultisme dans *Consuelo*," 155–58, cites other sources that she consulted.

24. Letters of June 1843 to Pierre Leroux; *Correspondance,* 6:179, 161.

25. See in this connection Rétat, "Parler aux yeux," 367–86.

26. See the editor's note in Sand, *Consuelo,* 3:506n2.

27. Eighteenth-century France also knew the so-called Lodges of Adoption, the female parallels to the male Masonic lodges. But what is unique about Sand's novel is Consuelo's initiation into a primarily male society. See in this connection Watrelot, "Femmes et sociétés secrètes," 387–400.

28. See Sophie Guermès's informative introduction to her critical edition: Charles Didier, *Rome souterraine* (Geneva: Droz, 2007), 7–134, here 42.

29. For the general historical context see ibid., 63–82.

30. Ibid., 112–13.

31. Eugène Sue, *Le Juif errant,* ed. Francis Lacassin (Paris: Robert Laffont, 1983), 389 (my translation).

32. Sue's novel is the principal literary example cited in Geoffrey Cubitt, *The Jesuit Myth: Conspiracy Theory and Politics in Nineteenth-Century France* (Oxford: Clarendon, 1993), which analyzes the hostility toward Jesuits among liberals on the political left as analogous to the fear of Freemasons on the conservative right.

33. Lacassin, in the preface to his edition of Sue, *Le Juif errant,* 6.

34. I have found no reference in works on either writer to one's awareness of the other.

35. Edward Bulwer-Lytton, *Zanoni* (Boston: Little, Brown, 1896).

36. The allegory is set forth in "Zanoni Explained By—" appended to the novel, 537–40. The explanation was actually written by his friend Harriet Martineau, who felt that the book was too foreign, too German, to be immediately comprehensible to English readers; and Bulwer-Lytton agreed to include it in his appendix. See Marie Roberts, *Gothic Immortals: The Fiction of the Brotherhood of the Rosy Cross* (London: Routledge, 1990), 171.

37. See Richard A. Zipser, *Edward Bulwer-Lytton and Germany* (Berne: Herbert Lang, 1974), 68–69.

38. Roberts, *Gothic Immortals,* 182. Elsewhere Roberts concludes that it is "the underlying problem of the Rosicrucian novel that the immortal hero may be spiritually redeemed only through death" (208).

39. See Roberts, *Gothic Immortals,* 160–61; and Zipser, *Edward Bulwer-Lytton and Germany,* 126–27, 140.

40. Leslie George Mitchell, *Bulwer Lytton: The Rise and Fall of a Victorian Man of Letters* (London: Hambledon, 2003), 142, reports that many of these works—some

heavily annotated but others with the pages still uncut—are still in the author's library at Knebworth.

41. Roberts, *Gothic Immortals*, 173.

42. Ibid., 156–61.

43. Ibid., 170; Roberts calls *Zanoni* "a[n] explicitly Rosicrucian text" and refers throughout her otherwise extremely perceptive analysis, 170–86, to Zanoni, Mejnour, and Glyndon as Rosicrucians. But Zanoni himself, as we have seen, claims membership only in an Order that antedates Rosicrucianism and any other more recent societies.

44. Mitchell, *Bulwer Lytton*, 143.

45. See Zipser, *Edward Bulwer-Lytton and Germany*, 181–207.

46. I refer by volume and page to the annotated edition, based on Gutzkow's own abbreviated 5th edition of 1869: *Die Ritter vom Geist*, ed. Reinhold Gensel, 3 vols. (Berlin: Deutsches Verlagshaus Bong [1912]); reissued as vols. 5–7 of Gutzkow's *Werke*, 7 vols. (Hildesheim: Olms, 1974). On the reception see the editor's introduction, 1:34–35.

47. Letter of August 5, 1850; *Der Briefwechsel zwischen Karl Gutzkow und Levin Schücking, 1838–1876*, ed. Wolfgang Rasch (Bielefeld: Aisthesis, 1998), 92.

48. On Gutzkow and Sand see Kerstin Wiedemann, *Zwischen Irritation und Faszination: George Sand und ihre deutsche Leserschaft im 19. Jahrhundert* (Tübingen: Günter Narr, 2003), 127; on Gutzkow and Sue see Gert Vonhoff, *Vom bürgerlichen Individuum zur sozialen Frage: Romane von Karl Gutzkow* (Frankfurt am Main: Lang, 1994), 236–42; on Gutzkow's ambivalent view of Bulwer-Lytton see Lawrence M. Price, "Karl Gutzkow and Bulwer-Lytton," *Journal of English and Germanic Philology* 16 (1917): 397–415; and Zipser, *Edward Bulwer-Lytton and Germany*, 197–98.

49. See in this connection Peter Hasubek, "Karl Gutzkow: *Die Ritter vom Geist* (1850/51): Gesellschaftsdarstellung im deutschen Roman nach 1848," in *Romane und Erzählungen des bürgerlichen Realismus: Neue Interpretationen*, ed. Horst Denkler (Stuttgart: Reclam, 1980), 26–39.

50. Achim Ricken, *Panorama und Panoramaroman: Parallelen zwischen der Panorama-Malerei und der Literatur im 19. Jahrhundert dargestellt an Eugène Sues Geheimnissen von Paris und Karl Gutzkows Rittern vom Geist* (Frankfurt am Main: Lang, 1991).

51. In his *Unterhaltungen am häuslichen Herd*, as cited by Hasubek, "Karl Gutzkow," 26.

52. Herbert Kaiser, *Studien zum deutschen Roman nach 1848* (Duisburg: Walter Braun, 1977), 9, calls the novel "ein erstrangiges Dokument der Geschichte des liberalen Bewußtseins."

53. See Scott Abbott, *Fictions of Freemasonry: Freemasonry and the German Novel* (Detroit: Wayne State University Press, 1991), 89–11, esp. 67–107.

54. See Eitel Wolf Dobert, *Karl Gutzkow und seine Zeit* (Berne: Francke, 1968).

55. On the stages leading to the order see Vonhoff, *Vom bürgerlichen Individuum zur sozialen Frage*, 169–99.

56. On the spectrum of political views of the novel see Kaiser, *Studien zum deutschen Roman nach 1848*, 9–56, esp. 18–31.

57. Ralf Klausnitzer, *Poesie und Konspiration: Beziehungssinn und Zeichenökonomie von Verschwörungsszenarien in Publizistik, Literatur und Wissenschaft, 1750–1850* (Berlin: De Gruyter, 2007), 590–98, sees a parallel to the *Communist Manifesto*, which is mentioned in the novel, in Dankmar's intention to render conspiracy superfluous through public exposure of the movement's goals and means.

58. Julian Schmidt, in *Grenzboten* 11 (1852): 41–63; quoted in *Karl Gutzkow: Liberale Energie,* ed. Peter Demetz (Frankfurt am Main: Ullstein, 1974), 328.

59. "Karl Gutzkow," in Julian Schmidt, *Bilder aus dem geistigen Leben unserer Zeit,* n.s. (Leipzig: Duncker und Humblot, 1871), 432.

60. On Gutzkow's new understanding of the industrial proletariat see Vonhoff, *Vom bürgerlichen Individuum zur sozialen Frage,* 153–63.

61. Arno Schmidt, "Der Ritter vom Geist," in his *Die Ritter vom Geist: Von vergessenen Kollegen* (Frankfurt am Main: Fischer, 1985), 6–54, here 39–43. Schmidt, we recall, also sought to rehabilitate Meyern's *Dya-Na-Sore.*

62. The man named as Master of the Order, (Bernard Samuel) Matolay, a Swedenborgian mystic and alchemist, was historically Master of the Viennese Masonic Lodge "Zur gekrönten Hoffnung" at the time Mozart became a member of that lodge.

63. Christopher McIntosh, *The Rosicrucians: The History, Mythology and Rituals of an Occult Order,* rev. ed. (Wellingborough, Northamptonshire: Crucible, 1987), 76.

64. Eduard Breier, *Die Rosenkreuzer in Wien: Sittengemälde aus der Zeit Kaiser Joseph's II,* 4 vols. (Vienna: Jasper und Hügel, 1852).

CHAPTER SIX: Modern Variations

1. J.-K. Huysmans, *Là-bas* (Paris: Plon, n.d.), 252.

2. Georg Simmel, "Das Geheimnis und die geheime Gesellschaft," in his *Soziologie: Untersuchungen über die Formen der Vergesellschaftung* (Leipzig: Duncker und Humblot, 1908), 337–402.

3. Theodore Ziolkowski, *Modes of Faith: Secular Surrogates for Lost Religious Belief* (Chicago: University of Chicago Press, 2007). See also Fritz Stern, *The Politics of Cultural Despair: A Study in the Rise of German Ideology* (1961; repr. New York: Anchor, 1965).

4. David V. Barrett, *A Brief History of Secret Societies* (1997; repr. New York: Carroll and Graf, 2007), 194–211.

5. Stern, *Politics of Cultural Despair,* 223–27; Scott Abbott, *Fictions of Freemasonry: Freemasonry and the German Novel* (Detroit: Wayne State University Press, 1991), 126–29.

6. See Barbara W. Tuchman, *The Proud Tower: A Portrait of the World before the War, 1890–1914* (1966; repr. New York: Ballantine, 1996). Apart from a chapter on music Tuchman does not, however, discuss the intellectual, cultural, and literary life of the period.

7. "Ein Brief," in Hugo von Hofmannsthal, *Sämtliche Werke: Erfundene Gespräche und Briefe,* vol. 31, ed. Ellen Ritter (Frankfurt am Main: Fischer, 1991), 45–55, here 47.

8. David H. Miles, *Hofmannsthal's Novel "Andreas": Memory and Self* (Princeton, NJ: Princeton University Press, 1972), 202–10, discusses analogies to three other libretti: *Ariadne auf Naxos, Die Frau ohne Schatten,* and *Die ägyptische Helena.*

9. The fragmentary text and notes have been reproduced in Hofmannsthal's *Sämtliche Werke,* vol. 30, ed. Manfred Pape (Frankfurt am Main: Fischer, 1982), 7–218.

10. In his notes Hofmannsthal alludes several times to the analogy: for instance, "Malteser = St.G." See *Sämtliche Werke,* 30:160, also 145 and 161. In this connection see Jens Rieckmann, *Hugo von Hofmannsthal und Stefan George: Signifikanz einer "Episode" aus der Jahrhundertwende* (Tübingen: Francke, 1997), 149–51.

11. Hofmannsthal was impressed and influenced by Morton Prince's 1906 study of multiple schizophrenia, *Dissociation of a Personality* (New York: Longmans, Green).

12. Ferdinand Maack, *Zweimal gestorben! Die Geschichte eines Rosenkreuzers aus dem XVIII. Jahrhundert.* I am indebted for this observation to Abbott, *Fictions of Freemasonry,* 140.

13. This parallel was noted by Miles, *Hofmannsthal's Novel "Andreas,"* 110–11.

14. *Deutsche Erzähler,* selected and edited by Hugo von Hofmannsthal (1912; repr. Wiesbaden: Insel, 1955), 7.

15. See, e.g., Karl Gautschi, "Hugo von Hofmannsthals Romanfragment 'Andreas'" (diss., Zurich, 1965), 97; quoted in Miles, *Hofmannsthal's Novel "Andreas,"* 190. The sequence of the novel following the published fragment must, of course, remain conjectural.

16. Miles, *Hofmannsthal's Novel "Andreas,"* 110.

17. In his afterword to Hofmannsthal, *Andreas oder die Vereinigten* (Frankfurt am Main: Fischer, 1961), 139.

18. Both works, along with an informative history of the genre in German Romanticism, were published by Helmut Rogge, *Der Doppelroman der Berliner Romantik,* 2 vols. (Leipzig: Klinkhardt und Biermann, 1927).

19. Richard Albrecht, "Vom Roman der XII zum Kollektivroman Wir lassen uns nicht verschaukeln: Aspekte der literarischen Gemeinschaftsproduktionen in der deutschen Literatur des 20. Jahrhunderts," *Neohelicon* 14 (1987): 269–85.

20. See the publisher's preface, "Wie der 'Roman der XII' entstand," in *Der Roman der XII* (Berlin: Mecklenburg, 1909), 5–8.

21. In the notes to the work in André Gide, *Romans, récits et soties: Œuvres lyriques,* with an introduction by Maurice Nadeau and notes by Yvonne Davet and Jean-Jacques Thierry (Paris: Gallimard, 1958), 1571.

22. For a thorough discussion of the *acte gratuit* generally and in *Les caves du Vatican* in particular see Jean Hytier, *André Gide,* trans. Richard Howard (Garden City, NY: Anchor, 1962), 91–119.

23. See the editors' notes in Gide, *Romans, récits et soties,* 1567–69.

24. *Compte rendu de la délivrance de Sa Sainteté Léon XIII, emprisonné dan les cachots du Vatican de Pâques 1892 à Pâques 1893* (Saint-Malo, 1893).

25. Thornton Niven Wilder, *The Cabala* (New York: Boni, 1926).

26. See in this connection Theodore Ziolkowski, *Virgil and the Moderns* (Princeton, NJ: Princeton University Press, 1993), 195–200.

27. See Rex Burbank, *Thornton Wilder,* 2nd ed. (Boston: Twayne, 1978), 31.

28. *Der Geisterseher,* ed. by Hanns Heinz Ewers (Munich: Georg Müller, 1922), 518–30, here 529–30.

29. Arno Schmidt, *Dya-Na-Sore: Gespräche in einer Bibliothek* (Karlsruhe: Stahlberg, 1958), 53.

30. Marianne Thalmann, *Der Trivialroman des 18. Jahrhunderts und der romantische Roman: Ein Beitrag zur Entwicklungsgeschichte der Geheimbundmystik* (Berlin, 1923).

31. André Gide, "Preface to *The Journey to the East,*" in André Gide, *Autumn Leaves,* trans. Elsie Pell (New York: Philosophical Library, 1950), 227–34; repr. in *Hesse: A Collection of Critical Essays,* ed. Theodore Ziolkowski (Englewood Cliffs, NJ: Prentice-Hall, 1973), 21–24, here 23–24.

32. Thomas Mann, *Gesammelte Werke,* 12 vols. (Frankfurt am Main: Fischer, 1960), 12:32.

33. For the examples in this paragraph and others see Abbott, *Fictions of Freemasonry,* 158–61.

34. "Eine Bibliothek der Weltliteratur," in Hermann Hesse, *Gesammelte Schriften*, 7 vols. (Frankfurt am Main: Suhrkamp, 1957), 7:307–43, here 337.

35. On Hesse's fascination with India see Ziolkowski, *Modes of Faith*, 104–7.

36. For more extensive discussions of *Demian* and the novels mentioned below see Theodore Ziolkowski, *The Novels of Hermann Hesse: A Study in Theme and Structure* (Princeton, NJ: Princeton University Press, 1965).

37. "Ein Stückchen Theologie," in Hesse, *Gesammelte Schriften*, 7:388–402, here 389 and 402.

38. See Theodore Ziolkowski, *Fictional Transfigurations of Jesus* (Princeton, NJ: Princeton University Press, 1972), 151–61.

39. *Demian*, in Hesse, *Gesammelte Schriften*, 3:99–257 (my translation).

40. Hesse, *Gesammelte Schriften*, 4:240.

41. In a letter of Nov. 19, 1935 (*Gesammelte Schriften*, 7:595).

42. For a thorough analysis of the novel see Ziolkowski, *The Novels of Hermann Hesse*, 283–338.

CHAPTER SEVEN: Interlude

1. For an authoritative account of the history of the forgery see Norman Cohn, *Warrant for Genocide: The Myth of the Jewish World-Conspiracy and the "Protocols of the Elders of Zion"* (London: Eyre and Spottiswoode, 1967). Much of my information comes from Cohn's book and from volume 4 *(Suicidal Europe, 1870–1933)* of Léon Poliakov, *History of Anti-Semitism*, trans. George Klin, 4 vols. (Oxford: Oxford University Press, 1977).

2. Bernstein's work has been reprinted with an introduction by Norman Cohn (New York: Ktav, 1971).

3. Maurice Joly, *Dialogue aux enfers entre Montesquieu et Machiavel, ou la Politique de Machiavel au XIXe siècle* (Paris: Calman-Lévy, 1948).

4. The "Dialogue of the Dead," a genre created in the second century CE by Lucian and used principally for satire, was especially popular among writers of the Enlightenment from Boileau and Fontenelle to Wieland and Goethe for didactic-satirical purposes.

5. For representative examples see the preface to Joly, *Dialogue aux enfers*, x–xii; and Cohn, *Warrant for Genocide*, 275–79.

6. On Goedsche see Volker Neuhaus, *Der zeitgeschichtliche Sensationsroman in Deutschland, 1855–1878: Sir John Retcliffe und seine Schule* (Berlin: Erich Schmidt, 1980).

7. John Retcliffe, *Biarritz*, 2 vols. (Berlin: Verlag von Liebrecht, 1868–69), 1:141–93.

8. For a representative comparison of passages from the two works see Cohn, *Warrant for Genocide*, 275–79.

9. For the material in this paragraph see Cohn, *Warrant for Genocide*, 36–39.

10. Poliakov, *History of Anti-Semitism*, 4:57.

11. Eric Conan, "Les Secrets d'une manipulation antisémite," *L'Express*, Nov. 18, 1999, 60–63.

12. Poliakov, *History of Anti-Semitism*, 4:104.

13. On the broader historical context of anti-Judaism and anti-Semitism that made many Europeans susceptible to the message of the forgery see Wolfgang Benz, *Die Protokolle der Weisen von Zion: Die Legende von der jüdischen Weltverschwörung* (Munich: Beck, 2007). For the most extensive documentation of the impact of the *Protocols* after

World War II see Pierre-André Taguieff, *Les Protocols des sages de Sion,* 2 vols. (Paris: Berg, 1992).

14. Adolf Hitler, *Mein Kampf,* 2 vols. (Munich: Franz Eher Nachfolger, 1933), 1:337.

15. Quoted in Hannah Arendt, *The Origins of Totalitarianism* (Cleveland: Meridian, 1958), 360.

16. Ibid., 358, 360, 378.

17. Cohn, *Warrant for Genocide,* 144–47.

18. It was actually volume 1 of a four-volume series of tracts published from 1920 to 1922 under the title *The International Jew.* See Cohn, *Warrant for Genocide,* 156–64.

19. Nesta H. Webster, *Secret Societies and Subversive Movements,* 2nd ed. (London: Boswell, 1924), 402.

20. On Céline see Bettina L. Knapp, *Céline: Man of Hate* (University of Alabama Press, 1974), esp. 115–23.

21. Louis-Ferdinand Céline, *Bagatelles pour un massacre* (Paris: Denoël, 1937), 276–89.

22. Letter of April 12, 1933; cited by Ronald Hayman, *Thomas Mann: A Biography* (New York: Scribner, 1995), 405.

23. Stefan Heym, "Ein Interview mit den Weisen von Zion," *Der Simpl: Prager Satirische Wochenschrift,* no. 11 (March 13, 1935): 118–19.

24. I take the biographical information from Wolfgang Cordan, *Die Matte: Autobiographische Aufzeichnungen,* ed. Manfred Herzer (Hamburg: MännerschwarmSkript, 2003).

25. Wolfgang Cordan, *De Wijzen van Zion,* trans. Theo J. van der Wal (Hilversum: De Boekenvrienden "Solidariteit," 1934). The work seems never to have appeared in the original German or to have been translated into any other language.

26. I cite the French translation by Pascale Delpech: "Le livre des rois et des sots," in Danilo Kiš, *Encyclopédie des morts* (Paris: Gallimard, 1985), 125–64.

27. On this point see Cohn, *Warrant for Genocide,* 71–73.

28. In fact Goedsche might equally well have been inspired by scenes in Bulwer-Lytton's *Zanoni,* Sand's *Consuelo,* or various German lodge novels.

29. Umberto Eco, *Six Walks in the Fictional Woods* (Cambridge, MA: Harvard University Press, 1994), 117–40, here 134–39.

30. *Il cimiterio di Praga* (Milan: Bompiani, 2010). I cite the American translation by Richard Dixon (Boston: Houghton Mifflin Harcourt, 2011). By stating in his afterword that "the only fictitious character in this story is the protagonist, Simone Simonini" (439), Eco implies that the portrayals of character and actions of the historical figures are historically accurate. But unlike most historical novels, in which a fictitious protagonist is inserted into a historical situation that remains plausibly close to actuality, Eco in many cases alters history itself, attributing to his protagonist many actions actually carried out by others.

31. See also Svetlana Boym, "Conspiracy Theories and Literary Ethics: Umberto Eco, Danilo Kiš, and *The Protocols of Zion,*" *Comparative Literature* 51 (1999): 97–122.

32. Will Eisner, *The Plot: The Secret Story of the Protocols of the Elders of Zion* (New York: Norton, 2005).

33. *Protocols of the Elders of Zion: A Fabricated "Historic" Document,* report prepared by the Subcommittee to Investigate the Administration of the Internal Security Act and Other Internal Security Laws to the Committee on the Judiciary, United States Senate, 88th Cong., 2nd sess. (Washington: U.S. Government Printing Office, 1964).

34. Benz, *Die Protokolle der Weisen von Zion,* 87, believes that Eisner's work, which as a graphic novel depends on stereotypes and oversimplifications, constitutes "less a contribution to enlightenment than a forum in which, for all its noble intentions, clichés are practiced and strengthened."

35. See Robert S. Wistrich, *Antisemitism: The Longest Hatred* (London: Thames Methuen, 1991), 195–267.

CHAPTER EIGHT: The Playfulness of Postmodernism

1. Karl Popper, "Towards a Rational Theory of Tradition," in his *Conjectures and Refutations: The Growth of Scientific Knowledge,* 3rd rev. ed. (London: Routledge, 1969), 120–35, here 123.

2. Dieter Groh, "The Temptation of Conspiracy Theory, or: Why Do Bad Things Happen to Good People? Part II: Case Studies," in *Changing Conceptions of Conspiracy,* ed. Carl F. Graumann and Serge Moscovici (New York: Springer, 1987), 15–37, here 15; and George Johnson, *Architects of Fear: Conspiracy Theories and Paranoia in American Politics* (Los Angeles: Tarcher, 1983).

3. See Theodore Ziolkowski, *Fictional Transfigurations of Jesus* (Princeton, NJ: Princeton University Press, 1972), 225–69.

4. See Theodore Ziolkowski, "The Veil as Metaphor and Myth," *Religion and Literature* 40 (2008): 61–81.

5. Jorge Luis Borges, "Tlön, Uqbar, Orbis Tertius" (1940), trans. James E. Irby, in Borges, *Labyrinths: Selected Stories and Other Writings,* ed. Donald A. Yates and James E. Irby (New York: New Directions, 1964), 3–18, here 15.

6. For a fuller discussion see Scott Abbott, *Fictions of Freemasonry: Freemasonry and the German Novel* (Detroit: Wayne State University Press, 1991), 162–64.

7. See John Barth, *The Friday Book: Essays and Other Nonfiction* (New York: Putnam, 1984), 62–76.

8. Thomas Pynchon, *The Crying of Lot 49,* Perennial Fiction Library (New York: Harper and Row, 1986).

9. Debra A. Castillo, "Borges and Pynchon: The Tenuous Symmetries of Art," in *New Essays on "The Crying of Lot 49,"* ed. Patrick O'Donnell (Cambridge: Cambridge University Press, 1991), 21–46, which does not mention this striking parallel.

10. On such postmodern elements as the semiotics, metaphorics, and epistemology of the novel see, for instance, the contributions in O'Donnell, *New Essays on "The Crying of Lot 49."*

11. Ishmael Reed, *Mumbo Jumbo* (New York: Atheneum, 1988), 5.

12. Reed's text actually reads: "Someone once said that beneath or behind all political and cultural warfare lies a struggle between secret societies" (18).

13. Robert Shea and Robert Anton Wilson, *The Illuminatus! Trilogy,* omnibus ed. (London: Constable and Robinson, 1998).

14. On the particular prominence of the Illuminati in postmodern conspiracy theories see Johnson, *Architects of Fear,* 25–27, 31–67, 211–12, and passim.

15. I take my information on the composition from http://en.wikipedia.org/wiki/The_Illuminatus!_Trilogy (retrieved June 13, 2010).

16. Umberto Eco, *Foucault's Pendulum,* trans. William Weaver (New York: Ballantine, 1997).

17. "Eugène Sue: Il socialismo e la consolatione," in Umberto Eco, *Il superuomo di massa* (Milan: Cooperativa Scrittori, 1976), 35–77. Here Eco deals almost exclusively with *Les mystères de Paris.*

18. Umberto Eco, "Borges and My Anxiety of Influence," in his *On Literature,* trans. Martin McLaughlin (Orlando: Harcourt, 2004), 118–35.

19. Ibid., 125.

20. Some scholars—notably Peter Bondanella, "Eco and the Tradition of the Detective Story," in *New Essays on Umberto Eco,* ed. Peter Bondanella (Cambridge: Cambridge University Press, 2009), 90–112—place Casaubon in the tradition of the detective stories of Dashiell Hammett and Raymond Chandler, and certainly the quest bears a certain resemblance to the detective's investigation. But the analogy of the lodge novel helps more, I believe, to explain the significance of the goal itself, the self-conceived "Plan," and the huge amount of background material on other cults, orders, societies, and conspiracies.

21. Norma Bouchard, "Eco and Popular Culture," in Bondanella, *New Essays on Umberto Eco,* 1–16, here 14.

22. Yorick Blumenfeld, *The Waters of Forgetfulness: An Augustan-Age Memoir* (London: Quartet, 2009).

CONCLUSION

1. Umberto Eco, *Foucault's Pendulum,* trans. William Weaver (New York: Ballantine, 1997), 620.

2. Marie Roberts, *Gothic Immortals: The Fiction of the Brotherhood of the Rosy Cross* (London: Routledge, 1990), 18–21, here 18. See also David Punter, *The Literature of Terror: A History of Gothic Fictions from 1765 to the Present Day* (London: Longmans, 1979).

3. See Theodore Ziolkowski, *Ovid and the Moderns* (Ithaca, NY: Cornell University Press, 2005), 147–225.

4. Roberts, *Gothic Immortals,* 18.

5. Jonathan Z. Smith, "The Devil in Mr. Jones," in his *Imagining Religion: From Babylon to Jonestown* (Chicago: University of Chicago Press, 1982), 102–20, here 112–14.

6. C. G. Jung, "Archetypes of the Collective Unconscious," in his *The Archetypes and the Collective Unconscious,* trans. R. F. C. Hull, 2nd ed., Bollingen Series 20 (Princeton, NJ: Princeton University Press, 1968), 5.

7. See Joseph Campbell, *The Hero with a Thousand Faces,* 2nd ed., Bollingen Series 17 (Princeton: Princeton University Press, 1968), 30.

8. Northrop Frye, *Anatomy of Criticism: Four Essays* (New York: Atheneum, 1966), 186–206, here 187.

Index